REDEMPTION: EARTH'S CRY

REDEMPTION: EARTH'S CRY

MELECH AND EARTH'S TALE

EDWINA FORT

Copyright © 2018 by Edwina Fort

All rights reserved. No part of this publication may be reproduced, distributed or transmitted in any form or by any means, including photocopying, recording, or other electronic or mechanical methods without written permission of the publisher, except in the case of brief quotations embodied in critical reviews and certain other noncommercial uses permitted by copyright law. For permission requests, write to the publisher, addressed "Attention: Permissions Coordinator," at the email address below:

Author Edwina Fort P.O. Box 346 Keithville, LA 71047 www.authoredwinafort.com

Publisher's Note: This is a work of fiction. Names, characters, places, and incidents are a product of the author's imagination. Locales and public names are sometimes used for atmospheric purposes. Any resemblance to actual people, living or dead, or to businesses, companies, events, institutions, or locales is completely coincidental.

Redemption – Earth's Cry/Edwina Fort. – 1st edition ISBN

❃ Created with Vellum

ACKNOWLEDGMENTS

As always, I'd like to give all honor and praise to the Heavenly Father. Without Him I am nothing, my pen belongs to Him. I'd also like to thank my husband, my children, my family and Team 2019. But I am nothing without my fans! Thank you, guys, you are the best!

Welcome Back Redemption Fans, May I present Level 2…

THE PROLOGUE

EARTH

My mother started teaching me to play the violin before I took my first step. By the time I was four, I could perform a full concerto with cadenzas in the first and last movements. I was the only child in the ghetto with a violin.

My mother, who had at one point in time had a very promising future, fell in love with the wrong man, who was also her band's manager and my father. Being a black female violinist made her very popular, and when she began to complain to him that she was too tired to perform so many shows because she was a new mom, he introduced her to cocaine.

At first it seemed like the answer to her prayers. The drug made her feel like a machine, she didn't need much sleep and didn't need much to eat. She was able to compose and perform and still spend a good amount of time with me.

But over time her powdery hero began to take a toll on her

gift. And the more my father pressured her to get herself together, because she was causing him to lose money, the more of the drug she did until finally he couldn't take it anymore and walked away from her, the band that was no longer getting booked for gigs, and me.

That's when things really got hard. My mother could barely hold a job, which meant she could no longer afford her cocaine habit, so she had to settle for its cheaper cousin, crack. Piece by piece I watched her sell away all our nice things.

Until all that was left was her precious violin that was named Earth's Cry. It was a mahogany beauty that sat on its stand in our living room in front of the windows. Every morning the sun shined on it, kissing it with its rays. When I was a little girl I would sometimes sit on the floor next to it and just stare at it, imagining that I could hear it weeping.

My mother loved the violin so much that she had named me Earth after it. She said when she was fourteen she saw a homeless man sitting at a bus stop with no shoes on in the dead of winter. She had felt so bad for him that she had given him the money her mother had given her to pay for her eighth-grade field trip.

In return he'd handed her the violin and told her its name was Earth's Cry. She took it home and taught herself how to play it. I always believed it had special power, because anytime my mother played it within hearing range, the music called to me, bringing me to a complete stop from whatever I was doing. It seemed as if it seeped into my soul and resonated in my bones.

One night when I was twelve years old my mother woke me up with tears in her eyes. She said she had to go away and that a very good friend of hers was going to take care of me until she came back. She packed my suitcase and to my surprise, she gently laid Earth's Cry in it on top of my clothes.

I picked up my violin that she had bought me a few years

back, but she took it from me tossing it to the side before bringing her hand to gently caress the deep mahogany wood of Earth's Cry.

"This is yours now." She spoke softly as she silently wept, lifting her shaking hand to try and wipe away her tears. "Maybe… it was always meant to be yours." She muttered more to herself than me.

"I was never worthy of it. It never sang for me."

I shook my head confused. She made beautiful music with the violin, what was she talking about? Why was she crying? Why was she packing my stuff?

"Where you going, mama?" My heart was racing so fast I felt that it would beat right out of my chest. There was too much happening at once and my brain wasn't awakened enough to process everything. She was leaving, no…*I* was leaving. She was giving me *Earth's Cry*.

"Mama sick. I need to go get help." Her hands shook very badly as she gently closed the lid on the suitcase. When she was done she took my coat down out of my closet.

"Here, just put this on over your pajamas. Sista Dinah is waiting in the car for you downstairs." I smiled, I liked Sista Dinah and her husband Brother Abraham, they were nice people that brought us food sometimes.

"When you coming back?" I asked my mother as she hurried me down the stairs. "How long do I have to stay with them?"

She tried to wipe the tears from her eyes, but it did no good. "I don't know, baby. Not that long…" Sista Dinah got out of her car when she saw us coming. The smile on her face was sad as she waved at me.

I got a bad feeling, turning to face my mom I squeezed her hand. "When you coming back?" She didn't answer, she just pulled me into a hug that made me feel like this was the last time I was going to see her. Tears burned the back of my eyes.

"Promise me, that when you have children you won't repeat the same mistakes I made, promise you're going to break the chain!" Frowning I opened my mouth to ask her what she was talking about, but she only squeezed me tighter, clutching my coat with desperate fingers.

"Promise to break the chain!" Her anxious voice rang out into the night.

"I promise," I muttered through my tears. She nodded her head lifting her mouth in a one-sided smile.

"Earth's Cry was always yours, she's going to sing for you, baby." With jerky movements she rubbed her hand through her hair that had one time been very beautiful, but was now a matted mess on her head.

"You just wait…it's going to sing for you." Then she turned and walked away.

Sista Dinah put her hands on my shoulder, I don't know if it was to stop me from running after her or to simply relay the message that she was here, and she wouldn't let me fall, but either way I needed it. Together we watched her until she disappeared down the street and around the corner. That was the last time I would ever see my mother.

I told myself that night that I would do as she asked and break the chain. But sometimes, no matter how hard we try, we unwittingly end up repeating our parents' mistakes.

1

THE KIDNAPPING

"History informs us of past mistakes from which we can learn without repeating them. It also inspires us and gives confidence and hope bred of victories already won."

— WILLIAM H. HASTIE

15 YEARS LATER...

EARTH

"Are you sure that's the *little* brother?" Brianna, my best friend asked. "Dang! He is fiiiinnnee!"

I took in the authoritative man that the maître d' was showing to the corner table that had been reserved for my dead husband's younger brother. Yes, he was very handsome. His powerful strides crossed the floor in a way that made me feel as if he was the ruler and we his subjects. The way the maître d' walked next to him with his head bowed only reinforced that feeling.

"Yeah, I'm pretty sure. The reservation had been made for Mike Black for 2 o'clock." I looked at my watch. "It's 2 on the dot."

"If they Indians, why they ain't got names like Running Bull or Dances with Wind?"

So lost I was in my head I didn't even hear her question. My nerves were a wreck and my palms were sweaty. I was seconds away from cowering and running for my life.

Many times my late husband Mitch warned me never to come in contact with his family. They were a powerful group that had generated their wealth through a string of casinos that had been in their family for decades. My husband was Native American from the Seminole tribe, he said his immediate family had long lost all the things that made them human and were a heartless bunch that destroyed innocent people like me and our daughter Rain for the pure sport of it.

He also told me many times that his family's power and influence knew no bounds. And that there was none as powerful as his older brother Melech, who was in control of their family's vast wealth.

Bria shook her head slightly. "I don't know, Earth. He don't really look Indian to me or like a little brother."

This time her ignorant words penetrated my thoughts. I punched her in the arm.

"Ouch! Bit--" She hissed grabbing her arm mean mugging me.

"They not Indians, Bria. Indians live in India... They Natives..." I rolled my eyes at her. "And yeah, you right, he don't look like either."

The man who had just sat at the table was darker than Crazy Larry and he wore his authority like a garment. It made the custom-made grey suit he sported pale in comparison. Unlike Mitch, who looked like a full-blooded Native, the baby brother looked to be of mixed heritage. Although he was very dark and could easily pass as an African American, his high cheek bones proclaimed his Seminole lineage.

For just a moment as he was undoing the button on his jacket so that he could sit, his gaze fell on me. I inhaled. The raw uncut strength that came from his eyes was breathtaking. Quickly I looked away pretending to straighten out the cloth on the table next to us. Brianna and I were dressed very similar to the waitresses here, not enough to rouse the suspicion of the employees, but enough to trick the eyes of the guest.

In reality, neither Bria nor I could afford to use the restroom in this establishment. We had come to kidnap a man. To be exact, my husband's little brother Michael. My gaze went back to the corner table. I had not expected his little brother to be so…so…

"Dominating." Brianna said as if she was in my head.

"What was that?" I asked her.

"He's so dominating. I don't think we have enough dope to put out that big body. Did Larry give you enough? We're going to need an elephant tranquilizer."

"We have enough, and we need to move fast before we draw the attention of the maître d'." We quickly made our way to the server's hall. I took the drugs that I had acquired for this purpose out my pocket. My hands shook as I emptied the whole pack into the pitcher of water. Using a spoon, I gave it a good stirring.

"Are you supposed to use the whole thing?" Bria asked from where she stood at the door keeping look out.

"I don't know! I think—" I exhaled trying to calm my nerves. I couldn't remember how much of the drugs Larry said to add.

Goodness! I couldn't believe I was doing this. I couldn't believe I was getting ready to kidnap this man. Please Heavenly Father, forgive me, but they left me no other choice. They were trying to take my Rain from me and I couldn't let that happen.

I couldn't let her go to a home where there was no love. Mitch said he came up in a cold, loveless environment. His parents were mutli-billionaires and didn't know the meaning of love. They had raised Mitch and his two brothers to be machines, as cold as them.

And now they were coming after my Rain, all because they found a little weed in my pee.

I tried to hand Bria the pitcher of water. "Here go, pour him some water."

She looked at me as if I had gone lame. "You crazy as hell if you think I'm going anywhere near that man. He look like he will get up from that table and just..." She searched for the words. "Step on you. I don't want to get stepped on, Earth!"

Her response flustered my already frayed nerves.

"Dammit, Bria! What did you even come for?" She gave me that better-you-than-me smile as she patted my shoulder.

"For moral support, my sista." I rolled my eyes at her as I knocked her hand off my shoulder.

Dammit!

I took several deep breaths. *Okay, I can do this. I can do this.*

I had no other choice. They were trying to take my baby. So, in exchange I will take theirs. Mitch said his brother Melech, who was the head of that heartless clan, actually had a soft spot for their younger brother Michael. I would just use that soft spot to get Melech to sign over his rights to Rain.

I know, it sounds crazy.

Believe it or not, it was a crazy Jamaican who gave me the idea. My boss and landlord Larry. Or rather, Crazy Larry. After my last court date, when the judge told me I had one month and thirty days to say my last goodbyes to my daughter before I had to turn her over to the Blacks, I came home and cried and yelled out my frustration at the injustice of the whole situation to Larry.

I was not a bad mother. I loved my child and took care of her because she was all I had. I was losing her because I was poor and could not afford a good attorney that could go against the team of overpaid vipers that had come to represent the Blacks. I don't know whose idea it was to drug test me, but once the results came back positive for weed, the Blacks' attorneys made it seem like I was out on the street selling a$$ for rocks.

The judge didn't even grant me visitation rights. He said he felt it would be better for the child to cut all ties to me and begin a new life with her father's side of the family. After he adjourned the case, one of Black's lawyers asked him if they were still on for lunch.

"This would have never happened in Jamaica. We would have extracted our own form of justice to deal with the boars." Boars is what Larry called any government figure.

"What would you have done?" I asked him. At that point I was desperate. Rain was the only good thing in my life. Without her, I might as well be dead.

He'd looked at me through a sea of ganja smoke. "It's simple, you take the younger boy for ransom."

And so, the idea was born.

That night I tossed and turned in my bed thinking about it. I mean, what did I have to lose? I figured I had a fifty-fifty chance of pulling this thing off. It was a far better percentage than watching my daughter be carried away to strangers who didn't even bother to show up to court in person.

Brie touched my shoulder again bringing me out of my thoughts. "You can do this!"

I nodded. "I don't have a choice."

After squaring my shoulders, I quickly crossed the room to Michael's table. I walked with a purpose, carrying the pitcher in one hand while placing the other behind my back like the other servers did.

The closer I got to the table the more the power that exuded from this man enveloped me... suffocating me.

"Would you like some water?" I asked. I couldn't help the fact that my voice trembled a bit. I was almost crippled with my fear. There was no doubt in my mind that Mitch had been right when he said he was the only one in his family that was not dangerous.

This man felt extremely dangerous. Slowly his deep midnight eyes rose to mine... and oh ya'll! It felt as if somebody snatched the breath straight out of my body. Being this close to him gave me the same rush one would feel if they were standing on the tracks in front of an oncoming train.

"Are you my waitress?" His deep baritone was like smoke. It slowly traveled up my body to pool in my belly, stirring up the butterflies that were already there.

I did my best to smile, but I know my lips quivered.

"No, I'm not. I just came to offer you water. Your waitress will be here momentarily."

He smiled and I'm telling you, that pitcher nearly fell from my hand. Saying he was handsome was an understatement. It looked as if he was fresh from the barber. His low fade, beard, and mustache were trimmed perfectly around his angled dark face. His good looks coupled with the authoritative power that clung to him was enough to be any girl's undoing.

I stood here about to drug this man so that I could kidnap him, and the only thing I could think was, when was the last time I made love? It had been over five years.

"In that case, sure, I would like some water." The way he was looking at me was unnerving, so unnerving that I had to focus on not shaking as I poured his water. But it did little good, because I was shaking so badly a little of his water spilt out on the table cloth.

His sharp gaze took in my action, missing nothing. Slowly it rose up my arm, my breasts, my neck, and lips to settle on my eyes.

"Nervous?"

His voice was so deep I could feel the bass of it in the soles of my feet.

I gave him an awkward smile. "It's my first day. Your waitress will be here directly." I turned and walked back towards the break down station. I had to force myself not to run.

"He's drinking it!" Bria whispered excitedly when I walked past her to pour out the rest of the liquid in the sink. After I was done I washed it out the best I could before laying it down on the floor. Hopefully whoever came in here behind us will see it on the floor and take it to the dishwasher.

A server hurried in balancing two cups of tea on her tray. "Oh!" she said startled.

"Are you guys new?" Bria shook her head.

"We just needed ice." She picked up an ice cube and chugged it in her mouth. "See."

The waitress slowly nodded looking confused, but we didn't wait around to try and explain things further to her. Quickly we crossed the room, being careful not to draw Michael's attention and left out the front doors.

"Wow! That was easy. What do we do now?" I looked at the bright smile on Bria's face and wanted to slap her. Sure, it was easy for *her*, she's not the one who had to walk the tight rope over a fire pit.

"Now we wait!"

When we got back into my little broke down Corolla, I

reached up and pulled the wig off my head. Bria, who was not just my best friend, but also my beautician, had braided my long thick hair into really cute cornrows that fell to the center of my back. While that style was super fresh on the block, I wore the wig because it would have drawn too much attention in that uppity restaurant. I doubted real seriously if it attracted the kind of people that wore braids.

A few minutes later, two more men joined Michael. I took the binoculars I'd borrowed from Larry out of my bag to get a better look. One of the men looked to be Native American and the other was white. The handsome Native American man looked younger than Michael. Maybe he was a younger relative or something.

"What's happening?" Bria asked leaning over my shoulder. I shrugged trying to dislodge her, but it did no good.

"Nothing yet."

"Gurl, I ain't never seen no black Ind—" She caught herself when I turned to look at her. "I mean I ain't never seen no black Native American before, but damn he fine! And he built too. Was Mitch as handsome as his brother?"

"Yeah." I told her, but it was a lie. Mitch couldn't hold a candle to his baby brother. They favored each other, you could tell they were siblings. But where his brother wore that air of authority very well, Mitch had none.

However, to an eighteen-year-old girl it appeared at first as if he had plenty. When I first met Mitch, I thought he was Puerto Rican, he talked like he was from the hood and he dressed like he was from the hood. I had no way of knowing he was Native American.

He'd approached me after hearing me play the violin at an event that Larry was catering. He said I was so sexy playing *that thing* that he wanted to put me in a music video that he was shooting for one of the rap artists on his label.

REDEMPTION: EARTH'S CRY

At first I waved him off, offended that he wanted to hire me for a music video and not to go in the studio and play my instrument. Then I realized he didn't even listen to me play, he had not gotten past my looks and was just trying to spit some lame game my way, like I ain't heard the record label script before.

I mean, I ain't claiming to be the prettiest girl in the world, but I know I'm attractive. Men have been coming at me since I was like ten. So it was safe to say when you heard one pick up line you heard them all, but he insisted, showing me a business card with his label's information on it.

At the time I was working two jobs as well as going to school so that I could help Sista Dinah and Brotha Abraham pay the rent. Brotha Abraham's back pain prevented him from getting the hours he used to get down at the city dump, which meant Sista Dinah and I had to make up for the loss, so I really could've used the extra cash.

"How much does it pay?" I asked him.

"Two-hundred dollars a day."

"How many days will I have to do?"

"One, maybe two."

"Do I have to get naked or near naked?" He paused before he answered the question. At the same time his gaze raked slowly over my body. I could see that he was attracted to me and was trying to size me up and see what kind of girl I was.

Curious to see if this guy, who was not of my race could read what kind of woman I was, I kept my mouth closed. Slowly his eyes took in my natural hair that I wore pulled back into a pony tail and braided down my back. Then they lowered to my green tank top, then down farther to the army print cargo pants I wore, and then finally they settled on my Timberland covered feet.

I held up an eyebrow when his gaze finally made its way back up to mine.

He shook his head. "Naw, not a girl like you. If you agree to do this, I will make you the star of the video."

I was impressed, so I agreed. True to his word, he was shooting a video. It was an artist I had never heard before, but the gig paid two-hundred dollars. After it was done he asked me out on a date and I agreed because he was treating me like a queen.

As the months went by, I would learn that he was a hard worker and very ambitious. He was building the record label from the ground up with no help from his powerful family. He carried feelings about that. To me it seemed as if he wanted to become a big name just so that he could say he was better than his older brother.

He believed Melech was trying to hinder his success, which was why when he went to him for money he refused. Apparently, Melech handled all the family's business and had the final say on where any monies went.

"Look! He's leaving!" Bria screeched from beside me, bringing me back to the present. I lifted the binoculars and watched as Michael stumbled to his car. The drug was working. Right then a horrible thought came to mind.

"Oh no! What if he tries to drive?" She and I both jumped out the car at the same time. Kidnapping is one thing, murder was a whole other ballgame. We hurried across the busy street to the restaurant parking lot just in time to see Michael sit down heavily in the driver seat of a car that looked like it came from another planet.

"Damn, that's a nice car!" Bria said sounding winded. We slowed down to a walk waiting to see what he was going to do next. He never lifted his legs into the car.

"I think he's out, come on!" Quickly we crossed the parking lot.

"Help me get his legs in." I cried as I tried to lift them with no success. Bria went around to the passenger door and pulled while I pushed.

"You ladies need a hand?" A deep voice asked from behind us.

We whipped around to see a dark man in a cowboy hat that cast half his face in shadow leaning casually against a tree watching us. He looked like a bonified black cowboy.

"Ummm," I opened my mouth to tell him this was my brother and he was drunk. But for some reason I couldn't lie to him. It was something about him I couldn't put my finger on. He straightened and came towards us. Bria and I moved out his way as he leaned in and effortlessly lifted the sleeping man moving him into the passenger seat.

"Thank you," I told him when he stood back up out the car. He tipped his hat.

"You're welcome, daughter." He lifted one side of his lips in a smile before he just moseyed on away. Both Bria and I stood there for a second staring after him, astonished that the stranger had just made this kidnapping breezy.

"What the hell was that?" She asked after a while.

"A blessing!" I said snapping into action. "I'll drive him, you take my car."

"Wait!" She called after me. "How we gon' get him up the stairs to your place? We couldn't even get his legs in the car."

"Larry should be there, he can help us." She nodded before turning to head back to my car. I slid behind the wheel and for the first time in my life, experienced pure luxury. Don't get me wrong, Mitch had a nice car, but it was nothing like this.

At first sight I thought it was a Jaguar, but now that I was in it, I saw that it was a Benz by the logo on the steering wheel.

"Michael, you have a really nice car here." I told the sleeping man as I reached over him to put on his seatbelt before putting on mine. As I led the way back to the hood I couldn't help but give the car a little gas to see what it could do, but then I thought better of it bringing it back to the speed limit. Last thing I needed was for the police to pull me over.

When we got to my place I pulled the car around back in the alley. My small apartment was located over Larry's Afrocentric Book Store and Juice Bar.

"Wheeew! Look at this ride!" He said in his heavy Jamaican accent coming out wiping his hands on a towel. The sounds of Bob Marley's Redemption Song followed him out the door. Larry was a middle aged, ganja smoking Rastafarian, who wore his long dreads wrapped in a head wrap, because he didn't believe in letting them go free in the heart of Babylon, which is what the Rastas called America.

"Hey Mon, you can look later, I need you to help me get this mon upstairs to me place." I said mimicking his Jamaican Patwah.

He shook his head. "No mon, me don't want to be an accessory to this crime."

Folding my arms, I looked at him as if he had gone crazy.

"Are you kidding me? Don't forget this was your idea. Also, don't forget that you made the little elixir that I poured in his drink."

He stood there for a minute looking at me through his blood shot eyes.

"Oh!" Was all he said before he came and helped get the man out the car.

It took Larry, Bria and I damn near an hour to get the big body upstairs. The whole time Larry complained that his heart was going to give out due to lifting such heavy weight with a chest full of ganja smoke.

"What now?" Bria asked as we all breathing heavily stared down at the body sprawled on my kitchen floor. The man was big, even passed out he carried an air of authority, making my little apartment feel even smaller.

I chewed on my nail as I thought about it. Rain was at Bria's mother's house, who wouldn't be bringing her back till morning, which meant I had all night to try and convince Michael here to give his big brother a call and tell him to release his hold on my child if he ever wanted to see him again.

"Help me get him up in the chair." Together the three of us got him in the chair. Larry went back down stairs and came back with rope. After we had him tied securely I let out a sigh of relief.

"I can't believe I went through with this." I told my two friends as we stood staring down at the man who still slept.

"Me cant' either." Larry muttered. "Well now ladies, I will leave you. The interrogation is all yours." I reached for his hand.

"Thank you, Larry."

"Don't thank me yet. There is a good chance you will end up in prison for this." Bria's mouth fell opened as she shook her head.

"Why would you say something like that? If this man get free I doubt if he calls the cops. He seems like the type that handle things like this on his own. It's a good chance she gon' end up floating at the bottom of the Bay for this."

Larry looked back at the sleeping man. "You know what Bria Bria, me think you're right."

"Thanks guys for all your votes of confidence. Get out, Larry." I went to push him out the door.

"Will you be showing up for work tomorrow?" He asked on his way out.

"If I'm not dead or in jail." I shut the door in his face. "Okay, let's wake him." I told Bria clapping my hands together. I was ready to get this over with and this man out of my small space.

"Wait!" Bria screeched. "What's the plan? I mean, we got to get our tough faces going right? We got to be intimidating." I nodded.

"Yeah we do, let me see what you got." She frowned her face up really good.

"Wake up, fool, you being kidnapped!" As she spoke she grabbed the front of her pants.

"Umm, Bria…What you grabbing?"

"My gat, fool!" I shook my head as I went to my kitchen drawer to take out the matches. We were in trouble.

2

MELECH

The acrid smell of smoke brought me to. I jerked up in the chair blinking as the two beautiful women came into focus. When the hell did I go to sleep? The last thing I remember was suddenly feeling very tired, so much so that I had to tell Michael and his business partner Jeff that I will have to meet with them another day to go over the proposition for the hotels they wanted to open in the East Bay area.

I remembered Mike telling me I needed a vacation as I stood. I chuckled telling him he was right, I was just thinking that very thought this morning. It had been nearly ten years since my last vacation. After that I don't remember much else. I think I must have been drugged.

"The waitress." I muttered.

I had been so caught up in how breathtakingly beautiful she was that I let the fact that she was awfully nervous slip my notice. I narrowed my eyes on the light-skinned woman with the cornrows. She had been the waitress. She must have been wearing a wig. But it was something else about her. Even earlier when I saw her she felt familiar. I knew that beautiful face from somewhere.

They were both doing something strange with their faces. It looked like they were trying to give me threatening looks. That's when I realized I was tied. My first response was to burn the rope, but something made me pause.

I just remembered where I knew the pretty light-skinned girl from. Her name was Earth and she was Mitch's wife. How could I forget that when I secretly lusted for her the whole time they were married?

"What's going on, why do you have me tied to this chair?" I raised my voice a bit and took in the fact that it frightened both of them.

What the hell? Now I was good and curious.

Earth inhaled, gathering her courage before she took a cautious step forward.

"Listen, Michael. I'm going to give you some instructions and you're going to follow them, no questions asked."

She thought I was Michael

I nearly smiled as I settled back in my chair. Just this morning I had been thinking that my life has gotten mundane and I needed a new scenario. I looked around Earth's apartment. It was small, but cozy. It had stamps of her personality all over it. From the colorful curtains, to the mud cloth pillows on her couch. A couch that was old, but still looked quite comfortable.

The apartment screamed of somebody making do with what they had. She had taken her lemons and made a pleasing-to-the-eye cup of lemonade.

"Whatever you say, ma'am. Just don't hurt me." Why not have a little fun with it? She drew herself up and I nearly laughed out loud when her little friend gave her a look that said. *Yeah, you told him!*

"Now, I'm going to pick up this phone and dial your older brother's number. And you are going to tell him to release the hold he has on my daughter Rain."

I had no idea what she was talking about. "What hold?"

"Custody. Your family's lawyers took me to court to get custody of my daughter." I shook my head.

"Are you sure? 'Cause I know nothing about it."

"Well, maybe they don't tell you everything, with you being the youngest, but it's true. I was married to Mitch and he and I had a daughter. He died before she was born. I've been raising her by myself for the last five years." As she spoke her beautiful eyes flashed with the passion of her words. My gaze fell to her full lips. It was those plush beauties that had caught my attention the first time I saw her picture. I licked mine as a ravenous hunger to taste hers fell over me.

"Somehow your big brother found out about her and sicked his lawyers on me. The judge ruled in his favor and told me I have thirty days to say my last goodbyes. To my child!" She yelled the last of her statement.

"Do that sound right to you? I'm not a bad mother. I mean no, I can't afford a mansion." She gestured to her humble apartment around her. The way she opened her arms caused her shirt to draw tight over her full breast.

"But Rain has everything she needs. Her room is full of the toys and clothes that I bought for her. How is it fair your family can now show up out of nowhere and take her from me?!" She was getting herself good and worked up.

This woman was amazingly beautiful. When I first saw her I wondered, how in the hell had my screw up of a brother found a woman like this? She wasn't his type at all. Mitch was known for going after the fast girls. What was it about this innocent beauty that had caught his eye? No doubt knowing Mitch, it was for a nefarious reason.

"It's not fair." I told her.

Her eyes brightened as a look of relief settled on her face. She was very naive. She had no clue of what she'd just done. Hell, even I was having a hard time wrapping my mind around it. This woman had just given herself to me. She'd flat out fell right into my hands.

"So, you'll do it? You'll make the call?" I lifted one side of my mouth in a grin. The girl woman next to her put her hand on her chest.

"Gracious!" She muttered to herself. But I didn't look away from Earth's beautiful gaze. She was Mine!

"No!" I finally spoke.

3

IF ALL ELSE FAILS

EARTH

I tilted my head slightly, completely taken off guard. "Excuse me, did you say no?"

I couldn't help the surprise in my voice. I had not expected him to say that.

Looking as calm as if he was sitting on the beach watching the sunrise he nodded his head.

"I did."

His voice was so deep and sure, strength poured from it to strangle me. I opened my mouth to say something but snapped it back shut when I realized I didn't have anything to say. I had practiced my response to a hundred scenarios, and him flat out refusing to call was not one of them.

I cleared my throat, careful to keep my threatening face in place. "If you will excuse me, I need to have a word with my associate."

With a one-sided grin on his face that didn't reach his hard eyes, he nodded his head. "Not a problem."

That irritated the hell out of me, did he just give me permission to leave the room? I narrowed my eyes at him.

"I wasn't asking your permission." His look never changed.

"Of course not, you're in charge." It didn't feel like he really understood that.

Slowly I walked towards him, careful not to get too close. I couldn't shake the feeling that although he was tied, he could get free if he wanted to. And if he got free, Bria and I didn't stand a chance.

"Don't you forget it." I growled in my Clint Eastwood voice as I pointed at him.

Clearly suppressing a grin, he nodded. "I won't."

"Good."

Turning I grabbed Bria's arm and practically dragged her down the short hall to my bedroom. It took everything within me to walk normal and not show the fact that I was freaking out on the inside. As soon as my bedroom door closed, we both looked at each other and spoke at the same time.

"He said no!"

Bria's eyes were rounded in fear, letting me know that she was trying not to panic as well. I began to pace, as all the bravery I'd just faked in the kitchen faded away. In desperation I may have made a foolish decision. Up until this moment, I thought I would do anything to get my baby back, even if it meant going to jail. At least she would know what all her mama was willing to sacrifice for her. But now that I was right here faced with the possibility, I didn't feel as brave as I did before.

"Oh man, I'm going to jail!" I stopped pacing as an even scarier thought came to me. "Maybe he said no, because even as we speak there's a group of mobsters heading this way." I raked my hand back across my braids as Mitch's warnings came to my mind.

What had he told me about Melech? Something about him being terribly feared amongst his people. He said that the folks in their tribe called Melech the devil. And I think I just realized why.

"His older brother owns casinos. There is a good chance Melech is some kind of mob boss and we've gone and kidnapped his younger brother!"

Bria frowned. "An Ind—" she began, but my frown caused her to correct her statement.

"A Native American mob boss?" she shook her head. "Naw, I ain't never seen that."

"Just because you ain't never seen it don't mean it don't exist. A man with that kind of power ain't no stranger to killing people."

She shook her head. "You're jumping to conclusions. How can they be headed this way if they don't even know we have him? Our plan is a good one, don't start messing it up with your doubt."

I nodded my head needing to grasp on to something. "Yeah, you're right."

She puffed out her chest. "I know I'm right, now we just need him to make the call to his brother to convince him to release his rights on Rain and also not to kill us. We already have the fact that he too thinks what they did to you was wrong on our side."

I nodded, yeah, we did have that. Michael said he didn't think it was right that they were taking my baby from me, so maybe he'll speak up for us and convince Melech not to kill us, or call a hit on us, or whatever men who own casinos did.

"But how are we going to get him to make the call?" I asked her.

She thought about it for a minute before she snapped her fingers. "I got it! Let's make him call by gunpoint."

I exhaled as all my hopes died. *Heavenly Father, give me the strength.*

"It's just one problem…I don't have a gun." It took everything within me not to scream the last of my words at her.

I was getting ready to lose my cool. He was not supposed to say no! I began pacing again. Now what was I going to do with him? As long as I had him we were safe. Bria was right, nobody will come for us if they didn't know we had him.

Well, nobody knew except for the dark man in the cowboy hat, and something was telling me he wouldn't rat us out. Something about him felt…familiar, paternal.

I shook my head, I was losing it…

Bria went to her overnight backpack that sat in the corner of my bedroom, squatting, she began to rummage through it.

"I know you don't have a gun," she said before she came to her feet. "But I do."

Turning around she held a pretty little chrome and pearl .22 in her palm.

My mouth dropped. "Where did you get that from?"

A clever grin came to her face. "You remember that dude I used to talk to that worked over there at that car wash on Sycamore Street?"

I nodded my head, even though I had no idea who she was talking about. I was happy to see the gun, but it was making my skin crawl. I had never been in the presence of one before.

"Well, he went and bought himself a nine that looked like this and I was like, *eww, I want one*. He got me the matching .22. So, he and I could be on some Bonnie and Clyde kind of sh*t. It's nice ain't it?" As she spoke she did a little dance.

I smiled nodding my head. It was nice, but most importantly it was a weapon that can be used to get Michael to see things my way. I began to mimic Bria's little dance. Once again, my girl had come through and saved the day.

"He didn't buy me no bullets though." Her words brought my movements to a halt.

"What?!"

She shook her head. "We ain't got no bullets, but that ain't going to matter, cause Ol' boy out there don't know we ain't got none."

Hmmm…

You know, there comes a point in every friendship when one friend must accept the truth about the other. Brianna was mentally disabled. I mean, don't get me wrong, I have been suspecting this about her for some time now.

She and I had been best friends since I moved in with Sista Dinah and Brother Abraham when I was twelve years old. Sista Dinah and Brianna's grandmother are sisters. Having Brianna in my life made it a little easier to deal with the fact that my mother had left me. Whenever the pain from that became too much to bear, Brianna and her crazy tactics were always welcomed.

But now that I was older, and the pain of losing my mother had long since faded, I had to face the facts about Brianna, she wasn't right in the head.

"You want us to go out there with that little itty-bitty, bite size gun without any bullets?" I spoke slowly to make sure she and I were understanding each other clearly.

She looked at me like…duh!

"First of all, this," She held up the little toy-sized gun. "Ain't all that little. And to a scared man, it's gon' look like an AK-47."

For just a moment I just stared at Bria with my Kevin Hart face. "An AK-47? Is that what it's going to look like?"

She nodded. "Ol' boy so scared right now, this gon' be all it take to tip him on over and get him to make that call."

I thought about the man who sat tied to the chair in my

kitchen. Nothing about him said he was even a little bit afraid of us. It almost felt as if we were entertaining him.

"He didn't look all that afraid to me." I muttered.

She waved away my statement. "Girl, he's terrified. You don't know how to read men like I do. The only guy you ever been with was Mitch. You don't have the eye."

I smacked my lips. "What eye? You need to quit it, your mama and grandma was just as strict as Sista Dinah, they didn't let you date either."

She held her little gun in the air. "They didn't have to let me, I did it anyway, unlike you. You was too big of a chicken."

I didn't respond to her. Bria would never understand. It wasn't that I was a chicken, I just didn't want to make Sista Dinah and Brother Abraham regret taking me in. I didn't want them to give me away like my mom did. So, I made sure I was never too much of a burden on them.

They said they didn't want me dating till I was eighteen, and I did them one better, I didn't date till I was nineteen. It just so happened to also be the year I met Mitch. Secretly at first, but six months later when we found out we were pregnant, we snuck away and got married. He bought a place for us an hour away in Tampa. I was ecstatic, because that was my first time ever leaving Kissimmee.

However, Sista Dinah and Brotha Abraham was not all that thrilled with my choice of husband. They didn't like the fact that he never came around. They had only met him once, the day we went to the house and told them we were married and I was moving out. They were not happy about that, not in the least, but once they found out I was pregnant, they were at least glad he was doing the honorable thing and marrying me.

Although I wouldn't say life was good after that, it was tolerable. Mitch did have his problems. But then, five months later, Mitch died in a car accident. One of his family's lawyers came to visit me the next day. He told me that not only was Mitch broke, he was in debt. Thankfully the family was willing to take care of the debt so that I wouldn't have to, but in the same breath, there was nothing left for me.

Then he informed me that they were taking Mitch's body to bury him in the way of their people and that I was basically not invited. Because at the time I wasn't showing, I didn't bother telling him about the baby. I just wanted to be away from those people. Mitch was right, his family was heartless. I said my goodbyes to him and then packed up my measly belongings and moved back to Kissimmee.

When I got back, I didn't bother going back to Sista Dinah's and Brotha Abraham's, although they wanted me to. I would soon have a baby, and they were getting up in age and deserved some peace. So, I lucked up and found this place over Larry's Bookstore…The rent was five fifty a month, but he sweetened the deal by offering me a job at his store. I jumped on it.

Plus, I liked to read and Larry didn't mind if I borrowed books and read them. He even allowed me to bring Rain to work on the days she had off from school. So, I had a steady place to live, a steady job, and plenty of cultural books to read. I couldn't beat that.

However, the one thing I haven't had time for was men. So maybe Bria was right. She on the other hand have been in several relationships since she's turned eighteen.

"I don't know, it might just be crazy enough to work." I begrudgingly muttered.

Her face brightened. "It will work, if not, I got a plan B."

Rubbing my sweaty palms on my pants I nodded. "Good, it's always good to have a plan B."

My gaze went to Earth's Cry sitting on its stand in front of my bedroom window where it sat untouched for a little over five years. My fingers twitched, now needing to play it about as much as I needed to breathe, because I was crazy nervous.

Earth's Cry had always been my go to whenever my emotions were unstable, like they were now. But the last time I played it was on the night I'd found out Mitch had been killed in a car crash, it had sung for me for the first time.

I know that sounds strange to you guys; it being a violin should sing what you play. Except that's not what happened with Earth's Cry that night.

It felt as if something took over my hands and they played what it wanted them to play. The song intertwined around me, taking me to a different place. And what it showed was so horrible that it left me crying and shaking on the floor. The vision I was shown affected me so much that it caused me to go into early labor with Rain. I wondered when my mother said that one day it would sing for me, had she known what its song would be.

"Earth!" Bria huffed waving her little gun in front of my face.

"Will you snap out of it? Now isn't the time for you to get lost in your magical violin. Let's do this."

I wish I never tried to tell Bria what had happened to me that night. Ever since then, she's been teasing me about being afraid to use my magical violin.

I blinked looking away from Earth's Cry. "Yeah, you're right. Let's do this."

MELECH

Mitch's widow showed more bravery today than Mitch had in his whole entire pathetic life... She is a bit naïve, but brave. Leave it to him to have not set up his wife and child to be taken care of should something happen to him, causing her to result to such desperate measures to try and save her child. I'd been so busy keeping my stepfather's legacy thriving, I had not even been aware that they had a kid.

When it was first reported to me that Mitch had gotten married, I requested the file on his bride so that I could make sure he hadn't done anything foolish, like get involved with any of my enemies that was always looking for a way in so that they could take what was mine. The file had included a couple of pictures of her.

After confirming that she was nothing for me to be concerned about, I took the time to study her photos. My investigator had caught her at the library. She had a pile of books in front of her and was taking notes on what she was reading. I remembered she had a red lollipop in her mouth. The pictures were taken at different stages of her sucking the candy in and out of her enticing lips. I could remember getting an erection so powerful it hurt.

It surprised the hell out of me, because it was an erection that would not be ignored. I had to call my mistress at the time to get relief. As I drove into her, it was Earth's face that I saw, her lips I imagined wrapped around me the way they had been wrapped around that lollipop.

After I emptied myself, I hadn't thought any about her, writing her off as a silly fortune hunter who fell for Mitch's silky lies. No doubt he had sold her on one of his many endeavors that never worked out, because he didn't have the fortitude to see anything through, and she had bought it. I could remember thinking, what a shame for such beauty to go to waste on a gold digger.

Like I said before, I am a very busy man and don't have time to worry about little things like wayward family members, I left those kinds of things in my step aunt and uncle's capable hands.

I know that sounds cruel… seeing as to how Mitch was my brother.

The fact was, Mitch was a screw up and had been one since we were kids. He and I did not share a father. I didn't share a father with any of my brothers, who had all been sired by my stepfather, Frank. The fact that Frank died, leaving his chain of casinos to me has always been a source of friction between my brothers and me.

Well, all except Mikey, my youngest brother who didn't even pretend he wanted the responsibility. Frank had a son by his first wife, who was the same age as I, Hawk. Hawk, like Mitch, who was Frank's oldest son by my mother, felt as if the business should have been left to them since they had come from his loins. Mitch had been easy to deal with, he's a screw up, leave him to it and he will be the cause of his own destruction, as you can see.

However, Hawk was a different story altogether. When Frank had called the four of us to his office to tell us his decision to leave the business to me, Hawk had not taken the news well.

"Are you serious?!" He all but yelled as he suddenly stood causing his chair to tip over backwards.

"You going to give what should rightfully be mine to your whore's nigger bastard?!" I shot out of my seat at him, but Frank made it to me first.

"Please son, calm yourself, please!" He looked me directly in the eye and pleaded with me not to kill his son. Grinding down on my teeth I tried to control my rage, but I was losing it. The drapes burst into flames and so did the chair Hawk had caused to fall to the floor.

He jumped away from it when he felt the fire kiss the back of his legs and hurried to the door. When he looked back at me, there was real fear in his eyes, but there was also determination.

"Our people are right about you, you are the devil! And my father has gone and left you my birthright!" His eyes filled with tears.

"That's twice you've taken what I should have inherited." His voice was barely over a whisper. "The power you carry should have gone to the first born, my father is chief of this tribe, it should have been mine... and now—" He shook his head.

"And now you've gone and taken my wealth as well. You may scare our people and obviously my coward of a father, but I will find a way to beat you and take back what's mine. I won't stop till I do!" And then he was gone from the office.

"Melech, listen to my voice. Fight it son, please, fight it."

Frank spoke calmly, trying to soothe me. Balling up my fist, it took every last bit of restraint I had learned from my grandfather not to imagine the halls burning as Hawk headed for the front door.

"If you don't relax you will kill us all. Please relax, son. Here, take deep breaths with me."

I took those breaths, but had it not been for Frank and the love and respect I had for him, I would have fried Hawk's ass.

I don't take kindly to threats, no way, no how, never did and probably never will. Now that Frank and my mother were dead, it was open season. If Hawk ever resurfaced, I was going to bury him.

My thoughts were cut short by the sound of the bedroom door opening. The girls had foolishly disappeared in there, leaving me in here by myself for a good while, long enough for me to get free from these ropes and slit both of their throats if I was so inclined to.

My eyes settled on Earth, who had just licked her lips nervously, leaving the delectable beauties moist in the wake of her tongue. It just so happened that I was not inclined to go anywhere, not till I get my taste.

And I will be getting my taste...

In fact, I'm going to be getting more than that. I will not be satisfied until I'm buried deep within in her womb.

"Alright Mikey boy, now you getting ready to play my game." The friend said as she walked around Earth pointing a very tiny gun at me. I tilted my head slightly to the right as my gaze fell on the gun.

"I don't take kindly to threats."

Her mouth opened in surprise as a scream tore from her throat. The sound of her flesh being singed by the suddenly scorching hot handle of the gun filled the room before she let it fall from her hand.

"Ouuuchhhhh!!!!" She howled, waving her burning hand through the air.

EARTH

"Bria, what happened?!" I cried as I tried to comfort my friend, who was jumping around holding her hand as if it was broken. There were tears running down her face.

"My hand!" She yelled. "Owww! My hand!"

"Let me see!" I tried to reach for her hand, but she snatched it out of my grasp, howling in pain.

"Bria, be still so I can see what happened!" My mind raced. I know the gun couldn't have fired because there were no bullets, did she somehow pinch her skin in it?

"Be still!" I yelled at her still trying to catch her hand. After about another twenty seconds of her jumping around and crying she finally was still long enough for us to get a look.

"Oh my God!" Her hand was badly burned. It looked as if she had touched an iron and just let her hand rest on it.

I pulled her to the sink and turned on the cold water. "Hold your hand under there while I call Larry." I told her as I rushed to the phone. A minute later, Larry was walking through the door.

"Wah gwaan?" He asked when he noticed Bria crying and carrying on at the sink.

"I think she burned herself on her gun!"

Larry's eyes widened when I mentioned gun. "Wha, Bria Bria a Quaeffa now?"

He asked me if Bria was a killer now. I shook my head. "No mon, that's the problem."

Larry never really moved too fast to do anything, maybe it was because he was always high or maybe it was just him, but Bria was keeping up so much racket, it actually made poor Larry hurry. Lifting her hand, he turned it this way and that before nodding.

"Sekkle yuhself, mi sue cum back." He told her before he hurried out the door. Her desperate gaze came to me to translate. Sometimes when Larry got too high, he forgot to speak in a way us Americans could understand him. The only reason I understood him is because I've worked for him for the last five years.

"He said be easy, he'll be right back." She nodded before putting her hand back under the water, the way she was moving from one foot to the other showed how much pain she was in. How in the world had she done that? There was really no telling with Brianna.

I exhaled, but swiftly drew my breath back in when I remembered my house guest. In all the commotion, I'd forgotten I still had a man tied to the chair just a few feet away. Goodness, he had not uttered a word in all the mayhem.

The next few minutes were the most awkward of my life. With Bria at the sink lost to her pain, it kind of just left me by myself to deal with Mr. Man. The way he looked at me made me aware that I was still dressed in the ugly black slacks and the white buttoned up shirt that I'd owned since my junior year in high school.

His intense gaze traveled slowly over my body, causing me to feel hot all over. This look of his was past inappropriate.

"Is your friend alright?" His deep voice nearly caused me to jump. I took several deep breaths needing to gain back the control of this situation. I felt like I was losing the upper hand.

"Don't you worry about her." I snapped putting my hand on my hip. "You need to worry about yourself and what I'm going to do to you if you don't make that call!"

One of his eyebrows rose as if he was intrigued. Goodness yall, this man was so damn handsome, he was breaking me down. I was having a full-blown hissy fit inside my head. *Why did he have to be so fine? Why? Why? Why?* He licked his lips and my inside self just melted into a pool of butter.

"I must admit to being more than a little intrigued by the thought of you doing anything to me."

What the hell?!

Before I could tell him off, Larry came back with a bandage and some homemade ointment in a tin jar. My boss was good with plants and herbs. Whenever Rain or I got sick, Larry would have us feeling better in no time.

We all watched as he slathered Bria's hand with the ointment before wrapping it in the bandage. He gave her some pills to take when she got home before he told her idiots shouldn't carry guns. She looked at me to translate.

"He said… you should feel better by morning." I lied. Larry went to deny he'd said that when I gave him a hard look silencing him.

"Earth, I'm so sorry," Bria whined coming to stand next to me. "I need to go home girl. My hand is killing me. Are you going to be able to handle this without me?"

I wanted to scream the word no to her. The man had only been here for a few minutes and he already made me a nervous wreck. And to top it all off, I was more than positive he was sexually attracted to me. I did not want to be left alone with him.

Hell no, I couldn't do this by myself!

But right then her eyes filled with more tears. She was in pain.

I nodded. "Yeah, I got this. Go ahead and get some rest."

"You sure?"

I chuckled, even though I felt like crying. "Of course, get on out of here. Next time you see me, I'm going to have this mess all cleared up." Wrapping her uninjured arm around me she hugged me. For just a second, I clung to her.

"Larry, can you give me a lift home?" She asked turning to look at the older Rasta.

Okay, so let me give yall the rundown about Larry and Bria. They were both my very best friends, but they didn't like each other that much. In fact, they argued a lot. Larry could barely tolerate Bria, because he thought she was simple minded. The way he was now looking at her bore witness to that fact. Bria however, thought Larry looked at her that way because he liked her. In Bria's world, all the men wanted a piece of her.

"Rassclaat." Larry muttered under his breath.

"What was that?" Bria asked him.

He exhaled. "Yeah mon, me tak you home." When she left the room to get her things, Larry turned to look at me.

"Why do you hang out with her?"

I shook my head. "Forget that mon, me ave bigger problems, don't you know?" I gestured to the man tied to the chair.

For just a moment, he looked surprised. In all the mayhem even he'd forgotten the man who sat quietly observing us.

Chuckling he shook his head. "Yuh cyaan duh noh'n bout it fi now, memba seh wen chubble kech yuh, pikni shut fit yuh."

Larry had a saying for every situation. He'd basically just told me: desperate situations call for desperate measures. And ain't it the truth?

As they were leaving out, Larry pulled me to the side.

"Mi don't think you ave much to worry about. That mon wants you. If all else fails, there's always that."

I followed them out to the hall and to the stairs, trying to prolong not being alone with Michael.

"I know you not suggesting I sleep with him?"

Larry chuckled as he followed Bria down the stairs. "Wen chubble kech yuh, pikni shut fit yuh." He called back up.

4

ALONE AT LAST

EARTH

I leaned my back against my front door taking in my prisoner.

My prisoner???

One of the things I discovered about us humans is most times we let our vanity make a fool of us. We get these images of self and when something happens to prove that our self-image had been all a figment of our imagination, we shatter.

This strong black man looked too powerful to be at the mercy of anyone, let alone me. He stared back at me with a hard gaze that made me feel that the only reason he was here tied to my chair was because he wanted to be.

Could that be the case?

My vanity told me that he was here because I had drugged him and then bound him before he woke, taking away his ability to leave. But he gave off an air of such authority that it felt impossible to hold one such as this, unless they wanted to be held.

He embodied everything one would think of when they thought of a strong African warrior. His beautiful head sat on a strong, thick neck that was connected to a pair of broad shoulders so wide that they made my kitchen feel small. My eyes traveled down his mighty legs that were covered by a pair of black slacks. His feet that were in a pair of expensive black boots were spread wide apart, firmly planted on the ground.

The whole time I watched him, he watched me back.

Vanity my dear friends is an undefeated foe. I couldn't help but feel slightly high at the thought of having this powerful man under my control.

Or was it I that was really under his control. I did a little fishing to find out.

"Why does it feel like you're here because you want to be?" I asked, my voice barely over a whisper.

He chuckled. It was a very sexy sound. "Maybe…" He paused as his eyes raked over my body making his thoughts clear. "You feel that way, because I choose to be here. And you know deep down that if I didn't there is nothing you would be able to do to hold me."

But then again maybe he was bluffing, and he was just trying to throw me off my game.

I pushed off the door determined not to let him. "Well, that's too bad you don't realize who really have the upper hand here. Your family trying to take my baby from me and I need to do what I have to do to stop it."

He casually nodded, as he watched me walk over to the gun Bria had dropped.

"I agree, you have to do what you have to do. The question is, what do you have to do?"

I reached down and carefully touched the gun with my

finger, quickly snatching it back so that I didn't get burned. When I felt that it wasn't hot to the touch, I slowly picked it up. Turning it this way and that, I tried to see what had happened to cause the weapon to burn Bria.

"I know what I have to do." I told him before I pointed the gun at him. "The question is, do you?"

One side of his mouth lifted in a grin. "I do, and the more time I spend with you, the more I'm determined to see it through."

"Make the call, Michael."

"No."

I thrust the gun toward him. "Make the call or I will shoot you."

He settled back in his chair. "I guess you'll have to shoot me then."

Balling up my fist I wanted to hit him with something. A sound of frustration came from my throat.

"Why?!" I yelled at him.

"Why what?" He asked still speaking as calmly as he had before, which was even more irritating.

"Why, won't you help me if you believe what your family is doing to me is wrong?"

"I didn't say I wouldn't help you, I just said I can't call Melech."

My shoulders slumped as I lowered the gun. Dammit, I was too tired for this. I had not gotten a good night's sleep since the judge first ruled in the Blacks' favor. At this point, I was just operating on fumes. It was pure desperation that kept me putting one foot in front of the other.

I exhaled. "How are you going to help me then?"

If ever the devil smiled, it had to resemble this man's. "Well now, that all depends."

Even though I knew I was going to regret asking, I did it anyway. "Depends on what?"

He licked his lips before he spoke. "It all depends on how long it takes me to convince you to allow me to make love to you."

My mouth fell open in shock. I knew this man was attracted to me, but I didn't think he was going to just come out and say it like that, especially with me pointing a gun at him.

"Can't you see how twisted that is? I was married to your *brother.*"

He shrugged. "So?"

He said that so matter-of-factly it caused me to blush. I looked away so that he couldn't see it.

"That's very wrong, Michael."

He chuckled. "In my culture, if one brother dies without having a son to continue his name, it then becomes his brother's duty to marry his wife and have a son by her to keep the deceased brother's lineage going."

I made a sound with my lips that was a half snort half chuckle. "I don't think so. I'm not having any more children and I'm definitely never, ever, marrying again, so you can forget that." I kicked my shoes off.

Although I wanted to get this whole situation over with so that I could have my life back, the truth was, I was just too doggone tired to try and figure this thing out right now. This man was talking foolishness. Although I knew he wasn't serious about the marriage thing and getting me pregnant with a son to continue his brother's memory and whatnot, he was for damn sure serious about wanting to sleep with me.

Larry was right, that was something. Stockholm syndrome could work in my favor should this whole thing go south. Of course I had no intentions of sleeping with him. However, I could use his lust against him some way, I was just too tired to think of exactly how I could do it right this moment. I needed to buy myself some time.

Meanwhile, a little light flirting wouldn't hurt to keep him interested. As long as I had him tied up I was safe, because I was in control. And like I said earlier, having all that muscled man under my control was a little hot, I ain't going to lie.

"So, being married to Mitch wasn't all that great, huh?" His question was low.

Being married to Mitch wasn't even close to being great. Mitch was ambitious and easily distracted at the same time. He never finished anything he started, and I was pretty sure he was obsessed with becoming a bigger and better man than his older brother, Melech. Plus, he and I were only together a little over a year and in that short time he cheated on me several times.

But I didn't tell Michael any of that.

"He was your brother, I'm sure you know the answer to that. I'm going to bed. Maybe a night sitting up in that chair will make you more agreeable by morning." I walked past him and turned off the light.

"It's just one problem." His deep voice was like smoke in the darkness.

I stopped without turning to look back at him. "Oh yeah? And what's that?"

"I have to tinkle."

I could hear the laughter in his voice. Whipping around I flipped the light on, studying him to see if he was serious. I had not factored this into the equation.

"Are you serious?"

He chuckled. "As serious as a heart attack, and unless you want me to decorate your nice clean floor, you might want to get serious about it too."

Don't panic, Earth! Don't panic!

I began to pace again. I had no idea what the hell I was supposed to do now. I couldn't call Larry because he had taken Bria home and no doubt he would go and visit his lady friend when he left there, and who knows when he'll be home after that?

I could just leave him sitting there and call his bluff. *But what if he wasn't bluffing?* There was no way I should be untying him without Larry here to help me.

"Ummm," I rubbed my hand back across my braids with the same hand that held the gun.

"Is this your first time kidnapping someone?" He asked as he calmly watched me pace.

I chuckled without any humor. "What do you think?" I couldn't keep the sarcasm out of my voice.

"Would you like my advice?" I stopped and stared at him.

"Why, have you ever kidnapped someone?"

He had the nerve to look smug. "A time or two."

I waited for him to show any sign that he was kidding. He showed none.

"Okay, what's your advice?"

"Well, first of all, remember you have the gun, so you have the power."

He was right, only I knew it wasn't loaded. Note to self, use the gun more.

"Also, it's a huge mistake to leave your victim in a room without a lock. And an even bigger mistake is to leave a victim my size anywhere that you can't personally keep an eye on."

Damn it! He was right again, what was I thinking? I told y'all I was too tired to think straight, I was getting ready to leave him in here by himself while I slept. If he escapes, I'm screwed and Rain will be lost to me forever.

Come on, Earth! Get your sh*t together! You can't let him get away!

"Okay," I said pointing the gun back at him. "I'm going to

untie you. And then you're going to walk to the bathroom really slow and tinkle with the door open."

MELECH

Don't get hard you bastard!

She got on her knees right in front of me. If I wanted to, I could have her neck within my grasp and broken in the matter of seconds. But that's not what I wanted.

No, my body wanted something altogether different, and if she didn't hurry, it was going to show her.

When she got my feet unfastened, she stood to untie my arms. Damn, she smelled so good. As she worked on the knots she chewed on her bottom lip. Everything this woman did was sexy as hell. Her pictures didn't do her any justice. Earth is gorgeous. Period.

She was concentrating so hard on what she was doing she didn't even realize she'd left the gun on the floor by my feet. Once she had the ropes undone she reached down to get it, bringing her head within a hair's breadth of my untied hands.

Damn! Crime was not her strong suit.

"Okay, get up slowly." She said pointing the gun at me. I lifted my hands carefully in the air as I stood. Holding the gun in one hand, she bent down and retrieved the ropes with the other.

"Don't try anything funny, just walk to the bathroom."

I did as she said, chuckling to myself when she actually posted up outside the door and looked everywhere but in. I can't believe the hoops I'm jumping through for a piece of—

"Why are you still peeing?" She asked sounding exacerbated.

Me peeing with the door open had her red in the face, I started to turn around without putting myself up, but as timid as she is, that may make her have a damn heart attack.

"Sorry, sweetheart, I guess that's what happens when you're

poisoned." Just as I figured that caused her to look away, ashamed.

After I zipped myself up, I washed my hands. She surprisingly motioned for me to go toward her bedroom. I lifted an eyebrow in anticipation. Can I hope she'll hold that little toy gun to my head and force me to pleasure her?

"It's not what you're thinking. You were right earlier, I can't leave you in the living room by yourself."

"Damn." I muttered as I looked around her bedroom.

It was neat and pleasant, like the rest of her little place. The room had a very comforting feel about it, especially the bed that was covered in a fat, plush white blanket and a bunch of useless pillows that women for some strange reason loved to pile high on their beds.

The sheer white curtain on her window blew gently in the breeze that heralded the coming storm. In front of the window being caressed by the curtain was a beautiful violin that sat perched up on its stand. I had never in my life seen anything like it; the instrument looked way too expensive to be sitting in a little apartment in the heart of the ghetto.

"Do you play?"

Her gaze followed mine and for a split second, there was longing in her eyes. "I used to."

My eyes narrowed on her face, I wondered what happened to make her not play anymore when she clearly wanted to. But I sensed that it was a topic she was not opened to discussing.

"What now?" I asked turning toward her with my hands still in the air.

I wanted her to feel like she was in control all the way up until it was time for me to strike. The more comfortable I can get her to feel around me the better. Soon she'll let down her guard completely and then she was mine.

Chewing on her bottom lip, she looked around her small room trying to figure out what to do with me. I could see her mind racing.

She gestured to the bed with the gun. "Lay down in the bed on your back."

"Can I take off my jacket?"

She thought for a minute before she nodded with jerky movements. I shrugged out my suit jacket.

"What about my boots?" She nodded. When I was done I lay down in the bed on my back.

Still pointing the gun at me she gestured toward the brass head board. "Hold your hands up towards the bars."

I did as she told me. She was a nervous wreck, trying to figure out the best way to tie my hands. The way she decided on doing it surprised the sh*t out of me. She sat the gun on the night stand and straddled my stomach. With hands that shook, she tied my wrists to her bed, never once did it cross her mind the danger of sitting her gun down and straddling me.

However, I knew well the danger of her straddling me like this. There was an awakening predator that was growing even more awake as we spoke. When she was done she exhaled and collapsed back into the bed, arms and legs spread with a huge grin on her face, breathing heavily like she'd just won the race.

The fact that this woman thought that she was safe because my hands were tied was amazing. Like I said earlier, crime was not Earth's strong suit.

"What now?" I asked, trying my best to sound unnerved.

She threw her feet over her head, rolling out of the bed and onto the floor, and then popped up with a grin on her face that made her look like a pixie.

"Now, my not so good friend, we sleep."

As she walked to her drawers to take out her night clothes,

she looked back at me with an impish grin on her face. Now that I was back tied and she was no longer a nervous wreck, her mischievous side was trying to come out. I was getting peeks of this playful nymph that I found myself wanting to entice out of its hiding place.

She left out the room and minutes later I heard her brushing her teeth in the bathroom. My gaze went to the gun that still sat on the nightstand only inches away from me. I shook my head. She may just very well be the sexiest woman alive, but she was the world's worst kidnapper ever.

However, all thoughts fled my head when she reappeared dressed in a pair of old gym shorts and a pink t-shirt that revealed the fact she wasn't wearing a bra. The fabric clung to her full breast in a way that left nothing to the imagination.

I have had women throwing themselves at me my entire life, it kind of came with the territory. Some were bolder than others, you get used to it. Up until this very moment, I'd thought I'd experienced it all. But as my gaze raked over the prettiest breasts I have ever seen, I was struck dumb.

Surely this sweet little temptress wasn't trying to seduce me. I licked my lips, wanting to taste her so bad. Was she aware of what her outfit was doing to me?

Naw, of course not.

After flipping off the light, she crawled into bed and under the covers settling down between me and the wall.

"Good night, Michael, tomorrow I need you to call your brother. Or else I'm not going to be able to let you go."

Sh*t, don't let me go, baby.

I cleared my throat. "Sweetheart, I need a huge favor." She stiffened.

"I'm not sleeping with you."

I beg to differ. "That's not the favor I need." I said out loud.

She sat up and then reached over me to turn on the lamp on

the nightstand next to the bed, pressing her soft breasts into my chest.

Well I'll be damned!

She was trying to seduce me.

This little minx knew exactly what she was doing, flirting with me and trying to use her feminine wiles to tempt me. She had it in her mind to use my lust against me.

Oh, hell yeah! This is what I'm talking about. Let the games begin.

"What do you want?" She asked looking down at me with her flirty gaze.

Goddamn! This girl was going to be the death of me!

"I can't sleep in this stiff shirt. Can you help me take it off?" I tried to sound as sincere as possible. If I let on to the fact that I was aware of what she was doing, she would pull back and stop her little enticing games, and where was the fun in that?

For just a moment fear came to her eyes. "I'm not untying you again."

"Maybe you can think of another way to get it off then."

She thought for a minute before her face brightened with an idea. Then the little temptress climbed over me, letting all that soft warm flesh of hers rub against my hardness.

Chuckling to myself, I shook my head. When I get a hold of her I'm going to make her pay for being the world's biggest tease. I was going to have her panting and begging me for release. Damn! The idea of it almost made me burn these ropes from my wrists.

Pace yourself, Melech, the prey will soon be yours.

She went to her dresser and came back to the bed with a pair of scissors.

"Let's see what we can do about that stiff shirt." She purred before she straddled me again. Taking her time, she began to undo my buttons. Although she was curious to see what lay underneath my shirt, she was also a little afraid. It was almost as if she couldn't believe how bold she was being.

When she had my shirt undone, she ran her hands over my tank top clad chest. The way she touched me let me know she wasn't even aware of what she was doing. I swear this made every hour I spent working out worth it.

Carefully she picked up the scissors and cut my shirt off. When she was done she exhaled smiling down at me.

"Good job, Minx. Now, what about my pants?"

She opened her pretty mouth at a loss for words before she erupted in laughter shaking her head down at me. "I don't think so, mister!"

After placing the scissors on the nightstand not too far from her little gun, she eased back down underneath the covers with her back towards me.

"What about me? I don't get any covers?" Now I was just picking on her.

"Will you call your brother?" She asked without turning to look at me. Her voice muffled by the covers.

"Nope."

"Well then no, you don't get any covers. Goodnight."

You guys are going to think I'm kidding, but in a matter of minutes, she was out cold. I chuckled. Leave it to me to get kidnapped by the world's worst kidnapper. Exhaling, I settled down into the soft comforter. It's crazy that this day unfolded like it did. My grandfather always told me that there is no such thing as a coincidence. He says The Great Spirit places us in situations and we're judged by the way we handle them.

I could say that it was purely coincidental that just this morning I was thinking how much I needed a vacation, so much so that I was considering just getting on my plane and telling my pilot to fly anywhere as long as it was far away from any casinos.

Granted, I didn't quite imagine taking my vacation in the

heart of the ghetto, but Earth has created something here in her little piece of the world that was far better than any place else. There is no where I would rather be than right here playing this little game of cat and mouse we've started.

No, this was no coincidence. The Ancient of Days was stirring up my life, the question is, *why?*

5

MEET THE HOBBIT

EARTH

"Minx, wake-up. There's a hobbit watching us."

I snuggled against my warm, soft, yet firm bed, letting my hand caress the muscled flesh underneath my palm. It was nice. Michael's voice sounded good in the morning.

"Minx, wake-up."

I opened one of my eyes and smiled at Rain. "Hey, sweetie." I mumbled bringing my hand from under the white tank top to gently push her braid that had fallen in her face behind her ear.

"Did Mrs. Tina drop you off?"

She nodded resting her head on her raised hand. Her elbow was propped up on the bed right in front of me.

"Crazy Larry let me in."

I grinned closing my eyes again, I just wasn't ready to leave my warm cocoon. "Now Rain, what did mama tell you about calling that man Crazy Larry?"

"Don't call him that to his face." She responded in her five-year-old serious voice. My bed chuckled. I smiled half way drifting back to sleep.

"Good girl."

"Mommy?"

"Hmmm," I brought my hand back down and slid it back under the wife beater to gently caress the beautifully muscled chest and stomach.

"Who is this man you touching?"

My hand froze as my eyes flew open. "Oh sh*t!" I squeaked before I jumped straight up in the bed. However, my foot got tangled in the covers and I ended up falling back out of the bed tumbling to the floor.

"Damn it!" I whispered, in no hurry to get up from the floor. I was so embarrassed. It wasn't bad enough I was sprawled all on top of the man, my hand had somehow found its way underneath his shirt and I was lying there rubbing his chest and stomach.

I slammed my head down into my hands. Oh man, I wish I could just melt through this floor, but then I remembered Rain and the gun on the nightstand. Slowly I peeked up over the bed. Maybe he was still asleep and hadn't notice.

Ha! Yeah right!

Not only was he awake, he and Rain were both looking at me with goofy grins on their faces. I exhaled. It was nothing to do at this point but to pretend it didn't happen. I hopped up from the floor.

"Baby, you're home early!" I cried opening my arms so that she could run into them. Hugging her close my concerned gaze went to the gun on the nightstand. Michael's gaze followed mine and bless the man, he used his elbow and knocked the gun off the nightstand to the floor between the bed and the stand.

"Thank you." I mouthed. He winked at me.

Goodness, this man was fine.

"Yeah, Mrs. Tina had to bring me home early 'cause she needed to take Bria Bria to the doctor." I sat at the foot of the bed bringing Rain in front of me so that she couldn't see Michael. Of course it was too late for that, but hey, a five year old's attention span was nothing to write home about.

I reached up and took her book bag with her night clothes and toys off her back.

"Oh yeah? Was it Bria's hand?"

Rain nodded. "Mmmhhhmmm…Mrs. Tina said Bria ain't got good sense. She say it's a wonder she still got a hand."

I nodded. "Mrs. Tina is right about that. Baby… go in your room and put your clothes and toys away for me while mama make us some breakfast."

Rain didn't move. In fact, she leaned down so that she could peek at Michael underneath my arm.

"But who is that man back there?"

I turned around and looked at Michael as if it was my first time seeing him. "Oh him?" my mind raced for an answer.

"That's---"

"Your uncle." He told her coming to my rescue. Rain's eyes brightened and she broke away from me and ran back to her original place which was just inches from his head.

"You my daddy's brotha?" She asked super excited.

He nodded. "I sure am, Hobbit."

She giggled. "Why you call me Hobbit?"

"Well, because you're about the size of the last one I saw."

Her eyes rounded in wonder. "You saw a Hobbit?"

"Mmmmhhhhmmm…and I'll tell you all about it after you go and do what your mother said."

No other words had to be said, Rain ran, scooped up her back pack and was out the door in seconds.

I jumped up from the bed and started pacing to keep from freaking out. Oh man, I hadn't counted on Bria's mom dropping Rain off so early. I was not prepared, everything was a mess—

"Earth, calm down, this is perfectly doable." The deep quiet voice came from the bed.

I stopped pacing and stared at him. "Oh yeah, and how is that? What am I supposed to say? Hey baby, mommy has kidnapped your uncle and I'm holding him for ransom?"

He chuckled. "First, you need to calm down. You can't think clearly if you're panicking. Second, you need to come and pick up your weapon and put it in your pocket. I know it's there, so I won't try anything. Then, you need to go and see if Crazy Larry has some zip ties. Come on baby, nobody uses rope to tie anybody up anymore, get with the program. Once you get the zip ties, secure my hands with them in front of me, then go ahead and cook breakfast, that was a great idea. While you do that, I'll take a shower. Also, see if Crazy Larry has some clean clothes for me to put on."

I stood there staring at him in utter astonishment. Did I just get kidnapping shamed? It was obvious he had told the truth last night and had in fact done this a time or two.

"Who are you?"

He chuckled. "It's a little too late to be asking that question, don't you think? Whoever I was, it doesn't matter, I'm yours now. Quickly, do as I said, the Hobbit is coming back."

I jumped into action, doing exactly what he told me. After sliding a pair of jeans on over my shorts I grabbed the gun from the side of the bed.

"You remember I have this in my pocket, so no funny business." I told him in my Clint Eastwood voice before I stuffed it in the back of my pants like I'd seen on a movie. I turned around to show him.

He nodded. "I won't forget, Minx." I started to head for the door.

"Minx!" He called after me.

"Yeah?"

"Put a shirt on over that one. You wouldn't want to be the cause of some poor fool's death now would you?" Frowning I opened my mouth to ask him what he was talking about, but right then Rain burst in the room.

"Okay, tell me the story about the Hobbit!" Quickly I grabbed my sweat shirt.

"Just a minute, baby, we need to go ask Larry a question." I told her catching her before she threw herself at Michael. I couldn't believe she was this friendly with him. Rain never opened up to strangers.

"Aww, mama, can't I stay up here with him?"

"No, Rain, we'll only be a minute. Come on." I had to practically drag her out the room.

"I'll be right back, Uncle!" she yelled back into the room. I heard him chuckle before his deep calm voice followed us out.

"And I'll be right here waiting for you, Hobbit."

Before we left I stopped by the bathroom to take care of a few essentials, I had to silently threaten Rain not to go back in the room with the man I'd kidnapped. The whole way down to the juice bar she gushed about him calling her Hobbit. I frowned down at her. All this time it had just been Rain and me. I never considered she might want to have a father figure around.

I mean we had Larry... but it was true, he was crazy. Most time Rain was the mature one if they were in a room together.

As we walked down the stairs the sound of Reggae music floated up to greet us. A lot of people told Larry he was crazy for opening an Afrocentric bookstore and juice bar in this neighborhood where most folks ain't thinking about reading or eating healthy. But Larry was determined to be amongst his people and be there to help the ones searching for a different way.

I thank the Most High I found him. This building was the

answer to my prayers. There were three apartments over the store and restaurant. One belonged to Larry, one belonged to his ex-wife Betty... *don't ask*, and their son, Willie who was away at school. And of course the other belonged to me. Everybody in the building was like family, so I didn't have to worry about locking my doors or whether Rain was going to be okay going back and forth to the juice bar, the bookstore and our apartment.

The only time I had to lock my doors is when Larry threw his Wednesday night parties in the bar that sometimes doubled as a little after set lounge for the cultural community. Everybody who was rocking natural hair and throwing their fist in the air didn't have good intentions.

"Ahhh! Top shotta just walked threw mi door!" Larry called out when we came down the stairs that let out into the restaurant kitchen. This was the only way to the upstairs portion of the building besides the fire escapes that ran up the back of the building. Legally, I don't think Larry is supposed to have apartments up there, but nobody came this deep in the ghetto to investigate stuff like that.

"Hey, Mon." I greeted as Rain broke away from me to jump in Larry's arm.

"Weh yuh ah deal wid dis mawnin?" He asked her as he hoisted her up in his arms. Rain, who had been around Larry her whole life had no problem understanding his patois.

"Guess what? My uncle is upstairs tied to mommy's bed. He gave me a new name!" Larry's gaze came to me before he looked back at her and smiled.

"Eh, an wah name did him com up wit?"

"Hobbit!" She declared clapping her hands together. Larry held his head back a bit and pretended to study her closely.

"Yuh know, dat is a perfect name. Yuh muma most change it pan di age paper."

"No, I will not be changing your name on your birth certificate." I told her when she turned and looked at me expectantly.

"Stop it!" I hissed at Larry. He knows dang on well she will bug me to death about that. Chuckling he sat her on her feet.

"Go now and taste de blueberries, fresh from de market."

"Yay, I love blueberries!" Rain yelled jumping away.

"Mi kno." Larry called after her shaking his head. "Eff mi had a lickkle of her energy, I would go upstairs and make sweet luv to Betty."

I waved that away. "You would have plenty of energy eff you was only making sweet luv to Betty and not half the women in town." He drew himself up as if I'd insulted him.

"Mi deserve all di queens."

I shook my head at him. "You ain't Bob Marley, negro. Anyway!" I hit the counter. "Mi didn't come down here with you to shoot the breeze, I need some zip ties and some clean clothes for the mon upstairs."

"Zip ties? Fi wah?"

"Larry, Larry, Larry..." I put my hand on his shoulder. "Ain't nobody using rope no mo. Real killas use zip ties."

"An weh di real killas?"

I turned around to show him the gun in my back. "You looking at a real killa!" He looked at me for a second before he threw his head back and laughed. And I ain't talking about no little laugh, I mean he was grabbing his belly.

I drew myself up insulted. He was acting like it wasn't me that had that big ol' mon tied upstairs.

"I don't know what you laughing fo, I'm holding this thing down." He laughed harder as he headed toward the basement stairs, before he went down he turned to look back at me growing quiet as he considered me. Do you know that bastard erupted in laughter again?

"Forget you, Larry!" I yelled after him.

A few minutes later, what sounded like pots and pans banging around could be heard coming from the basement before a few curse words from the Rasta. Rain looked over at me and put her hand over her mouth hiding the fact that she was laughing at him. About ten minutes later, Larry came back up with a pack of big zip ties in one hand and a brown paper bag in the other.

"It a fi yuh lucky day." He said as he came up the stairs turning to kick something back down. I shook my head, Larry was a work of art.

"Mi get dem yah a few months ago." He pulled one of the zip ties out the bag, the thing was huge.

"For what?"

"To reinforce di back gate." I took them from him and the bag of clothes before standing on my toes to kiss his cheek.

"Once again, Larry, you are my hero! Come on, baby." I said to Rain as I headed back for the stairs.

"Emmmhhhmmm… Yuh coming to wuk todeh?"

I paused at the foot of the stairs looking back at him. "Yeah, if you babysit my prisoner for me." He thought about it for a minute before nodding his head.

"Yeah, wah mek nuh." I clapped my hands together.

"Thank you, Larry, you're the best boss and landlord in the whole world."

He grinned, nodding his head. "Mi kno."

This was perfect, if Larry sat with Michael for a while this would give me some time to figure out what I was going to do. I think I was on to something with this flirting thing. I mean, if I made him believe I would sleep with him after he makes the call, there really ain't no harm in that.

The way I figure, all is fair in love and war.

* * *

I HAD JUST PUT the plate with the stack of pancakes on my table when Michael walked out of the bathroom, and I'm telling you I damn near dropped it.

Tell me why this man walked out of my bathroom looking like my own personal sex slave. Okay wait, let me break down to y'all what I was dealing with. Larry had given him a few pairs of jeans and a pack of black boxer briefs that were unopened with a couple of t-shirts.

When I got back upstairs and untied the ropes from around Michael's wrist at gunpoint, he then walked me through taking a few of the zip ties and forming something like shackles around his wrists. It left him with enough room to do things like use the bathroom and bathe himself, but not enough room to open his arms wide enough to let's say strangle me.

Because his hands were shackled, I had to take my handy dandy scissors and cut that wife beater away from his beautiful, muscled, chocolate chest and stomach. And let me tell you, that took strength. A weaker woman would have succumbed and just threw herself at him, trust me.

He went into the bathroom and started the shower and I heard him mumbling to himself about how small the damn shower was. Poor rich bastard wasn't used to such modest accommodations. At one point, there was a loud bang and then a few curse words followed.

Rain, who was in the living room watching Sesame Street put her hand over her mouth and giggled as if she had said the potty word. I don't know why she did that, but that's what she did whenever someone cursed in her hearing.

I went to the door and asked him if he was alright.

"This damn shower is not big enough for an adult human being!" He yelled out. "It was made for Hobbits!" Rain erupted in laughter.

"I shower in there just fine." I told him. He mumbled something I couldn't understand clearly. Shaking my head I went back to cooking.

Rain wanted pancakes, which were her absolute favorite. I fried up some turkey bacon and eggs as well. Since I didn't know how much Michael ate, I made the whole package of turkey bacon and the whole dozen of eggs, I figured we could have the leftovers for lunch.

Anyhow, where was I? Oh yes, the sex slave.

So, I'm putting the pancakes on the table with the rest of the food and out walks Michael in a pair of jeans that's riding low around his waist leaving the top of his black boxer briefs showing. No shirt because he couldn't put one on with his hands in cuffs and his chest and stomach still moist from his shower.

Mercy!

I don't know how long I stood there staring at that man with my mouth hanging open, but eventually I snapped out of it when he asked in that sexy deep voice if I liked what I saw.

I shrugged nonchalantly. "I guess you aight…come on, Rain, breakfast is ready." He chuckled at my answer as he took a seat at my small table.

By the time we were all seated I was feeling very uncomfortable about how small my table was. He was so big that it seemed as if he was guarding Rain and me. I know that sounds crazy, but that's how it felt. It was too intimate.

As Rain ate she drilled him with questions about the hobbit he'd seen and he patiently answered them all. I was more than positive he was making up most of what he was saying. However, I couldn't help but watch for signs that she was irritating him and believe it or not, I saw none.

Meanwhile the man's appetite was monstrous. On his first plate he piled high pancakes, a whole heap of bacon and plenty of eggs. I thought to myself as I worked on my two pancakes that it was no way he could finish all that food.

Please...

This brotha not only finished off that plate, but after asking us if we would be having any more, he piled the rest of what was left on his plate and finished that off as well.

"You eat a lot." Rain told him as she too watched him use his fork to cut a pancake in half before putting it in his mouth.

"It's because your mommy cooks so good." He told her before he put the other half in his mouth.

"Why does mommy have you tied up?"

My hand froze as I looked across the table at him. He had everything worked out, so I just waited for him to tell her.

"Well... because we're playing a game."

Her little face bunched into a frown. "What kind of game?"

He held up his hands so that the zip ties showed. "Mommy bet me a hundred dollars I couldn't wear these the whole time I was visiting you guys."

With her head resting in her little hand and her elbow resting on the table, Rain continued to drill him with questions.

"How long are you going to be visiting?"

He chuckled. "Well that all depends."

"All depends on what?"

His deep dark gaze settled on me. "It all depends on how long mommy will let me stay."

It took everything within me to keep cool. I couldn't believe he'd just said that. Rain turned her excited gaze to me.

"Mommy, can he stay forever?" I nearly spit out my juice.

"Rain, baby...I—" I was at a loss for what to say. I shot a disapproving glance across the table to Michael, who was now smiling at me like a Chester cat.

He blinked with fake innocence. "Yeah mommy, can I stay forever?"

"No!" I snapped at him. Rain's face fell as she sat back in her seat folding her little arms in a full-blown pout.

"Why can't I have a daddy? Bria Bria got a daddy and Jennifer got a daddy."

My mouth dropped as I looked at my daughter. She'd just sucker punched me right in my gut. Where was all this coming from? Her words hurt so bad it nearly bought me to tears.

"Baby, it's just been me and you, we've been alright…right?"

She shook her little head. "No mommy! I want a daddy too!"

"Well, I'm sorry to hear that. Not everybody have daddys. I didn't have one…and--," I started to say, and look how I turned out, but I caught myself. The only thing more painful than when my dad left me was when my mom left.

Poor Rain, I thought that she would be better off because she never knew her father, and all this time she had secretly been longing for him. Feeling myself about to lose grip of my emotions, I stood and began removing the dishes from the table, carrying them to the sink I made dish water and began washing them.

God knows I've done everything in my power to break the chain and be a good mommy to her. I know she didn't have a dad, so I went out of my way to make up for her loss. Tears burned the back of my eyes. My mother asked me to do one thing and I was failing at it miserably.

I couldn't believe I was having this breakdown right now in front of my prisoner, that just so happened to be my late husband's brother. That just so happened to be a part of the family that wanted to take my baby away because they felt I couldn't provide the things that she needed.

When I'd gain control of my emotions a little better, I turned to the table to get more dishes, but came up short at the sight of my daughter sitting on Michael's lap and him whispering something in her ear.

Panic shot through me as visions of him hurting my baby to

get me to let him go flashed in my head. Opening my arms, I signaled for her to come to me.

"Rain baby, come to mama."

"Go ahead." Michael told her putting her on her feet. She walked to me looking up at me with sorry eyes.

"I'm sorry I hurt your feelings, mommy. I didn't mean what I said." A tear ran down my cheek as I squatted down hugging her close, so relieved that he didn't try anything with her.

Damn it! I was making all the wrong decisions.

"It's okay baby, mommy know you didn't mean to hurt my feelings."

But I knew she meant what she said about wanting a father. My gaze went to Michael, who watched me with eyes that saw too much as he lifted his glass of juice and finished it off.

"Go on and finish watching Sesame Street while mommy finish cleaning up the kitchen. Crazy Larry coming up here to sit with your uncle while you and I go to work, how does that sound?" Rain fist pumped the air, she loved going to work in the bookstore.

"Yessss!" She did a little dance to the living room.

My apartment was really small, the kitchen opened up into the living room, and then there was a little hall off to the left where Rain's and my rooms were located as well as the bathroom. So Michael was able to see both Rain and I from where he still sat at the kitchen table.

I ignored him as I went back to washing the dishes. I didn't need the opinion of any of my husband's family, who had been M.I.A for five years and now all of a sudden wanted to show up having all kinds of negative effects on my life.

"Have you been in a relationship since Mitch's death?"

Without turning around to face him, I chuckled with no humor. Leave it to him with his smooth, sexy, deep voice to just come right out and point out the elephant in the room.

I put a plate I'd just washed and rinsed in the drain tray. "That's none of your business."

"Sure it is."

I shook my head. "I don't think so, brotha."

What happened next happened so suddenly it snatched my breath away, I opened my mouth to scream, but nothing came out. I didn't hear him move or cross the kitchen floor, but he'd done it and ended up behind me bringing his strong arms over my head and around me, locking me to him.

When finally my mind registered what was happening and my vocal cords loosened so that I could raise the alarm, his hand was over my mouth cutting off my scream. He was pressing my back into his front so good it was hard to tell where I ended and he began.

He wasn't hurting me, but he had me, and the fact that I couldn't move a muscle let me know how good he had me.

"I don't like to see you hurt."

His words were low and calm, he spoke so close to my ear that his warm breath caressed my skin causing a shiver to go through me so strong that I know he felt it. His arms tightened around me.

"You are strong and you've been doing a damn good job with Rain, anybody say different will have me to deal with. But you are wrong about one thing. What happens to the two of you is my business. The sooner you accept that fact, the easier your life from this moment on will be."

His lips lightly caressed my ear before he took my lobe in his mouth and sucked on it. I closed my eyes tight as a spasm shot through my center so strong it stole my breath.

"I will never hurt you, Minx, and I will never hurt Rain, that's my word. I will lay down my life for you both, because the both of you are mine."

He removed his hand from my mouth, but with the same

hand he gripped my chin turning my face to his. His lips took mine in a kiss that made my toes that were barely touching the floor curl. A moan escaped my lips when he deepened the kiss.

I had never in my life been kissed this way. He held me in his iron grip and forced me to surrender to his dominant mouth. In his kiss was the promise of pleasures to come. My lips softened under his as I willingly surrendered needing him to—

"What you doing, Uncle?" Rain's little voice came from somewhere next to us. Just as quickly as he grabbed me he released me. Raising his zip tied arms back over my head.

"Nothing Hobbit, just thanking your mom for a delicious breakfast." He walked past her scooping her up high in the air so that she could sit on his shoulders. She squalled with laughter as she wrapped her little arms around his head.

He held out his hands as he pretended he couldn't see. "Who cut off all the lights?"

Rain held back her little head and laughed, yelling out in excitement when he turned this way and that before suddenly dipping to sit in the Lazy Boy chair that I'd found at the Goodwill for sixty dollars. He lifted her off his shoulders and tried to put her back on the floor, but she climbed right back up into his arms.

Dear God...

As if he could hear my inner turmoil, Michael's deep penetrating gaze came back to settle on me, where I still stood clutching the sink with one hand and my chest with the other as I tried to still my racing heart.

His eyes took in everything about me in that moment. My hand clutching the sink so tight my knuckles were white. The hand that clutched my chest. The fact that I was still breathing hard. My lips that was still slightly moist and swollen from our kiss. When they finally met mine, he winked at me before Rain drew his attention pointing at something on the television.

6

THE BROWNIES

EARTH

I was so glad to see Bria walk through the bookstore doors that I jumped up from my seat and ran to her pulling her in for a big hug.

As usual she was dressed to the nines in a hot pink Nike jumper and a pair of pink and white Jordans. On her arm was her cream Louis Vuitton bag that she had paid crazy cash for. Her hair, like always was laid. Outside of the white bandage wrapped around her right hand, there wasn't a thread on her out of place.

I on the other hand had barely pulled this outfit together. After Larry had shown up to sit with Michael, I'd jumped in the shower to start getting ready for work, but the only thing I could think about was that kiss. I was so distracted that I had reached in my closet and pulled out the first thing I put my hands on, which was my cream Boho peasant blouse that hung off one shoulder and a pair of jeans. I damn near put on two separate shoes.

However, when I'd come out of my bedroom, you would have thought I was a Victoria's Secret model with the way Michael's gaze roamed over my body.

"Damn girl, I ain't dead!" Bria screeched drawing me back to the present. Goodness! I had been hugging her this whole time.

"I went to the hospital so I can get the good dope, not because I was in any real pain!" She cried trying to pull away from my arms.

"Figures, I should've known you had something up your sleeve." I closed and locked the door behind her. I know people around here didn't steal books, but they will come in to try and rob the register, which is why Larry installed the buzz in system. Customers rang a little bell and I buzzed them in if they were copasetic.

"How is your hand?"

She smiled big and goofy. "Much better, thanks to the Tylenol 3."

I gave her the side eye. "You need to stay off all forms of dope. How in the hell did you burn your hand like that anyway?"

She shook her head. "Girl, I have no idea. The only thing I can figure was that stuff I used to clean it with the other day. Some of it must have still been on it and I had an allergic reaction to it."

I frowned as I eased down into my chair. "Did you burn yourself when you first cleaned it?"

She sat on the stool next to me. "When I first touched the stuff it did burn my hands a little. So, I washed it off and put on some gloves to clean it the rest of the way."

"Why you cleaning a gun you ain't never shot anyway? You need to stop fronting."

She popped her collar with her good hand. "Don't hate."

"Hey, Bria Bria, look at my picture." Rain said getting up from the floor where she had been coloring her picture.

"Will you look at that, Candy Rain? It is a masterpiece. Did you draw this for me?"

Rain shook her head. "Nope, I drew it for my daddy."

I swallowed the wrong way and instantly started choking. Bria pounded me on my back with her good hand while giving me that *we got tea* look. I shook my head trying to signal for Rain to stop talking, but Bria was like a dog that had just picked up the scent of meat.

"Who is your daddy, lil bit?" Rain smiled.

"The man mommy tied up."

"Rain—" I hissed when I finally stopped choking. "Stop calling that man your daddy!"

She folded her arms again, but I was in no mood to argue with her and I let her know with the look on my face. Holding her head down she unfolded her arms.

"Why, mommy? He want to be my daddy." Bria and my eyes connected for just a second over Rain's head before my gaze lowered back to hers.

"Why do you say that, honey?"

"He told me." Both Bria and I leaned closer.

"When?" I asked.

"When you was at the sink crying." Bria gaze flew up to mine.

"I'll tell you about that later." I told her before my attention was back on Rain.

"What exactly did he say?"

She began to fiddle with the zipper on Bria's jumper and I had to physically restrain myself from telling her to spit it out already.

"He said for me not to worry, he was going to be my daddy

and for me to go and apologize to you for hurting your feelings. I said promise and he said promise."

Slowly Bria's hand came up to her mouth.

I patted Rain on her little butt. "Go on over there and finish your picture, baby."

As if she hadn't just flipped my world upside down, she happily trotted back to her crayons.

"What the hell happened after I left?"

I clutched my face with my hands. "I'm in so much trouble!"

Bria pulled my hands down. "What did you do?" She sucked in her breath. "Oh my God! Did you sleep with him?" She got super excited, patting her leg with her good hand.

"Please tell me you slept with that gorgeous piece of man. Eww, I bet it was good! Was it good?"

"Calm down, Horny Lady, I didn't sleep with him." I said dryly.

Her face fell. "Ugh! Earth, you so damn boring." She put her purse down on the floor and crossed her legs. "Go on, start from the beginning. What happened?"

I told her everything, from me using the gun to get him tied to my bed to me waking up lying on top of him with my hand underneath his shirt. I told her about breakfast and him grabbing me at the sink kissing me.

"Girl, I bet he got some good di—" I put my hand over her mouth pointing to Rain, who was all ears now.

Bria smile at her. "Diet. I bet he's on a good diet."

"Anyway," I told her. "I'll never know, because I'm not going there."

She shook her head. "You have always been such a scaredy-cat. You told me that you would do anything to get back custody. It seems to me that the only thing he wants to make the call is something that really need the dust knocked off it."

I opened my mouth insulted. "Don't worry about my dust."

She shook her head. "Somebody need to worry about it. What the hell you saving it for? Do you know how often the opportunity presents itself for a girl to be able to have somebody like that working it?"

I shook my head. "No, how often?"

"For some of us, never. Oh my goodness, stop tripping. If I was you I'll take that little piece—" Instead of saying gun she just made the symbol with her hand. "And point it at him telling him to get down on his knees." As she spoke she was making these sexy kitty faces that weren't all that sexy.

"Ummm—Rain," I said cutting Ms. Potty mouth off. "Go next door to the juice bar and see if Betty have some more of those blueberries you like."

Rain jumped up and ran towards the door that connected the bookstore to the restaurant. Once she was gone I looked back at Bree.

"Okay…go ahead." She laughed when she seen just how much of my attention she had.

"I would tell him to get down on his knees. Then I would make him take off all my clothes and then use his mouth to make me co---" I stopped her.

"I get the picture."

"Girl, you are tripping, if that's all you have to do to get Rain back, what are you waiting for?"

"Because, it's not that simple, it never is." I was not trying to get involved with no one from my husband's family, especially no one as dominating as Michael. I could only imagine what their older brother Melech must be like.

"You the only one making it complicated. You always over-think things. Trust me, a man like that probably used to banging models. You ought to be flattered he feeling you enough to call his brother if you give him some nooky." She gave me her duh look.

"Unloose the nooky, girl. Damn!"

It was so easy for Bria to make rash decisions like that, she didn't have children who could be affected by her mistakes. I mean yeah, Michael was sexy as all get out. And that kiss he gave me earlier, oh my goodness, you just know he knows what he's doing in the bedroom. I haven't been with a man since Mitch and he had been my first.

And let me tell you, he did very little to appease my sexual frustration. So I can't lie and pretend I'm not tempted. It's just that Michael wasn't anything like Mitch and he didn't feel like the type I could just use to help me work out a little frustration with and simply walk away.

"But what about what he said to Rain? About him being her daddy? I'm not trying to get in no relationship with him."

She waved her hand. "Girl, that's just game. Men know the quickest way to a single mom's heart is through her kid. He just don't know that you not looking for forever. Y'all really looking for the same thing. He want some nooky to help you and you're willing to give him some nooky to help. It's a win-win situation. At the end of the day, he goes back to his glamourous life, banging models…and you go back to your boring life staring at a violin you too chicken sh*t to play."

You know, sometimes Bria's words really hurt, but I think she may be on to something. Yes, Michael's words that he'd whispered to me today when he held me by the sink scared the crap out of me. But what if it was all game? What if he was saying that stuff just to get me to sleep with him? I guess he figured I was the kind of girl that was looking for forever.

That was the furthest from the truth. Rushing off and marrying Mitch had damaged me. Mitch was no Prince Charming and if I would have known then what I knew now, I would have never gone out with him. Michael was his younger brother, so I know he probably had a lot of Mitch's ways.

However, something he did not have in common with Mitch was his body. The short time I had been with him, Mitch complained about his body and was very self-conscious. Michael on the other hand looked as if he had been sculpted by the sculptor. He was taller than Mitch and stronger; and the kiss he had given me by the sink, goodness gracious! Mitch had never ever come close to kissing me like that. Truth be told I really didn't care for Mitch's kisses and tried to avoid them as often as I could. There were some things he was definitely better at than his older brother.

I couldn't help but wonder if he was better than Mitch at the art of lovemaking. I had lied to Brianna and told her that my husband had brought me to peak, but the truth was he hadn't. He told me it was something wrong with me, that I was too uptight and that's why I couldn't come. To this very day, I wonder if his words were true.

If there was ever a man that could do it, I bet it was Michael. If he couldn't, then Mitch would be right, I was broken.

Hmmm...

I was going to have to think hard about this.

An hour later, I showed Bria to the door, sitting out front waiting for her in a blue Cadillac truck was some guy she'd just met named Gregory. She says he's not much to look at, but she could look past it 'cause he had a nice car.

I shook my head as I watched them drive off; I don't know how our friendship lasted so long. She and I were like night and day. I rocked natural hair, she bought her hair. I read cultural books and studied my people's history, Bria looked at the pictures in Vogue. I was a home body and Bria would be at the club every night if she could.

Mitch had called me uptight and Bria said I was boring. And

although I didn't want to be nearly as adventures as she, I think I could stand to have a little fun with that gorgeous brotha upstairs. But I still had Rain and the example I needed to set for her to think about. I mean, I haven't decided if I was going to sleep with him or not, but I could probably loosen up a little bit.

* * *

I CLOSED THE STORE EARLY. The whole day we'd had a total of two customers. Because Larry was one of the very few Afrocentric bookstores in Kissimmee, most of the conscious community in the city came to us to get everything from fresh organic food to good books to read to incense to burn. But today was very slow, maybe because it was still two days till pay day.

"Thank you for keeping an eye on her for me." I told Betty as I picked a sleeping Rain up from the cot they kept in the kitchen for her.

"It is no problem. Rain is a good baby, she never gives me a hard time." Betty had been in America a lot longer than Larry, so she spoke English about as well as most of our people in this country.

I don't know why she and Larry couldn't make their marriage work. They were the best of friends, worked together and lived in the same building. But for some reason they had different opinions on fidelity. Betty wanted him to be true to her and Larry felt like he should have all the queens. His words.

"Larry tells me you've kidnapped a mon. Is that true?"

I nodded. "Something like that."

"Is he good looking?"

"Oh yes."

Her face brightened. "Good for you, my girl, you enjoy him."

I chuckled as I headed up the stairs, I had a strange group of friends, but one thing I could say, they were loyal. When I reached the second floor my steps slowed. I could hear raised male voices coming from my apartment.

Quickly I opened the door and came up short at the sight that greeted me.

Larry, his brother, Natty Dread, and Michael were in a heated debate about God knows what, but that wasn't what threw me. Michael stood in the middle of the living room speaking forcefully down at Larry, who was stubbornly shaking his head, and the zip ties that were connected to the zip ties around his wrists were gone. For all intents and purposes, his hands were free as a bird. He was also sporting one of Larry's palm tree button up shirts, only it was *un*buttoned.

They were in such a heated debate that none of them even noticed I'd come in. Because they were keeping up such a racket, I hurried to Rain's room and laid her down, pulling her door behind me.

"What the hell is going on here?" I had to practically yell over the men.

Michael turned to face me and it was then I saw that his eyes were blood shot red.

"Baby, you're just in time to clear something up. What do you know about the Seminole people?" I folded my arms.

"I know the one standing before me is high as a Georgia Pine. Larry!" I admonished turning to face the Rasta.

"How could you smoke weed up here and you know that's why this one's family is trying to take my baby away?!"

Larry came to his feet as if he was insulted. He too was high as a kite.

"Ow yuh cya tink mi wud duh sup'm like dat?" He asked putting his hand on his chest.

I walked over to Michael, who had sat back in the Lazy boy

and was in the process of popping some kind of baked good in his mouth. No doubt they all had the munchies.

"Exhibit A." I said using both of my hands to gesture to him and to Natty Dread who was laid out on the couch engrossed in a Sponge Bob episode. Michael had the nerve to smile up at me through his hazy gaze.

Let me tell yall, this man had some killer bedroom eyes already. Those eyes on weed just tipped the scale.

"Are you trying to make me lose my daughter, is that it?" I asked Larry.

His mouth opened in clear shock. The high fool. "Earth, yuh hurt mi heart. Who did there fi yuh wen yuh need a place to live an a job?"

I rolled my eyes...Here we go, a high Larry will preach your ear off, which was probably what he was doing to poor Michael before I came in.

"Who helped yuh kidnap dis mon?" He asked gesturing toward Michael who was popping another one of whatever Larry had baked into his mouth.

"Yeah, but you were supposed to come up here and keep an eye on him, not smoke weed with him!"

"Mi no smoke wit dis mon!" He looked at Mike. "Did mi smoke wit yuh?"

Mike shook his head grinning. "No, mon. Relax, Minx, I don't do drugs."

I put my hand on my hips and looked at all three of them, if they were sober, then I was Michelle Obama. Natty Dread still hadn't looked away from the TV and it was a commercial on.

"Look at dis mon!" I said gestured toward Larry's cousin. "He stuck! Look at this one!" I gestured toward Michael, who sat back in his chair and rubbed his hands down his face. The whole time there was a huge grin on his face.

"What is he grinning about? How did they get like this, if they didn't smoke any weed?"

Larry looked down at his cohorts before looking back up at me. "Mi just wa fi sey dat mi hurt yuh tink mi wud smoke ganja inna yuh place."

I crossed my arms and lifted an eyebrow at him, I wasn't buying his crap.

He grinned. "Mi bake di ganja inna di brownies."

Michael held up one of the brownies. "Wait, there's weed in these brownies?"

I nodded. He brought the brownie closer trying to look and see if he could spot the weed, before giving up and popping it in his mouth, then he sat up in his chair and pointed at Larry.

"That's what I mean, that was low down to give me brownies with weed in it. Where is the honor in that? But then you want to try and convince me that your people are somehow better than my people, who never saw slavery."

Larry ripped his scarf off his head causing his locs to rain down around his shoulders and slammed the cloth to the floor.

"Did yuh people cum to America pan slave ships?"

Mike nodded and was about to say something, but Larry spoke over him. "Den yuh people weh slaves!"

Goodness, I can't believe that's what they were arguing over. Let this be a lesson for you folks out there listening to my tale.

Just say no to drugs.

Michael shot to his feet, all humor gone. "That's what I'm telling you, man, yeah we came to America in slave ships, but my people fled South Carolina before the runaway slave was the in thing to do. We joined the Seminole in Florida and fought and died for our freedom. I am a direct descendant of Abraham the Great Black Seminole leader."

Okay, so that answers one of my questions about this mystery man. He was a Black Seminole, which meant he and

Mitch did not share a father. Mitch said his mother and father were both full blooded Seminole.

Larry poked his chest out. "An mi a descendent of Abraham Issac an Jacob."

I held up my hand. "You two are aware that you're the same people, right?" They both looked down at me.

"Both of your ancestors were probably on the same slave ship, they were taken from the same place. Which literally means the two of you can be descendants of two brothers, one who was dropped off in the islands and the other who was dropped off in the Carolinas. Which would make this whole argument you guys are having very foolish."

The both of them grinned when they realized just how stupid their conversation was.

I raised my hand again. "But I have a real important question. Where is this man's zip ties, am I the only one that has noticed his hands are free?"

Natty Dread looked up then. "Di shackles burn away from fi him wrist!"

I shook my head, this, and the fact it could cause me to lose my baby is the reason I no longer smoked weed. Michael leaned down wrapping his arm around my waist pulling me close.

"Don't you know, can't no shackles hold me, baby?"

I had to bite my cheek to keep from laughing at him. High Michael was a little bit of a nut.

Larry grunted. "Fi one ting yuh wa fi put dis black man inna shackles. Tis jus wrong."

My mouth dropped. "Oh my God, Larry, he could be dangerous."

Chuckling Michael sat back in the Lazy Boy pulling me down with him to sit on his lap.

"Cum now gyal eff dis man want yuh dead yuh wudda be dead aready."

"Him cya mek di fire cum from fi him hand. There no shackle dat cya hold him!" Natty Dread supplied passionately.

"Okay Larry, it's time for you and Natty Dread to get on home."

"Yeah mon, mi going to mek sweet luv to Betty." He said as he started gathering his things. Note to self, do not let Larry babysit the prisoner anymore.

"Don't forget your brownies." I told him handing him his plate.

"Wh...wait—" Michael said reaching to snag one more and popped it in his mouth. I shook my head at him.

"I thought you didn't do drugs."

"I don't," he said around a mouth full of brownie. Using his thumb, he pointed at Larry. "The Rasta tricked me."

After they left I tried to get up off his lap to straighten the living room back up, but he wouldn't let me.

"Can you believe that guy put weed in his brownies?" He asked trying to look serious, but was failing miserably.

Biting my lip to keep from grinning with him I pointed my finger into his chest.

"What I can't believe is that you escaped your shackles and found this awesome shirt."

He grabbed a hold of one side of his shirt. "Oh yeah, you like this? I think if I ever escape my fierce captor, I'm going to order one of these bad boys in every color."

That made me laugh, but when I noticed him watching me, I grew sober.

"What?" I asked.

"You seem lighter tonight. More at ease. What happened at work to make you more comfortable around me? Why aren't you waving your miniature gun in the air demanding I put my restraints back on?"

As far as the zip ties, I realized earlier how silly they were, seeing as to how he could have killed me when he grabbed me by the sink if he wanted to. Now, for the other half of his question about my mood...

Mmmm...

That was a little more complicated. I toyed with the button on his shirt, trying to think of how best to answer him.

"Your brother used to tell me all the time that I was uptight." My words were barely over a whisper.

Michael snorted. "That's because he was a screw up. Anybody that actually take care of their business would seem uptight to him. He's told me that on more than one occasion as well."

"Really?"

He nodded. "I know he was your husband, but you can't take sh*t he told you seriously." I continued to play with his button, just needing to look anywhere else but into his intense hazy eyes.

"Bria says I'm boring." He snorted again.

"Yeah well, she doesn't take me as the kind of person that got her sh*t together either."

Using his big finger, he gently lifted my chin so that our eyes connected. "Do you want to know what I think about you?"

Biting my lip, I nodded.

"I think you're amazing. You're strong, focused. You're raising an equally amazing little Hobbit all by yourself. And she's a good child, not like one of those little sh*ts that's so bad you just want to kick them and their parents"

I tried really hard not to laugh at that. "Oh, my goodness, Michael, tell me you're not going around kicking people's children."

"I mean no, I haven't actually kicked one, but I have met some that made me want to." I shook my head at him, he gave me the side eye.

"So, you've never met a little demon spawn that you found yourself wanting to lay hands on? Oh, it's just me."

Grudgingly, I nodded at him through my laughter. Note to self, never let Michael get weed again, he was really goofy on the stuff.

"Yeah, I know you have. Anyway, Rain is not like that. She's good on the inside, you can tell somebody has been teaching her morals and values."

I smiled at him from under my lashes. I do believe that's the sweetest thing anybody has ever said to me.

"Well I've been doing some thinking." I told him, back to playing with that button on his shirt. He licked his lips and my heartbeat sped up.

"Oh yeah? About what?"

"I was thinking that maybe if I give you what you want, you will give me what I want."

"And what do you want?"

"I—" I hesitated for a moment, suddenly super nervous. I licked my lips. "I want you to call your older brother and tell him what you just told me so that he can give me back custody of my baby. I have no life without her."

Using his finger, he lifted my chin again so that he could see my eyes.

"What if I can guarantee you will always be with Rain?"

"How can you guarantee that?"

Searching my eyes, he opened his mouth to say something, but then thought better of it.

"What if I can guarantee it?"

"Then I will give you what you want."

"Good, then I guarantee you will always be with Rain."

For some reason I believed him. I knew he was the little brother, but he had a domineering personality. He was the kind of person that said something and people just did it, because it seemed like he knew best. He is the kind of man that led. I know this is going to sound funny, but he came across as kingly. It wasn't hard pressed to imagine him ruling.

My gaze went back to my finger playing with that button. "And what do you want?" My question was a whisper really.

"I don't want you to call me Michael anymore. I want you to call me Black."

7

THE DELECTABLE MR. BLACK

EARTH

*A*lthough I didn't want to, I had to pull myself out of Black's strong arms. I could hear Rain up and moving around, it just wasn't a good idea to leave her to her own devices for too long. For just a moment he tightened his arms around me pulling me back into the warm cocoon I'd slept in.

Bria had been wrong about him, I had practically offered him the nooky last night on a silver platter, but the only thing he wanted was for me to call him by his last name instead of his first. Well, that and a few kisses when we made it to the bed last night.

I blushed as I thought about it. It had actually been more than a few kisses. And guess who else I found out was wrong last night?

Mitch.

I was not broken, Miche—I mean Black had done things to

my body that had not only caused my world to shatter, it caused it to shatter twice, the second time more powerful than the first.

I'll let y'all in on a little of what happened last night.

I sat on his lap amazed that after I'd practically offered him the goods he didn't take it. I could see that he was attracted to me, so why hadn't he jumped on it? So, ladies you know how we are, I had to put him to the test. Of course I couldn't just come right out and ask him why…No, that was just too logical. I decided to play a little game.

"Well, it was nice talking to you, but I'm tired…so, I'll bid you goodnight." I climbed down off his lap and when he started to rise after me, I put my hand on his shoulder stopping him.

"And where do you think you're going?"

He looked at me with the sexiest grin on his face. "To bed."

I took my hand off his shoulder and put it on my hip. "I don't think so, mister." I had to bite the side of my jaw to keep a straight face.

"Where am I supposed to sleep then?"

I turned and looked at the couch.

"But I slept in the bed with you last night."

"Well that was different, last night you were tied up." I went to the linen cabinet and pulled out a blanket and a pillow tossing it on the couch.

"No, Minx…I want to sleep with you."

I pressed my lips together. I couldn't believe this powerful man had this puppy dog look on his face. I committed the look to memory, because I know a sober Black would never be so silly.

I shrugged the shoulder that my shirt fell off. "Well… too bad." Turning I sashayed out of the living room.

When I got to the light switch, I looked back at him over my bare shoulder and caught an unguarded look on his face, a look that startled me and now that I think about it, I should have paid more attention and been more wary, but I didn't. A decision I would later regret. In that unguarded moment, a predator stared back at me. There was no other word to describe it. His eyes were hard and cold, it was like I was being looked at hungrily by a killer.

When he blinked, my playful captive was back. Exhaling I flipped the light off, leaving him sitting in the dark, his unguarded look forgotten. Now, what I did next could be considered low, but it all depends on how you look at it. After completing my nightly rituals in the bathroom, I slid on a pair of my really cute peach panties and a peach cami that hugged my breast perfectly.

Then I cracked my bedroom door and slid under the covers. It couldn't have been more than five minutes before I heard my door opening wider.

"If I let you tie my hands back up, can I sleep with you?"

I chuckled, he sounded like a scared little boy.

"Why do you want to sleep with me, Black?"

He walked towards my bed looking so powerful standing over me. My bedroom window was open so that I could get that night time breeze, in the distance the sound of thunder could be heard. It rained all the time in Florida, but I loved it.

Slowly he went down to his knees next to my bed. "Say my name again, Minx."

I bit my lip nervous as heck to have him this close to me. "Black." I whispered.

He growled. "That sounds so sweet coming from your lips." He put his hands up on the bed next to me. "Here, tie me up. Do whatever you have to, just don't make me sleep on the couch."

I looked toward the ceiling biting my lip and pretended to think about it.

"Okay, I guess you can sleep with me." He grinned before he jumped to his feet and threw off the crazy Palm Tree shirt.

When he put his hands on the button of his jeans I looked away.

"Raasclaat!" He hissed when he pulled back the cover to get under and saw what I was wearing.

I burst out laughing. "Okay, somebody has been spending too much time with Larry."

"Damn gyal wah yuh trying to duh to mi?" He said speaking perfect patios. I turned to look at him surprised.

"I didn't know you spoke patios."

He chuckled leaning over to bury his head in my neck where he inhaled loudly, causing me to erupt in giggles from where his beard and mustache tickled me.

"I do a lot of traveling back and forward to the islands, we own several casinos there." He explained as he settled down on his back, bundling me up in his arms so that I lay on his chest like I had this morning.

All this time I thought he was struggling to understand Larry and Natty Dread, and here he understood them perfectly. Wow, Mr. Black was full of surprises. In that moment, he seemed so capable to me that I couldn't resist asking him the question that had plagued me since I thought about it earlier.

"Black..." I whispered as I traced the outline of his muscled peck with my finger.

"Mmmm..."

"I've, umm... never experienced—well it just that Bria talks about the pleasure of, umm..." *Goodness! I was messing this up.*

He lifted his head to look down at me.

"I mean I know that I've had a child and all, so obviously I'm not a virgin. But umm...I've never...You know."

The grin that came to his face couldn't be described as anything other than wolfish.

He nodded. "Yeah, I know. And it will be my pleasure."

He moved so fast then, the only thing I could do was laugh.

One minute I was laying on him and in the next he had switched our positions, and then my laughter died because he was kissing me. His chocolate tasting kisses were like morphine, I lost all my ability to do or think about anything other than how he was making me feel.

He took his time kissing me, cherishing my lips in a way I didn't think was possible. His hands gently caressed my stomach right above my panty line and it was driving me mad. That gentle caress and his kiss made a killer combination. But then his mouth lowered to my neck and he continued his gentle assault over the spot where my pulse beat, lapping at it with his tongue before he drew it in his mouth.

I hissed as a tremor suddenly shot through my center causing my softness to rub against his hardness in a way that made my back arch up off the bed.

He groaned. "You are so damn beautiful, Earth."

I bit my lip as his head lowered, when his tongue touched my belly button that peeked out the bottom of my cami, the breath rushed from my lungs. His hand was so big it covered my whole stomach.

"When I first saw you, I thought to myself, Mitch didn't deserve you."

As he spoke he slowly lifted my cami higher open mouth kissing every piece of skin he exposed as if he was a starved man and I was his food. I felt as if he was spinning a web of seduction around me. His soft words and gentle touch, the feel of his hardness pressed against my softness, the warm caress of his tongue and soft caress of his lips. It was too much, the pleasure from the combination was overwhelming.

"I wanted to taste you so bad," was the last words he whispered before gently pushing the cami up over my breast. The look of hunger on his face was breathtaking, I bit my lip as he slowly lowered his head. When his hot mouth closed around my nipple sucking it in, I lost it and for the very first time in my life, my world shattered.

He softly kissed my lips while I floated back down to earth. "Not fair, Minx." He whispered in my ear.

Breathing heavily I licked my lips looking up at him confused. What had I done wrong?

"What's not fair?"

"You came apart before I got my taste." I squeaked when he suddenly rose up over me on his knees snatching the cover completely off of us.

He shook his head, tsking. "You've got to do better than that, Minx. That kind of selfishness is not permitted."

"I don't understand." I gasped completely thrown by his behavior.

That predatory look was back on his face as he gently rubbed his big hands up my legs. When he got to my panties, his deadly gaze came back to mine.

Y'all, I ain't gon' lie, I was a little frightened.

"I want my taste!" He growled before he ripped my panties in two.

Mmmm mmmm mmmm…

The gentle Mr. Black had exited the building. When next my world shattered it happened violently, leaving me whimpering and shuddering as I clung to him trying to catch my breath.

"Shh baby, it's okay!" He whispered.

But I shook my head, it wasn't okay. I had never in my life experienced anything like it. Bria never told me it could be this way. For just a moment I thought I would die from the pleasure.

The last thing I remember before I succumbed to sleep was asking him what about him? He never got his own release.

"Next time. Tonight was just for you, Minx." I drifted off to the feel of him kissing my forehead.

And now, although I hated it, I had to pull myself away from him. He grumbled something trying to reach for me again, but he didn't waken. For just a moment I stood and looked at myself in the mirror, I felt like I had officially become a woman. My gaze went to the gorgeously muscled man that had rolled over to his stomach taking up my whole bed.

It was all because of him... The delectable Mr. Black.

With a satisfied smile on my face, I slid my arms into my robe tying the belt around my waist. Bending down I picked up my ripped panties.

Wow!

That had been so freaking intense. Whew!

After stuffing them in the pocket of my robe I went to my closet and opened it.

Hmmm... What to wear today?

I felt amazing and I wanted to look amazing. Today, I will be the girl in the yellow dress. It wasn't much, but it was my favorite. I had found it at the Goodwill for forty cents. In my opinion that had been a steal.

I don't know how the designer managed to capture the color of the Florida sun, but that's exactly what they did. But what I liked most about it was that the slightest breeze caused it to blow around my legs and ankles caressing my skin with its soft touch.

After gathering a few more things I hopped in the shower. Rain had just turned on her little educational shows, she'll be ready for breakfast in about thirty minutes, which gave me enough time to fix myself up.

When I was done showering, I took my time and moisturized my skin. Then I slid into my yellow panty and bra set that matched my dress perfectly. I took my braids down and using a little gel and water, I brush my hair into a ponytail that left a big beautiful afro puff to fall down my back. It was perfect because I'd had my hair braided. However, in this Florida humidity, it would be shrunken to half the size it was right now by noon.

I put a little eyeliner and mascara on and touched my lips with some gloss. Today, I was in the mood for gold, so I put my big gold like hoops in my ears and the matching gold like bangles on my wrists. When I was done I did a little turn in the bathroom mirror and smiled when the dress flowed around me, making me feel like a princess.

"You ready for some breakfast, sweetheart?" I called to Rain as I rounded the corner to the living room. However, the sight that greeted me caused a scream to rip from my throat.

Laid out on the living room floor next to Rain was the biggest black cat I had ever seen. My scream caused them both to look my way startled; I leaped over the thing and scooped my baby up in my arms.

In the next second before I could even blink, Mr. Black, clutching the sheet around his waist was there in the living room crotched low, ready to attack.

How in the hell did he move so fast?

"What's the matter?!" He asked looking around the living room, his eyes scanned right over the beast that was still laid out looking up at me as if I was interrupting its rest.

I pointed down at the monster.

"Do you see this...this beast!"

He exhaled coming out of fighter pose. "Damn woman, you scared the hell out of me." After giving me a disapproving look shaking his head, the jerk disappeared back into the bedroom.

"Wait...where are you going?" I squeaked, too afraid to take one step.

I minute later he came back out the bedroom with his jeans on, but then disappeared in the bathroom.

"Are you kidding me?!" I yelled this time when I heard the toilet flush and seconds later him brushing his teeth. The whole time the animal lay sprawled out on the floor with its tail swooshing back and forward in the air as if it owned the place.

When Black came back out, he casually draped his big body on the couch.

His eyes roamed over my body as he nodded, liking what he saw. "Wow, you look amazing today."

Was he insane?

"Are you insane? Or maybe you're blind. Do you not see that there is a monster on the floor in front of me!"

He chuckled, before patting the couch next to him. My mouth dropped when the huge majestic animal raised its slick black form off the floor, and after going down in a sublime stretch, gracefully leaped up on the couch next to Black before curling its body into his. The cat took up more space on the couch than he did.

"This is no monster, this Abner my kitty cat." He finally spoke as he roughly patted the belly of the thing.

"Kitty cat my ass, it's a black panther! It belongs in the jungle!"

He chuckled again. "Actually, Abner is a jaguar, don't you see the spots?" He used his hand to smooth out the animal's fur so that its spots were clearly seen.

"I don't care what Abner is, he's got to go!"

"Why mommy? He's my friend!" Rain cried as she tried to push herself out of my arms.

"No, baby, it's not safe." I tightened my hold on her.

"Abner is very safe, I've had him my whole life and he's never attacked anyone unless I told him to."

Oh My God! I can't believe what he was saying to me.

"Do you hear yourself right now? You're talking like it's perfectly normal for you to have a pet jaguar!"

He chuckled. "It is perfectly normal for me, I told you he's been in my life forever, what will you have me do with him?"

"I don't know!" I tried to wrap my mind around this. "Send him home."

He shook his head exhaling. "It won't do any good, he won't go."

"What do you mean he won't go?"

He opened his hands. "I mean he won't go. If I'm gone away from home too long, he's going to find me, no matter where I am."

"Wow!" Rain gushed, Black had officially become her hero.

"Are you serious?"

He nodded. "As a heart attack. But the good news is, he's harmless. Come over here so you can meet him." He patted the couch on the other side of him. "Come on."

I took the long way around to that side of the couch. Still holding Rain in my arms, I eased down next to Black.

"Give me your hand."

I shook my head. "I don't want to touch it."

"I do!" Rain yelped before she scrambled off my lap and into Black's.

"That's my brave little Hobbit!" he told her as he ruffled her hair that was in a serious need of a brush. I reached for her, but Black grabbed my hands stopping me.

"Hey, Abner." Rain said as she gently rubbed the thing's head, she didn't have any fear. I held my breath the whole time ready to leap and grab my baby if it moved a muscle. I couldn't believe she wasn't afraid of it. When I'd come out, the thing had been sitting on the floor next to her watching Sesame Street with her.

"Black, what you doing?" I squeaked when he took my hand that he still held and put it on the cat's warm body. I tried to pull it back, but he wouldn't let me.

"You're hurting Abner's feelings, he's going to think something is wrong with him if you keep acting like this."

Was this man insane? Y'all I was shaking so bad I could hear my teeth chattering. However, the longer he held my hand on it, the less afraid I became. I could feel a strong heart beat under my palm, and amazingly, as I began to rub him, he actually began to purr.

"Oh my God, he's purring like a real kitty." I said astonished.

"He *is* a real kitty, Minx. He's just a *big* kitty."

I snorted. That was the understatement of the year. This cat was past big. His face alone was bigger than the whole top half of Rain's body.

"I wanted a cat when I was younger." I admitted as I continued to rub Abner. The more I rubbed him the louder he purred.

"Why didn't you get one?" He asked quietly from where he was relaxed back against the couch.

"My mama could barely afford to feed us and Sista Dinah was allergic."

"Who's Sista Dinah?"

"She took care of me after my mama left." I told him, but I intentionally gave the cat more of my attention, not wanting to discuss my personal business with him. I had already said too much.

"Okay that's enough, you giving him all my loving." He said knocking my hands away from his pet.

I looked over at him with a grin on my face. "Really, Black?"

"Really." He said, completely serious.

Wow! This man was jealous of his own pet.

"Meanwhile, you sure look pretty today." He muttered, looking at me with his killer bedroom eyes.

He fisted his hand in my afro- puff and pulled my head back to him. I gasped and his mouth closed on mine. His minty kiss just like the one he'd given me by the sink made me feel drugged.

"Whatever that wet stuff is on your lips its driving me nuts." He growled nibbling on my lips. The sound of Rain giggling caused me to break away.

"Ewww, y'all was kissing." She said doing some goofy little dance on Black's lap. He chuckled ruffling her hair again.

But then the big cat moved suddenly and I froze in fear. It stood turning its body to face me. Rain scrambled of Blacks lap just in time because the thing put one of his monstrous size paws smack dab in the center of Black's stomach.

"Oh, come on, Abner!" He cried when the animal put all its weight on him causing his breath to whoosh from his body.

Rain giggled as the cat then settled its body down on Black's lap, taking up his lap stomach and chest as if it was the size of a house cat. But then it put one paw across my lap and settled its huge head on top. Without moving a muscle my eyes went to Black's.

He shook his head. "He's petty that way, he wants you to keep rubbing him."

"For real?" I whispered, still too afraid to move.

"Mmmhhhhmmm."

"Rub his head, mommy!" Rain squealed.

Squeezing my eyes shut tight, I slowly lowered my hand to its head and began to rub. This time when he started purring it vibrated through my whole body. I rubbed harder using both hands and he purred louder. His head was so big I could wrap my arms around it and hug him. Smiling, I looked over to Black, who I could tell was pleased I was welcoming his pet.

"He's like a big teddy bear, so huggable." I rubbed under his neck cuddling him to me. Then it started doing something with his huge razor-sharp claws where it was gently sheathing and then unsheathing them against my leg. That little motion along with its purring was quiet satisfying.

And I'll be doggone if it wasn't the most comforting thing I have ever experienced.

"Wow, that feels great." I muttered. I can see being lured to sleep this way.

"Yeah… enough!" Black said before he stood forcing the cat to jump to the floor.

He grinned down at his pet, the animal looked up at him as if to ask him what was up with that?

"My woman!"

The majestic animal licked his tongue out at him before he turned with his head proudly in the air and resumed his spot on the floor. Rain settled down next to him rubbing her little hands through his fur, and the two went back to watching Sesame Street.

"I'm going to go jump in the shower while you whip us up something delicious like you did yesterday. I'm sure Abner is good and hungry after his journey."

Chuckling I shook my head at him. "Brotha, I don't even have enough food to feed you, let alone your giant-sized pet. What does he eat anyway?"

He looked down at the animal and shrugged. "He'll pretty much eat anything you put in front of him."

"Does he eat cereal?" Rain asked.

"Yes, he does, Hobbit, his favorite is Frosted Flakes." Rain erupted in laughter when Black winked at her.

"Alright, I'll tell you what, when I'm done getting dressed we can go shopping for food and maybe go somewhere and have a picnic."

Rain jumped up and began to dance around. "I love picnics!" She yelled, her excitement level past the point that could be negotiated with.

I frowned. "Ummm, I don't get paid till Friday."

He looked at me as if I'd gone dumb. "You do know that I'm rich, right?"

You know…he was right. For some reason that little fact had slipped my mind. I guess it was because he seemed so content to stay here in my humble abode that it was easy to forget he's not from this environment. Outside of complaining about the size of the shower he didn't complain about anything else.

You would think a person that was raised in the lap of luxury would not ever want to sit on my furniture that all came from the Goodwill. Or lay in my bed that too came from a second-hand store.

I narrowed my eyes at him. "Why are you here?"

I know it was a little late to be asking that question, but let's be honest, he could have left anytime he felt like it.

At first he didn't respond, and then he chuckled shaking his head. "I'll be honest, I'm a little surprised by my reluctance to leave as well. I just—" He paused rubbing his hand down his head.

"I just really needed a vacation. You have no idea how bad I needed a new scenery."

Yeah, I was surprised about that. I put my hand on my chest. "And you decided to take it here?" His eyes fell to my hand that was over my heart.

"I can't think of a better place to be." He muttered before he turned and went back into the bedroom.

I sat for a minute trying to figure out where was he speaking of, my apartment or my heart.

MELECH BLACK

With my hand on the shower wall, I held my head down and let the hot water rain down over me. I knew she meant her place, but she'd put her hand on her heart, and in that moment, I realized that's exactly where I wanted to be.

Earth didn't understand what was happening, but I wanted her. I spoke the truth, I was surprised by the way my feelings were changing for her. At first I thought I would be satisfied with just sampling her body. But then after watching how perfect she is with Rain and seeing how nourishing she is, I realized I wanted all of her. Her mind, her body, and her heart.

I wanted her to take me into that place that she reserved for only those she loved. I felt like if I could get there, then I have truly accomplished something in this life, my past accomplishment to this point paling in comparison. This would be the real challenge because thanks to my brother, her heart was not going to be an easy thing to win.

However, I am determined and failing was not something I knew how to do. The conquest for Earth's heart has begun and the way I figured it, all was fair in love and war.

I exhaled...

She has been through so much, the right thing for me to do would be to walk away from her. She was too innocent for my world. She was the kind of girl that liked the simple things and there was nothing simple about my life.

Damn, the decent thing to do would be to walk away. I chuckled, it's a good damn thing I don't strive to be decent. Who had time for all that sh*t? I go after what I want and if it doesn't come to me willingly, then I took it. Earth would be no different. Unfortunately for her, I've become hooked on her taste.

She is so sweet, her taste on my tongue was like a drug. I've never sampled anything like it. It took everything within me not take her last night. Mitch, that selfish mutha f**** had never brought her to pleasure. That rotten bastard. Seeing her come apart for me was the most astonishing thing I have ever witnessed.

I needed to see it again. I needed to sample her arousal again. In just a short time she had become my addiction.

However, the clock was ticking and as much as I would love to, I couldn't spend much more time hidden away in this private little paradise. My cell phone was in the arm rest of my car, I know it's been blowing up. My men were probably tearing apart the city as we speak looking for me.

What the hell was I thinking?

I had a tribe to look after and thirteen casinos to run. My life was demanding, entirely too demanding for what I was doing now. But still, I couldn't bring myself to walk away, there was no place I would rather be. For once, I was doing something just for me, doing something that brought me pleasure. I couldn't remember the last time I just chilled and did nothing.

Even arguing minuet points with Crazy Larry last night had been relaxing. Seeing Earth come upstairs flustered because Larry had gotten me high was refreshing. I couldn't think of the last time somebody was concerned about my wellbeing. I am the one who protects and takes care of everybody else, nobody has to take care of me. She had been like a little angry mother hen clucking over her chicks.

The thing is, I needed to get her to fall in love with me before she realizes it's not a chick she's let into her nest… but a wolf. I feel like once she's let me in her heart, it will then be okay to tell her who I am. To tell her…

What I am.

Damn, she looked so good in that yellow dress, and that gloss on her lips made me want to just pick her up and take her back into the bedroom and do my very best to ruin her. I chuckled as I shook my head. Poor girl, she had no idea what she was dealing with. She was soon going to find out though. The trick was to get her to fall in love before she does.

Hell, I was doing a damn good job. I didn't even recognize myself. Being here in her world, without the pressures and the stresses of mine brought out another side of me that I didn't even know existed.

I wonder is this why the Ancient of Days led me here. Maybe

he still had use for me. Maybe there wasn't too much blood on my hands after all.

I shook my head.

Naw… I have never been good at lying to myself. My hands were covered in blood. I couldn't confess to knowing why the Great Spirit has decided to gift me with one of his rare daughters, but he had. And I'm not giving her up. Not for her or anybody else.

However, for her own sake, I pray she can adjust to having me around, I'm not a complete savage, of course it will be better if she did it willingly…but it isn't necessary.

"You guys ready?" I asked as I came out the bathroom dressed in a Crazy Larry special. Today I was wearing a pair of black jeans and another one of his island button up shirts. This is one thing about my little vacay I was not going to miss.

"Yay!" My little Hobbit whose mother had gotten her dressed and ready to go yelled before she leapt up in my arms.

The Ancient of Days had trusted me with two of his daughters. My grandfather always said that children were perfect tools for the Great Spirit. He said their innocence makes for a faultless dwelling place for the Rauch Ha Qodesh.

Rain had taken one look at me and decided I was hers. Unlike her mother, who was a tougher egg to crack, she saw what she wanted and went after it. My kind of gal. This little fire cracker already had my heart. And somebody in my tribe was trying to hurt her by ripping her away from her mother.

The only three people with the power to make such a call in my name, was my step aunt and uncle, Paul and Isabel, or my little brother Micky. I know Mike wasn't behind this, which leaves Paul and Isabel. Neither of them was big on children, which meant they were doing this because of money.

No doubt trying to stop Earth from later realizing what she was entitled to, being the mother of a tribe member and coming for it. I chuckled, they were getting ready to get the shock of their lives. Thanks to their little selfish act, Earth was getting ready to become the wife of the tribe's chief.

On our way out the door she suddenly stopped, turning to look at me.

"What about Abner? There is only one way out, Crazy Larry will have a heart attack if he walks past them." Because her lips still glistened with that gloss that was driving me to distraction, I leaned down and kissed her soft succulent mouth. I couldn't resist.

"Don't worry about him, he's only seen when he wants to be." She frowned trying to figure out what I meant.

My poor Minx, in the coming days she was going to find out things that were going to have her questioning all she thought she knew of the place she was named after. I gently kissed her lips again.

"You're going to have to learn to trust me, Minx."

8

THE TALENTED MR. BLACK

EARTH

When we exited the stairs into the kitchen, it was to catch Larry with his arms around Betty, whispering something in her ear as she stirred a pot on the stove. The smell of curry filled the room.

"Smells good!" I called out and the two of them broke apart as if they were teenagers caught in the act of stealing kisses.

"My Word!" Betty said when Black exited the steps behind me with Rain in his arms. He was so tall that he had to duck down a bit to clear the door frame.

"Earth, child, is this the man you kidnapped?" She put her hand on her chest opening her mouth looking around to see if anybody else was witnessing what she was seeing.

I stood to the side and looked at him, nodding proudly. "Betty, this is Mr. Black, Black this is Larry's ex-wife Betty."

Larry was not happy with my introduction. He turned to face

me. "Wah mek yuh wudda tell a mon dat excites mi wife like dis dat mi har ex?"

Betty pushed past him and held her hand out for Black to kiss, but he ended up shaking it. "Hi there, handsome, my name is Betty, and I'm his ex-wife." She emphasized ex.

He chuckled. "Nice to meet you, ma'am."

She patted his arm playfully. "Why are you calling me ma'am? I'm younger than Larry."

"Eff dat mon neva suh big mi wud tek him out fi dis." Larry said coming to stand next to me sucking on his teeth. I shook my head at him.

"Let this be a lesson. You never know when a mon come along that's going to steal Betty from you for good."

He shook his head puffing out his chest. One of the things Larry did not suffer from was low self-esteem, not even a little bit.

"No mon can tek Betty away from mi. Mi gi har sup'm no oddah man cya eva gi har."

I rolled my eyes at his vanity. "Anyway, we're going out for a bit, but we should be back before your party gets started real good."

Wednesday nights is when Larry turned the juice bar into a lounge, he moved all the tables to the side in the restaurant making room for a dance floor. With Natty Dread on the turn tables, he generally generated a pretty penny with charging five dollars at the door, two dollars for Red Strip, and five dollars for rum and coke.

He nodded. "Yeah, mek sure yuh nuh forget. Pretty bowy there a guh really attract di ladies."

Hmmm...

I think that made me feel some kind of way. I mean I wasn't bothered by Betty, I know she was just trying to make Larry jealous. But I think I was bothered by the idea of other women checking Black out. Was I?

I shook my head. "Nah."

"Wat's dat?"

I cleared my throat. "Nothing, just said we're going to head out, so that we can get back."

"It gud to si unu traveling as a fambly ."

I turned to look at him. "We are not traveling as a family. I don't have anything to eat upstairs so were going for food that's all."

It was Larry's turn to roll his eyes. "Yeah mon, tell me anyting…"

Ignoring him, I walked over to rescue poor Black from Betty.

"Wow! You must spend a lot of time in the gym." She told him as she rubbed her hand up his muscled arm. He chuckled, but his desperate gaze came to mine.

I took the hand Betty held in mine. "Okay, we'll talk to y'all later." I called as I pulled him the rest of the way out the door.

Betty followed us to the door, her eyes shamelessly drinking in Mr. Black. "Don't forget we're having a little get together down here tonight. When you get the little one in bed, y'all come on down and have a cocktail with us!"

"We will." I called back to her. Black reached out and grabbed me around my waist pulling me back to him.

"Why didn't you protect me from that woman?" He whispered in my ear, causing me to giggle because his face was buried in my neck and his beard and mustache was tickling me.

"I'm sure you can take care of yourself."

He looked back and sure enough, Betty was still looking out the window at him.

"I'm afraid."

I threw back my head and laughed at that. He should be afraid of Betty. She was one of the thicker sistas and crazy Larry say her appetite was hard to handle when they make luv. A lesser man wouldn't stand a chance against such skill. His words.

Taking my keys out my purse I led the way to my car.

"Ohh!" I cried out when Abner appeared out of nowhere rubbing his big body against my leg. "He'd just scared the heck out of me, where did he come from?"

I was now clutching Black's free arm.

He chuckled. "I told you, he's only seen when he wants to be." With a hand that shook slightly I rubbed the cats big head.

"I guess you're right."

When we got to my car Black stood and eyeballed it with a slight frown on his face. I stood back and looked at it through his eyes.

"She's a little beat up, but she's reliable."

"Yeeeaah..." He said as he looked around. "You guys didn't happen to steal my car when you stole me did you?"

I grinned big. "As a matter of fact, we did. Larry parked it in his garage."

His leery gaze went to the broken-down structure that was in back of the building. "Is that the garage?"

My smile got a little strained as I slowly nodded.

"You wouldn't happen to have my keys, would you?"

I reached in my purse and took out his keys, handing them to him

"Good, I'll drive."

As we walked to that garage I prayed hard that Larry didn't do anything to this man's car. As soon as he parked it, I made sure I got his keys from him, so I know he didn't take it for a joy ride or anything. But Larry used the garage for storage, which was why we all parked in the little lot out back. And as y'all already know, Larry wasn't the neatest brotha on the block.

The light in here didn't work so I hit the switch to open the garage door, and as the light shined in I exhaled when I saw it still looked like a shiny space ship in midst of all Larry's junk.

We had to step over a lot of empty Red Stripe boxes to get to the car. Leave it to Larry not to throw them away. Black popped the locks and put Rain on the back seat buckling her in. Then he opened the door for me, after I slid in, he and Abner fought their way to the other side, and after letting his pet in to take a seat next to Rain, he slid in the driver seat.

I frowned because he didn't close the door. Instead he reached down under my seat and came from under it with a gun that he was trying to hide with his big hand. Then he reached under his seat and got another one. When I looked up at him shocked, he shrugged with a little grin on his face.

"Don't have Hobbits riding with me too often." He joked before he got out of the car holding the weapons so that Rain couldn't see and putting them in the trunk.

As I sat back in my seat, the only thing I could think was that the Heavenly Father protected babies and fools. And let me tell you something folks, Bria and I ain't no babies. Had he got a hold of either one of those guns, that was way bigger than Bria's little .22, we would have been dead , and I was willing to bet my life they were loaded.

"Ready?" He asked all cheery as he got back in the car.

Seeing him with those guns started me to thinking. What do I know about Mr. Black, except for the fact that he's Mitch's little brother, and he ain't as mean as his older brother, who everybody in their tribe called the devil?

I mean how many levels were there under the devil to fear?

"Calm down, Minx, I can hear your brain working." He said as he backed up out of the garage. I put on my seatbelt; this man just whipped the car out of the garage. Okay, that was something else I knew about him, he wasn't a very cautious driver.

"I don't know what you're talking about, I'm just enjoying the ride." I lied.

"So, you're not over their wondering what kind of man rides around with two guns in his car?" Pressing my lips together I shook my head.

Yes!!!!

He chuckled as he drove out the alley. "Well I'll tell you what kind of man carries guns with him. The kind of man that people poison and kidnap."

I had to bite my lip to try and tame my grin. "Touché."

He reached over and chugged me under my chin. "Don't get scared of me now, Minx."

Wow, I was going to start calling this man The Talented Mr. Black. I don't know how he always seemed to know what I was thinking. It's amazing, I was with Mitch for over a year, and he didn't even know when I was upset.

I was married to a man that never took the time to get to know me, and here Mr. Black had been around me for only two days and he seemed to read me like a book.

Earth, don't do anything foolish like fall in love with this man.

I turned to look at his profile as he drove. Dang it! He was so fine. Even dressed in Larry's ridiculous clothes, *he was so damn fine.* He had a royal profile, strong and powerful. It wasn't hard to tell that he had in fact descended from the great black kings of the past. I inhaled when he turned and caught me staring at him.

Crap!

"What is it, beautiful?"

His deep voice almost made me moan. "I was just wondering where we were going."

"I know this little place on Main Street that has really good steaks, I figured we can grab a couple of those and head to the beach. Give Abner a chance to get some exercise."

I smiled. "That sounds good."

* * *

WELL, I found out something else about the talented Mr. Black. He was the jealous type. And I'm not talking like a mean look jealous type.

No… Mr. Black was the lay hands on a man jealous type. Yep, he almost broke a man's hand in the grocery store. Okay, I know you guys are wondering what you missed. Let me rewind things a little.

So, we did get the steaks. But do you guys remember when he said we were going to grab a couple. Well that couple turned out to be ten steaks. Now, this wasn't a cheap steakhouse. This place was on Main Street, the steaks were like twenty dollars a pop.

Cocoa Beach was about an hour away for a normal driver, Black got us there in like twenty minutes, I kid you not. Since it was really cloudy outside because once again, rain was in the forecast, he ended up finding us the perfect spot on the beach that was fairly empty except for one or two surfers that wanted to tackle nature and conquer the monstrous waves.

Rain and I ended up sharing one of the steaks and potato meals, the things were huge. Black ate one and guess who ate the rest?

Mmmmhhhmmm, Abner.

The same Abner we were bringing to the beach so that he could get some exercise. Smh! Let me tell you what Mr. Abner did, as Rain, Black and I played a game of football that Black cheated at horribly. He sat sprawled out on the sand, swishing his tail as if he owned the beach.

And when Rain, Black and I played a game of tag, what did Abner do? You guessed it, sat on his royal heinie and didn't move a muscle.

At one point I got tired and ended up laying my head on his soft belly, reaching my hand up to rub his chin so that he could start purring. For a while I watched Rain and Black play. She was trying to push him in the water, he'd let her believe she had it until they got right to the edge but then he'd stop, and she would be standing behind him pushing his legs going nowhere.

Then at one point as the sun was turning orange behind the clouds, Rain and I switched places and it was she who laid on Abner's belly while it was me that Black was threatening to throw in the water.

"Black, stop playing!" I yelled when he scooped me up in his arms and carried me towards the water. I wrapped my arms around his strong neck burying my head in his soft beard.

"Please, please don't throw me in." I whined in his ear.

He stopped at the edge before pretending to toss me. I screeched tightening my arms around him.

He chuckled, laughing at my fear. I looked up at him pouting. "That's not funny."

His chuckle turned to a grin. "I tell you what, tell me a secret about yourself and I won't toss you." I unwrapped my arms from around his neck folding them in front of me.

"No, you being a bully."

He shrugged and made like he was going to toss me in again, my hands came around his neck so fast.

"Okay!" I screeched. "What do you want to know?"

"Why don't you play your violin anymore?"

His question startled me. My mind raced for an answer, but the truth was I couldn't explain to him something I myself did not understand. Earth's Cry was not of this world, I was convinced. In all the time I'd owned it, I'd never had to polish or fill in any cracks in the wood. I've never had to replace the pegs or the strings. Even the bridge always remains in place, never shifting forward or backward.

The same thing with the bow, it's made out of the same strange wood as the violin. I have searched all over the internet trying to find out what kind of wood it is, but have yet to come across any like it. And so too with the hairs of the bow, like the string of the violin, I have never had to change it or even tighten it for that matter. Horse hair is used for regular bows, I don't know what kind of hair was used for Earth's Cry.

It's not human, it's not any animal I have yet to encounter. And believe me folks, I have searched for the answer far and wide. The hair is the color of pure spun silver. If you look really close it looks almost crystalized.

No...I have never seen anything like it.

But none of that is the reason I haven't played in over five years. I haven't played Earth's Cry in over five years because the last time I did it took over my body.

And I know that sounds crazy, but it did. It showed me things, horrible things that have happened on the Earth, things that it had witnessed. I could not wake up, I couldn't do anything but weep as image after image of atrocities played out before my eyes.

With me still in his arms, Black eased down on the sand next to a sleeping Rain and Abner.

"What could have happened so bad with your instrument to change your mood like this?" He asked quietly. I lifted one side of my mouth in a grin that didn't reach my eyes.

"Why are you always studying my moods?"

He shrugged. "You interest me."

I straddled his lap staring down into his handsome face. Lifting my hand, I gently caressed his bottom lips with my finger.

"I don't want to talk about my violin." I whispered.

"What do you want to talk about?"

I shook my head. "Nothing." I gently lowered my lips to his. He tightened his arms around me bringing me closer as he deepened the kiss.

This man was such a good kisser I didn't notice the seconds turning into minutes or the minutes turning into hours. I didn't even notice the fact that the sky had begun to darken. He and I sat on that beach and kissed till my lips were sore. He even made me laugh out loud as he held my head and forcibly put a hickey on my neck, but my laughter turned into panting when he had somehow managed to get the top half of my dress undone so that he could have access to my breasts and put a matching hickey on my tender flesh.

We sipped from each other until Rain began to stir. Quickly he helped me do my dress back up before she came fully awake and then we left and headed to the grocery store because they decided they wanted pancakes in the morning. Now it was there I learned a few more things about the talented Mr. Black.

One, it was not a good idea to take him grocery shopping. His patience was about as thin as Rain's. Granted, nobody really liked going shopping with me. I was a label reader and a number cruncher. I just wanted to make sure I was getting the best bang for my buck.

By the time we made it to the second aisle, Black stood looking at me as if he wanted to throw me over his shoulder and carry me out. "Minx, it's just bread, put it in the damn cart already." The fact that he actually growled his statement let me know how irritated he was with me.

"I just want to make sure I'm getting the best product for my dollar."

"But that's just it, it's not your dollar, it's mine, and I don't care which one you get. Just get it!"

I put my hand on my chest pretending to be offended. I really wasn't though, I was used to this. Both Bria and Larry have threatened to walk out the grocery store and leave me.

"Oh, my goodness, we've only been in here for like fifteen minutes. Relax."

Rain, who was grouchy because we'd had to wake her up to come in the store wasn't in any better condition. She too whined saying she was ready to go home. Poor baby, all that running on the beach had tuckered her out.

"Listen," I snapped at them both. "Y'all whining ain't gon' help this go faster. Why don't you take Rain and go taste some of the samples the ladies are handing out while I do this."

"Gladly! Come on, Hobbit, we might as well have some tasty treats since your mom insist on torturing us." He muttered before he scooped Rain up out the buggy into his arms. Shaking my head, I went back to doing what I do best...making sure I get the best bang for my buck...Or rather Black's buck.

Now, as you guys know, I spent a little extra time fixing myself up this morning, so it was safe to say I was looking kind of cute. There were a few men checking me out, but with Black's big self walking next to me, not for long. However, when he and Rain walked away the guys were a little friendlier. One guy in particular was friendlier than the others.

I was standing in the syrup aisle studying the syrups. I liked to get the syrup without the high-fructose corn syrup in it, but I liked to get that on a budget. Standing on my toes I reached up for the one I had gotten last time that was pretty good. But my hand froze when an arm reached over my head to get it for me.

Startled, I turned to see this guy standing really close smiling down at me.

"Let me get that for you. It's the least I could do since you decided to give us sunshine on this cloudy day."

Mmmm mmm, if he was trying to be charming he missed.

Before I could open my mouth to check him for crowding my space his eyes looked behind me and widened as if he was seeing a monster. Then a familiar muscled arm shot past me and grabbed the syrup and the man's hand at the same time.

"Thank you, brother, Sunshine and I appreciate that." Black's deep voice came from over my shoulder.

"Ahhh!!!" The poor guy cried, bunching up his shoulders in pain as the sound of his fingers cracking around the bottle could be heard in the small space the three of us stood in.

When Black let him go that fella didn't waste any time getting out of there, clutching his hand he literally ran from the aisle without once looking back. I turned to face the giant of a man next to me, who was calmly sitting Rain back in the cart. When he saw me looking at him he smiled like nothing happened.

"That was nice of him to get that down for us, huh, Sunshine?"

Biting my lip, I tried not to laugh at his silliness, knowing I shouldn't condone this behavior. But when he blinked in fake innocence it was too much and I erupted into laughter. However, when he smiled back, I wiped the laughter off my face.

Well...at least I tried. "That's not funny, you probably broke that man's hand."

"No baby, you are looking at this the wrong way. I taught that brotha a lesson. What do you think he's going to do the next time he sees somebody else's woman reaching for a bottle of syrup?"

"Hold his head down and keep walking." I said around my laughter.

He nodded. "He should be thanking me. The next man may not be as kind as I."

Mr. Black is charming if he's nothing else. The fact that he managed to make me laugh at his jealous act only testified to that. But once again, it's something I should have paid closer attention to. You see guys, I would soon meet the real man underneath all that charm. I would learn just how ruthless he could become in a matter of seconds.

And I guess when I look back at things, there were little hints and clues that gave away his true nature.

The cold, predatory, unguarded look I glimpsed last night. The way he'd come upon me at the sink without me hearing him and completely rendered me helpless before I even knew what was happening. The guns in his car. The encounter in the grocery store.

I ignored all those signs that pointed to his true nature, and instead found myself spiraling deeper and deeper into the web that was The Talented Mr. Black.

9

THE ALLURE OF THE YELLOW DRESS

EARTH

*A*llow me to explain the allure of the yellow dress, just in case there are some ladies out there that don't know the power it holds. You see, when a girl feels beautiful down on the inside, there ain't nobody in the world that can convince her different. She emits a certain chemical that causes everyone around her to see exactly what she sees.

If only for the day…

It's in the way that she walks, the way she lifts her hand to signal for a cab, the way she throws her head back and laugh at a joke. It's in the way she turns her head to look at an admirer, the way she turns and looks away just at the right moment.

The girl puts on the yellow dress because in that day, she feels beautiful. She's granted an intermission from on high, and in that day, no negative spirits are allowed to whisper any thoughts to her…thoughts that produce doubt.

In that day, she's not too skinny or too fat. In that day, she's not too dark or not dark enough. In that day, her hair is not too curly or too straight. In that day, her eyes sparkle just right, because in that day, she's just right the way she is and there is nothing anyone can say to make her feel different.

Now I don't know if it was my yellow dress or Crazy Larry's Rum and Coke, or a stimulating combination of them both, but I stood barefoot off to the side of the juice bar that had been temporarily turned into a night club and I moved my body in a way that reflected how I felt on the inside.

Today, I am the girl in the yellow dress and I am just right…

I felt beautiful. Sexy, feminine…

Closing my eyes, I let my head fall back as I offered myself to him, even though he stood across the room. In that moment, I understood that whatever it was down inside me would only appeal to him. I mean sure, other men looked at me with admiration, but he watched me with something more. He wanted what was at the very base of my core. He wanted something that went beyond my body, something that went beyond my mind. He wanted everything that made me…me.

And at this moment, that knowledge served as an aggressive aphrodisiac. The music felt as if it was a part of me. I moved my hips gently in a dirty wind to the beat.

Biting my lip, I inhaled as I imagined his mouth on me, touching me, tasting me in a way that is most intimate. In the way he'd tasted me last night, in the way he'd just tasted me on the beach. The delicious tenderness from the hickey on my neck and the tips of my breasts bear witness to that and serve as a constant reminder of his hungry kiss.

As I danced, images of him last night flooded my mind. He was so powerful and strong, using his mouth and hands to bring me to the heights of fulfillment somewhere far up into space close to the moon, only to cause my world to shatter with one last flick of his tongue and giving way from under me, making me feel as if I was falling and crashing back to the earth.

I remembered screaming my release in fear that I would fall to my death, only for him to catch me before I hit the ground pulling me into his arms and whispering to me that everything was going to be alright.

A shiver went through my body as I imagined what it would be like if he took me fully. If he could make me feel that way with just his mouth and hands, how much more would I feel with him inside of me?

I moaned as the tempo changed. Natty Dread had slowed down the rhythm and although my hips changed pace to match it, my heartbeat increased with the thought of sex with the Talented Mr. Black.

In my mind, it's raw, dirty and wet. In my mind, he causes me to abandon everything that makes me, me, as I become one with him. In my mind, he takes me completely and I forget to breathe. And he whispers...

Breathe, Minx...

I know the very moment the spotlight falls on me, but I don't stop dancing, because I'm dancing for him. I take courage in my Yellow Dress and I own it.

There are so many eyes on me right now, but it was only one pair that mattered. Although the lighting had been dimmed, I felt him watching me from across the room. I continued to sensually roll my hips as I slowly rubbed my hands up my neck and then back down, imagining him touching me that way.

"Look at the way he's watching her." Betty muttered to Bria from where they sat at the table behind me. "He looks like a predator, so dangerous and hungry. Damn, he's going to turn our little Earth out!"

Her words caused me to inhale sharply. I should stop. I was no match for Black... but I couldn't, instead, I threw back my head, rubbing my hands up my neck, wanting him to turn me out.

"Yes, he is. That's the kind of nigga that'll have a b**** stalking him, carrying his picture and a piece of his hair around, like no, nigga, it ain't over till I say it is." Bria said changing her voice to imitate what I'm pretty sure was Satan.

I couldn't help the smile that came to my face. Damn, I loved my friend, even though she's clearly mentally challenged.

"It's something seriously wrong with you. Are you aware of that?" Betty hissed at her.

"Look how he standing over there against the wall watching her. You can see every freaky dirty thing he wants to do to her in his eyes." Bria continued.

"Look at the way the other guys stand around him, as if just being close to him makes them look powerful." They both laughed at that, but I tuned them out because right then, I opened my eyes and instantly I'm wrapped up in the tempest of Black's midnight gaze.

He's leaned against the wall right across the room from me with one leg propped up on it behind him with his hands in his pockets. He looks casual, as if he's just chilling and enjoying the scene.

However, there was nothing in his gaze that said he was calm. He watched me with that same hungry look I'd spied last night. Only tonight, it didn't scare me like it did then. And I know that is because of Larry's Rum and Coke.

That look in his eyes should scare me. If I had good sense, I would not continue to tease him like I'm doing, but I don't have good sense. Holding his dangerous gaze, I continued to roll my hips, rubbing my hands up my body, gently raising them in the air above me, giving myself to the music, imagining giving myself to him.

Bria and Betty are right. The Talented Mr. Black stood across the room surrounded by Larry and several other guys that stood next to him trying to appear as majestic as he.

You see, y'all? That's the kind of brotha he is, other men surrounded him holding their heads high, drawing from the power he exuded. And yet the whole time, he stood watching me. There were quite a few women in the room, some of them dressed in far less material than I.

And yet...he stood watching me.

I licked my lips. I don't know if it was the fact that I had downed four Rum and Cokes or the fact that the red lighting that Larry liked to use for these parties cast Black in a sexy glow. But I was ready to give him what I'd never given another man outside of my late husband. I wanted him to make me feel good.

Melech Black

IT IS SAID that the Daughters of Sarah, rare entities indeed, are gifts from the Great Spirit to those men found worthy of being a chosen warrior of the Ancient of Days. These women, who are desired by many, becomes a curse to whatever man or being that tries to possess her who she was not created for. Many men, kings, angels, demons...have been destroyed for trying to obtain the unobtainable.

But to the man she is created for, she is worth more than rubies and gold. She becomes his peace, his tent, his comfort. She becomes proof that the Great Spirit has not forgotten about him, even if until this very moment, he thought he had.

This man, this warrior, will notice her instantly, because she was created just for him. When I first saw Earth's picture, something about her called to me. But at the time, she belonged to my brother and there was no way it could have gone any further than that.

What I couldn't tell from a picture is that there is a light inside of her that I am now convinced only I can see. It radiates from her skin and her eyes; I can see it coming from the strands of her hair, from the tips of her fingers. I saw it in the restaurant when she looked down at me and offered me water. I saw it when I awoke tied to her chair. When I touched her with my tongue, I tasted it.

Her taste…

A sweetness like I'd never sampled before…

But if I had wondered before, there is no longer a question in my mind. As I stood now and watched Earth dance for me…only me, it became clear who she is.

A Daughter of Sarah…

My eyes have never seen a woman more beautiful. Everything about her called out to me. Her beautiful brown skin, her long, graceful neck, the way she dances with her feet bare, looking like a mystical minx sent here to test my self-control I'd prided myself in till this day.

And I know like I know money, her beauty was created especially for me. Like I said earlier, I will never let her go. I'm not capable of it, I don't have the strength to walk away from her and all that she can offer me. There are angels and demons who have fallen because of these special daughters. Kings…

I… well, I am just a man.

That being said, possessing one of these rare jewels comes with great responsibility. If the Ancient of Days has gifted her to me, then I know that he in turn will require my existence. And that's the part that scares me the most. I have come a long way from the old way. The values my grandfather taught me are now childhood memories. That faze of my life is long gone.

I am now deeply steeped in the game of making money, and I

can't see myself giving all of that up to submit to the will of the Ancient of Days. My gut's telling me my life now is way easier than what my grandfather convinced me I had been born to do. Even then, I rejected his words; I don't know that I'm ready for that kind of responsibility.

Why me?

Right then, Natty Dread positioned the spotlight so that it's shining down on Earth, her head falls back, exposing her long, graceful neck and my mouth waters. She is moving her hips gently in a controlled way that lets me know that she's purposely not giving away too much, but just enough to call to me. However, for all those looking, it's clear that she could do more if she so chose to.

I watch her rub her hands up her neck while swaying her hips to the beat and my hands twitched, wanting to touch her, needing to touch her. Then she opens her big beautiful eyes to look at me. Like mist, all of my previous thoughts of not being ready to submit to the will of The Great Spirit evaporate.

A growl came from my throat as I watched another man approach her, drawn to her allure like a bee to honey. I know then that whatever it is that's required of me, I will do to keep her.

EARTH

"Dance with me, sista." A guy that frequented these parties asked as he held out his hands to the sides of me, winding his body in a way to match mine. I forgot his name, I think it was something like John or Josh maybe.

I wanted him to leave instantly. He was like a bucket of cold water. He didn't carry the kind of strength I needed. His smell wasn't the smell I was looking for. His hands are not the ones that are capable.

Right when I was going to just stop dancing, a big hand palms John's chest and shoves him out of the way. I smile because I know that hand. It's the hand that's causing me to throw my head back and moan, imagining it touching me.

Black's strong arm wrapped around me and pulled me against his muscled body. Instantly I feel relief as his scent and strength surrounds me. He doesn't even look behind him at the angry man he'd just shoved out of the way. He's not even worried. John stood for a moment, sizing Black up, but must have decided against trying to take him, because he turns and walks away shaking his head.

I looked up into the eyes of the Talented Mr. Black and although there is amusement in my gaze, I slowly shake my head at him, the confidence he exudes is like a drug. Or maybe I'm being drugged by the way this powerful man is looking down at me as if he wants me and only I will do.

I let the music take over and turn in his arms so that my soft behind is rubbing against his hardness in a most carnal way. And as if on cue, Natty Dread drops a grimy beat that draws several couples to the floor. Betty looks at me and nods as if to tell me to gon' and show the Talented Mr. Black how we do things around here.

I think about it for only a moment...

What the hell? Why not?

As soon as the bass drops, I began to show this brotha how the dirty wind is done. I feel him groan, surprised I had these movements in me. Its deep penetrating rumble washes over me, causing me to really get into it. Betty watches me from our table like a proud mama as I expertly execute the moves she'd taught me.

The beat is grimy and I dip my hips while rolling them. I can feel Black's body changing behind me. I don't think he's doing much dancing, but he has his big hands on my hips as he is watching me do my thang, while somehow managing to use his body to block me and my movements from the other men in the room.

Larry pulls Betty on the floor and she and Bria dance with me, hyping me through the dancing that I know is driving the big man behind me crazy. Yeah, I may be boring and a book worm, but thanks to Betty, I could be the Dance Hall Queen if I so chose. I can wind the hell out of my hips.

I inhale sharply when he suddenly grabs me, pulling me up close in front of him, my bare feet are barely touching the floor. Closing my eyes, I damn near moan when I feel his mouth on my ear.

"Damn, Minx! What are you trying to do to me?" His words are a little over a growl. "Who the hell do you think you playing with?"

Oh, my goodness! He is so feral. Wild...untamable. So damn hot! With a smile on my face, I reached up and removed his hands from me, slipping through his fingers like butter.

I want him!

Everybody else in the room just seemed to disappear.

Without turning my body to face him, I just turn my head to look back at him. My eyes go from his boot covered feet, up to his bowlegs, tapered waist and ripped abs that look amazing in the t-shirt he's wearing. I took in the beautifully muscled chest, the column of his strong neck, the pair of lips that are nestled nicely between his trimmed beard and mustache, the high cheek bones that give his handsome face the dangerous feel...and lastly, the pair of dark eyes that can't hide the fact that this man is a savage.

"Meet me upstairs in fifteen minutes..." I tell him, amazed at myself and my brazenness.

The grin that came on his face had to be the exact one the Wolf wore when Little Red invited him to look into her basket. I should be afraid at what that look promised, but I wasn't. This man was not my late husband. Black's touch was going to become my new addiction.

Hell, it already was, and he has yet to take me fully. I didn't need that kind of complication in my life right now. Rain needed me to make the right decisions.

But what about what you need?

Yes, what about what I needed? I needed what only this man can give. I needed to feel really good, if only for the night. I needed to know what it's like to be made love to by a real man... a man like Black.

He reached out and grabbed my hand bringing it to his lips and instead of kissing the back of it, he held it up and gently kissed the inside of my wrist where my pulse beat. I closed my eyes when I felt his warm tongue, the shiver that went through me was so strong, I knew he felt it.

"You're sure you want to do this?" His deep voice was even more drugging than his kiss.

Oh, hell yes!

But to him I just nodded. "I'm sure." I whispered before I turned and slowly walked away, working the hell out of my hips and this yellow dress. I could feel his eyes on me like one would feel the rays from the sun or drops of rain.

When I reached the stairs that led up to my place, I paused for just a moment to look over at him. He still stood where I left him watching me like a hungry wolf, not caring in the least that all eyes in the joint were watching him watch me.

No, he didn't try to curb his hunger one bit. And just like last night, I couldn't help but feel as if a predator stared back at me. But unlike last night, that look didn't scare me, it excited me.

With one hand on the rail and one bare foot on the steps, I licked my lips before lifting an eyebrow. My message was loud and clear...

Show me?

That dangerous grin appeared on his face before he slowly nodded, his answer just as clear.

I will...

By the time I let myself into my apartment, my bravado had fled a little and my nervousness had somehow worked its way back in. However, my anticipation kept it from causing me to punk out. Gently as not to waken her, I widened the crack in Rain's bedroom door to check in on her.

Abner lifted his head to look at me from where he had been lying on the ABC rug in front of her bed. Smiling I waved at him. Black convinced me that Abner was a great babysitter. Still out of habit, I ran back and forward up here to check on her several times over the last hour and a half.

Surprisingly, each time I had, Abner had been in his place right in front of her bed watching over her.

"Thanks for looking after her for me." I whispered.

He swooshed his tail once through the air before laying his big head back on the floor. Chuckling I pulled the door back up, leaving it cracked just a bit so that he could come out if he wanted and made my way to my bedroom.

If you would have told me yesterday around this time that I would be letting a pet Jaguar babysit Rain, I would have called you a liar. What a difference a day makes.

Shaking my head, I opened my underwear drawer. With hands that shook both from nervousness and anticipation, I looked through it for something sexy to put on.

This was a problem, because I didn't have anything sexy. I mean, why would I? I'd been celibate for six years. Exhaling in frustration, I desperately searched through my things. What kind of woman didn't own at least a couple of pieces of lingerie just in case?

The kind of a woman that needed to spend money wisely and not waste it for things that will get no use.

I pulled out a pair of pink lace panties I had found at Walmart for a dollar. They were nice and the sexiest pair I owned. The original price was fourteen dollars before they went on sale. I racked my brain to figure out what to partner them up with, not brave enough to wear them alone.

Opening my other drawers, I looked through them and found nothing. I went to my closet. Nothing...

Then I remembered the little pink halter top Bria had bought me from Victoria's Secret. They had a sale, buy one and get one free; she got one for the both of us. Standing on my toes I took the pink and black bag down from the top of my closet shelf.

Showed you what I thought of this sexy item, I hadn't even taken it out of the bag. When she bought it for me, I gave her the side eye.

"Where in the hell am I supposed to wear this?" I'd asked holding the little t-shirt that looked as if it was Rain's size up to my chest.

She smacked her lips. "Why you got to be so old-fashioned? How about you wear it anywhere, so you can find yourself a man?"

"The man I catch wearing this ain't going to be nothing but a headache later."

"Dammit, Earth, you so boring! The man you catch in them granny panties ain't gon' be nothing but a great disappointment to your clitoris later."

My mouth opened, shocked by the words my best friend had let come out of her mouth. But I didn't know why I was, Bria always said crazy stuff. Anyway, I stood arguing with her for another minute, trying to get her to keep the shirt for herself, but she refused to take it back. So, I'd just thrown it back in the bag and tossed it up on my shelf.

Now I could kiss my crazy, stubborn friend. Because of her, I was getting ready to work the hell out of the t-shirt and panty look. At least that's what I told myself.

After a quick shower, I moisturized my skin really good with my fruit fusion body butter. I liked this blend because not only did it smell edible, it left my skin glowing beautifully. With only about a minute before Black was due to come up, I tried to figure out where was the best place to be when he walked into the room.

Should I lie down in the bed like Eartha Kitt?

Naw, that seemed kind of desperate.

What about sitting on the bed?

I shook my head, that seemed kind of amateurish.

By the time he gently opened the bedroom door, I stood leaning against my dresser hugging myself, subconsciously trying to cover up my exposed belly as I bit nervously on my thumb nail.

Can you guys say, Huge Fail?!

He chuckled as he closed the door behind him.

"Well look at you. Aren't you sexy in pink?" His deep voice was so confident.

The nervous giggle that left my lips only bore witness to my fear.

"You look afraid, Minx." He said coming to stand in front of me, he took my hands in his and slowly pulled my arms away from my body so that he could see it fully. He groaned.

I swallowed, not being able to bring my eyes up to meet his intense gaze, so I just stared at his chest and nodded. "I am a little."

"Why?" He asked in a hush tone before he slowly lowered himself to one knee in front of me, his easy movement showing the strength in his big body. He lowered himself so that his head came to about the level of my breast, forcing me to look down into his eyes.

"Why are you afraid?"

I bit my bottom lip as I shrugged. "I've never done this with anybody besides Mitch. I almost feel like a virgin."

He leaned in and gently kissed above my belly buttoned where my tight pink shirt stopped. My stomach quivered under his lips.

"Mmmm, you smell good."

I licked my lips. "Thank you."

"I don't want you to be afraid of me." He quietly said as he continued to open mouth kiss my stomach and belly button.

"I just want to kiss you at first. Is that okay? We won't do anything until you're no longer nervous. For now, just let me kiss you. Okay?"

I nodded looking down at him as he hooked his fingers in my panties and slowly slid them down tossing them to the side.

"Would you like me to taste you?" He asked in between placing gentle kisses on my inner thigh. Biting down hard on my bottom lip I nodded again as my breath began to come out in shallow puffs from my body.

"Say it…Tell me what you want, Minx."

"I--," swallowing my words cut off…I have never dirty talked before.

"Come on, baby…tell me what you want. Where did my brave little Minx from downstairs go, my beautiful lady that danced for her man?" The whole time he spoke, he used his hot breath and lips to drive me crazy.

"I want you to taste me, Black." I finally said, not being able to take anymore of his teasing. Every nerve in my body felt aroused and on the edge.

"Good girl, I want to taste you too. It's all I've thought about since we left the beach." He wrapped his hands around my waist and lifted me until I was sitting slightly on my dresser. Then he halfway opened two of the drawers and probed my feet up on them.

"Hold on baby, can you do that for me?"

I nodded, clutching the edge of the dresser so tightly my knuckles were white.

He smiled the smile of the hungry wolf. "Good girl."

Black caused my world to shatter twice, back to back. By the time he carried me to my bed and gently lay me on its surface, I was more than ready for him.

I wanted him to take me fully.

However, when he joined me on the bed without his clothes, I had a moment of doubt. There was nothing about his body that was like my late husband's. I mean really, they had nothing in common, if you get my drift.

And for just a minute, I felt panic, afraid that my body was not going to be able to accommodate him. I opened my mouth to express my concerns, but he only palmed my face with his big hands, holding my gaze captive in that dark abyss.

"Shhh, baby. Everything will be alright!" He cooed as he ever so slowly filled me, proving my thoughts wrong.

I exhaled a breath that I hadn't even been aware I was holding. At first, he didn't move. He just let me get adjusted to the feel of him. And then very gently, he made love to me on my bed all while palming my face, forcing me to look into his gaze.

Every time my eyes drifted closed, he'd whisper.

"Look at me, Minx. I want you to know who this is making you feel this way. Black…not Mitch. Black."

10

MEET THE GUARDIANS

MELECH BLACK

*E*arth felt good lying in my arms, I didn't know if she was asleep or like me, lying awake, thinking about the amazing sex we'd just had without a condom. I'd just sealed this woman's fate and I couldn't help but to wonder if maybe I'd done it on purpose.

When I became heir to my stepfather's small kingdom, one of the first lessons taught was never to let my seed spill in a woman that is not my wife. Any child that came from me is a child of the chief, therefore entitling them to a good chance at becoming chief of our tribe should I pass and a massive inheritance.

Over the years, I have been with many women, women who now seem faceless since Earth. And I have never gone into any of them without protection. A man in my position was always in danger of some gold digger trying to get pregnant with my child to weasel her way into the spot of wife to the tribal chief.

And like I said, although our kingdom was quite small as far as kingdoms go, it was still very much an empire, and a very rich one at that. You'll be surprised how many women wanted to get their go at it.

Earth had no clue that the position was now hers. I'd studied her closely over the last few days, and I was positive that when she found out, she was going to put up a fight. My money didn't mean anything to her. She wanted happiness; she didn't give a damn about wealth.

But what was even more amazing was the fact that I'd just made love to her and I wanted her again. Just the thought of how good her heat felt wrapped around me was waking up my hunger. There is no prettier sight than watching her unravel for me. I wanted to see it again.

I'd told myself I would let her rest, knowing she was probably a little tender. But then I kissed her shoulder and she moaned. I whispered in her ear, telling her how beautiful she is when she comes apart for me, and she moaned again, her hips moving slightly, invitingly.

I turned her in my arms so that she was lying on the bed next to me, gently easing my body down between her soft thighs, still telling myself that I wouldn't take her again so soon. Telling myself I would ignore the hunger this woman has caused to be a living, breathing thing inside of me.

I kissed her neck, my lips seeking hers. As soon as they touched those soft, well kissed beauties I was lost. Needing to feel her again like I needed my next breath, I took her. But this time not so gently. It damn near killed me to go slow the first time and there was no way in hell I could do it again.

She made me feel as if I was fighting not to lose control. I could not get enough of her. At one point, needing to feel her deeper, I put one hand on the wall and lifted her body with my other arm bringing her closer as I drove into her. Feeling like liquid fire in my hands, my brave little Minx wrapped her arms around my neck, holding on tight like a good girl, and I made her moans turn into screams.

Hearing her scream my name as she unraveled for me was a high like I've never experienced before. Shutters racked through my body to match hers when I felt my warm seed release from me and flow into her.

I've found my new addiction, and her name is Earth.

EARTH

Careful, so that I didn't wake Black, I slid out of his arms. I couldn't help but smile at the way he held me with not only his arms wrapped around me, but also his leg. I once read an article about the body language of men. It said that if a man slept with his arms and legs wrapped around a woman, it meant he had strong feelings for her and didn't want to risk losing her in his sleep.

I shook my head as I wrapped my robe around me. I didn't know if that was true or not, but it was kind of cute waking up to him sleeping that way. However, my smile disappeared when my thoughts went back to Black's sticky seed between my legs.

I couldn't believe I had sex with him not only once, but twice without protection. It was like in that moment where I could have stopped it, I just didn't. Yeah it felt good, real good...But that wasn't the only reason I didn't stop him.

Our joining felt spiritual.

And I know to many of you that probably sounds stupid, but it did. When I'd gotten pregnant by Mitch, it hadn't been anything like that. He and I actually wore a condom, but it broke. Nothing spiritual there, just an honest to goodness mistake.

Although it was a mistake, I would do it again if it meant getting my Rain. I couldn't imagine my life without Rain.

Needing to clean myself up, I made my way to the bathroom.

The funny thing was that the farther I got away from Black, the more I began to feel like what I'd done was in fact stupid. Goodness! Is it possible the man held some kind of power or something that drew me to him?

How could I let my late husband's brother come inside me?

I leaned my head against the bathroom mirror. *Oh! My! God!* I was getting ready to freak out.

Like I needed another child, another child by the same family who was trying to destroy my life. And Black was not like Mitch; he was way more assertive and domineering.

"What have I done?" I asked my reflection as I rubbed my hands down my face. Amazing how reality can wash back over a person, making them feel foolish.

Dammit! After making a huge mistake with Mitch, I prided myself in never doing anything senseless again. Even though I was constantly prompted by my reckless friend to let go and do something stupid, I'd managed not to.

Introduce the Talented Mr. Black and his ability to make my body crave his, and I've gone and did the ultimate stupid thing, sleep with him without a condom, not to mention the fact that he could have just given me some kind of disease or something. I know that I'm clean because I haven't had sex with anyone since my last checkup. Hell, I've been celibate since my late husband.

There was no telling how many women Black has been with. He was what most women in the world would consider the perfect catch, tall, dark, handsome…not to mention rich. He probably had women throwing their panties at him everywhere he went.

Crap!

After I was finished cleaning myself up, I headed into the kitchen to make myself a cup of tea, because there was no way I was going back to sleep with all this on my mind. Mid pour, I felt Abner's warm body rub against the back of my leg.

I reached down and rubbed his big head as I walked to the couch and took a seat with my cup in hand. As if he could sense the turmoil going on inside of me, he hopped up on the couch next to me and settled his big body against my side like he'd done Black earlier.

I rubbed his belly and he began to purr. Amazingly, that was quite soothing. "You are just the gentlest soul, aren't you?" I cooed.

"When he wants to be, there are many who would argue the exact opposite about him."

Black's deep voice startled me. I looked up to see him leaning against the hallway wall watching me.

"How long have you been standing there?" I asked with a bittersweet smile on my face.

"Long enough to see the battle you're fighting with yourself."

I grunted, not denying his words as I tucked my legs underneath myself, my feet ended up underneath Abner's warm body.

Shirtless in only a pair of jeans, Black eased down on the coffee table in front of me, his strong legs opened wide boxing me in. My gaze raked over his body appreciatively. Goodness, this man is gorgeous. It was impossible to see him this way and not think about how he'd just loved me, how he'd held me close as he filled me, forcing me to take his powerful thrusts.

And just like that, the hunger he'd introduced me to was awakened, wanting…no, needing him again.

"What's on your mind?" His deep voice was gentle, but it was his eyes that I was drowning in. I took another sip of my tea, not looking away from him.

"We had unprotected sex."

There was no need for me to beat around the bush. I was more than curious to see his response to that.

He exhaled as he slightly nodded his head, his eyes studying me. "We did."

The fact that he didn't even show the slightest sign of remorse threw me a little.

"That was dangerous…right?" My words were a little more than a whisper.

He leaned forward resting his arms on his knees, bringing himself closer to me. At first, he didn't speak, he just took my hand in his, playing with my fingers.

"What if I told you I've never done that before?"

I lifted an eyebrow. "I would say you're the most talented virgin I've ever met."

He chuckled. "No, I mean had unprotected sex. I've never had sex without a condom."

I studied him, my eyes searching his. He was telling the truth.

"Then I would have to ask, why now? Why me?"

He chuckled again as he nodded. "I want to be with you. I want to be Rain's dad. I want you to be the mother of my children."

I pulled my hand from his. "What? How can you know that? You barely know me?"

He reached out and took my hand again. "I know that you're a great mom. I see you with Rain, she's happy and smart. You take time to nurture her, teach her, and love her. I know that you're caring and brave. I know that when you love, you love strong. And I want that…I want you to love me. I want you to love our children."

He was pleading with me with his eyes. I opened my mouth to speak, but no words came out. What could I say? I wanted him too. To be desired by this kind of man was astonishing. What was it about me that attracted him? I wasn't bold and beautiful like Bria. All the men were always attracted to Bria.

"But I'm boring." I told him.

He shook his head. "I don't see that. I see the Minx you keep hidden under all your pain. Life has forced you to take it seriously. And that's not bad. I'm just glad it's something about me that brings the Minx out of you."

Wow! His words were true. He had caused me to step outside some of my norms, like dancing for him downstairs in a room full of people. I would have never done that, and also trying to seduce him when he first came.

"I'm not that pretty." I said, now curious to see what he would say to that.

He reached out and rubbed his rough finger along my cheek. "I've never seen a woman more beautiful in my whole life."

"I—I'm afraid…"

He nodded. "Me too…"

I gave him a look of doubt. "What do *you* have to be afraid of? You have everything. You're strong and powerful, not to mention smart. You're blessed, God is with you…"

He stared at me for a moment, taking in my words. I sat back, I don't know what made me say the last of that. The words just came to my mouth and spilled out. My words shook him. He let go of my hand and stood.

Surprisingly, he began to pace, reminding me of a caged cat. For some reason my words had caused turmoil in him. He stopped pacing all at once and looked at me.

"What made you say that?"

Chuckling to cover up my uneasiness, I gestured toward him. "Look at you, you're very muscl—"

He shook his head cutting me off. "Not that. You said God is with me…What made you say that?"

I bit my bottom lip. "I—I don't know…the words just came out."

He nodded again, as if he understood something I didn't. And then he took his seat back on the table in front of me, reaching for my hand again.

"That's just it, baby. I am afraid of some things." There was agony in his voice. I put down my tea cup and wrapped my other hand around his. I didn't like seeing him in agony, no way no how.

"Like what?" Surprisingly, I was ready to go to battle for him. I was ready to fight any demon that plagued him and caused him agony.

When he spoke, he looked down at our joined hands, and I knew that I was seeing a part of him I probably never would again. In this moment, in this hour of the night, he was vulnerable.

"I'm afraid that one day you will look at me like I'm a monster." His words were low. "I'm afraid that once you see the real me, you will want to leave. I'm afraid of what it means now that you're in my life. I'm afraid of the change that awaits me."

I reached up and gently buried my fingers in his beard, lifting his head so that our eyes connected. I don't know where this fierce need to protect him came from, but I couldn't stand seeing him vulnerable.

"I will never look at you like a monster. And my feelings for you are strong as well." I chuckled. "I'm surprised…When I kidnapped you, I never imagined that I would come to lo—care about you." I stuttered, not believing what I'd almost said.

"We'll take each day at a time." I continued. "I don't know what it means now that we're in each other's life, and yeah, change is always scary. But we have each other now and together, we can face whatever change brings our way."

The muscle ticked in his cheek as he listened to my words. I don't know what battle he was fighting within himself, only that he fought one. When I finished speaking, he leaned in and kissed my lips.

"You promise?" He growled.

I nodded as he stood lifting me in his arms. "I promise."

"Can I take you back to bed and make love to you again?"

I nodded. "I would like that very much."

"Can I have you completely?"

I knew what he was asking. He was asking if we could continue to have unprotected sex. I think it was that power he held over me whenever we were close that had me nodding my head.

"I would like that very much.

* * *

OVER THE NEXT FEW DAYS, Black and I made love like rabbits. We could barely keep our hands off each other. I'm not going to lie, I was falling in love with him. He was perfect with me and Rain. And I know for sure she loved him.

How in the world did this happened so fast?

Anytime I bring up the custody date that was getting closer and closer, he always waves it away, telling me not to worry about that.

"Nobody from my tribe is taking Rain away from you. That's my word."

And I believed him. I was able to breathe easily. I found myself laughing with him and playing with him. Last night we let Rain talk us into having a wrestling match, which turned into him tickling the both of us on the floor till I felt like I was going to pee my pants.

Abner jumped on his back knocking him off of us. And amazingly, the two of them started wrestling. Abner is a big cat; when he threw his body at Black it took him off his feet. And of course, that caused old grouchy Larry to call upstairs.

"Wah gwaan up there? Yuh killing dat bredda up there?"

I erupted in laughter. "No, he's trying to kill *me*!" I yelled out because right then, Black came up behind me swooping me up in his arms holding me in front of Abner.

"Get away from me or I'll take her out." He told his pet, causing me to erupt in another fit of laughter when he shook me up.

"It's gud to hear happeness inna yuh voice, Earth." Larry said into the phone sounding more serious than I'd heard in a long time. "Dat man brings out di gud inna yuh."

Larry's words stayed with me all last night and this morning too. Now Black and I sat on the couch as Rain watched her little shows that she liked to watch on Sundays stealing kisses when she wasn't looking.

Our kisses were slow and sensual, simply us enjoying each other's touch. We kissed until my lips were sore. I smiled thinking that this was a perfect lazy day.

Sometime a little later, Black and I lay dozing on the couch, Rain and Abner still on the floor, she was now using his body for a pillow. The phone rang on the kitchen wall and I didn't want to get up, but I dragged myself up anyway.

"Heads up, yuh parent figures coming up di stairs." Larry's voice came through the phone causing my heart to drop to the floor.

"Dang it!" I whispered hanging up. "This is not good."

"What's up?" Black asked from where he was still lounged on the couch.

"Brotha Abraham and Sista Dinah are here—" Before I could even finish they knocked on the door.

"Sista Dinah!" Rain cried joyfully jumping to her feet. Before I could even catch her, she raced to the door and opened it throwing herself in Sister Dinah's arms.

"Rain!" I admonished her.

Sister Dinah was getting up in age and she couldn't keep picking Rain's big self up like that. Black came to his feet as the two people who had help raised me walked through the door. My gaze shot to the floor to see if Abner was still lying in the middle of it and surprisingly, I looked up just in time to see his tail disappear around my bedroom door.

"That wild man is down there smoking that dop—" Sister Dinah began as soon as she walked through the door, but her words died a sudden death when she noticed Black standing there. He smiled at her.

"Sweet baby Joseph!" She whispered putting her hand on her chest just under her neck as her eyes raked down that tall lean body before coming back up.

"What's going on?" Brother Abraham asked as he walked around her to come farther into the apartment. Both of them were dressed in matching red and gold Afrocentric garbs today.

"Oh, wow!" Was all he said as he too took in Black.

I was so glad he was wearing one of Larry's t-shirts instead of one of those wife beaters that he looked so good in, or God forbid no shirt at all. Poor Sister Dinah would have probably had her first stroke.

I shut the door behind them, searching my mind for the best way to introduce them. I really wanted them to like him. They had taken one look at Mitch and decided they didn't care for him at all. Had I listened to them, I could have spared myself a lot of heartache. What if they didn't like Black, did I have the strength to walk away from him? Sister Dinah was a good judge of character.

"Hey guys, I'd like you to meet—"

"My Uncle Black!" Rain cut me off, she was so excited she was practically screaming her words as she pulled Sister Dinah over to my houseguest. "He is my first daddy's brotha, but he says he's going to be my new daddy. My mommy had him tied to her be—"

"Alright Rain, my goodness!" I spoke over her. Damn it! Children had big mouths.

"Nice to meet you, ma'am, I've heard so much about you."

Black said in a calm controlled voice and surprisingly pulled Sister Dinah into a hug.

"Oh My..." I heard her muffled voice come from somewhere in his big shoulder area.

Brother Abraham cleared his throat.

"And Sir, I'd like to shake the hand of the man that kept my Earth safe. It's so good to finally meet you." Black continued, releasing the older woman to shake her husband's hand. Sister Dinah was dark skinned, but I'm pretty sure she was blushing as she used her hand to fan her cheeks, her eyes still raking over Black's muscled body.

Like I had seen all men do when speaking to Black, Brother Abraham stuck out his chest a bit, lifting his shoulders as he nodded.

"It's good to meet you too, son." I exhaled after hearing him call him son, but my relief was short lived.

"Why is it that we're just now meeting you?" My worried gaze went to Black's. However, the cool, calm and collective look on his face helped release some of the tension that was building inside of me. He was so capable, the kind of man that controlled his environment.

"Sir, that is completely my fault. I surprised Earth by coming into town early. But we were just discussing getting together with the two of you to have brunch today."

"You were?" Sister Dinah asked sounding amazed that this man had thought of them.

"We were?" I asked.

He smiled. "We were, and I know just the place."

Black took us to a really nice restaurant and when I tell y'all he charmed the pants off of my parents, believe it. At one point, Sister Dinah and I excused ourselves to take Rain to the washroom.

"Oh, my goodness, Earth! That's the brother you were

supposed to be with, how in the world did you get tangled up with that other fella?"

"Sista Dinah! Don't talk ill of the dead…"

She humphed. "Baby, I'm just telling the truth. I'm sad Mitch is dead, but I'll be lying if I said I wasn't glad he is no longer in your life draining away your happiness. It's been so long since I've seen your eyes sparkle like they're doing right now." She took my hand in hers. "I was beginning to worry about you."

"I feel happy." I told her.

"I know, Black brings out the best in you. He's a keeper, I like him."

I looked over at her. "You do?"

She nodded. "Very much. Although I do have a question." Frowning slightly, she leaned in closer.

"What exactly did Rain mean when she said you had that man tied to your bed?"

Because I could never lie to Sister Dinah, I got really busy helping Rain wash her hands. When I lifted my gaze to look at the older woman in the mirror, she had a knowing look on her face, although she didn't press the issue.

Bless her heart, she probably thought it had been something kinky going on. If I told her it was because I had kidnapped him, she would never believe me.

MELECH BLACK

"When Mitch died, nobody from your family came forth to help Earth. She's been doing it all by herself. She wouldn't even accept help from us. Why is it that nothing was done to help her from your end?" Brother Abraham asked as soon as the ladies were out of hearing distance.

He didn't mince words, I liked that. I in turn will return the favor.

"Honestly sir, I didn't know anything about Rain. Mitch kept a lot of things from the rest of the family. Foolishly I'd assumed he had something set up for his widow. This is my fault, I should have been more astute. Now that I know, I'm going to do the right thing and make sure both Earth and Rain have all they need from this point on."

"What are your intentions toward her?"

"Well sir, if you give me your blessings, I would like to marry her."

For just a moment he looked shocked, whether from my statement or the fact that I'd asked for his blessings, I don't know.

"Earth has been through a lot." He told me. "Her mother walked away and left her when she was only twelve years old. My wife and I tried to show her all the love we could so that blow wouldn't scar her too bad. But then she met your brother and he only made the scar worse. She doesn't even play her violin anymore. Can you promise me that you will do all you can to help that wound heal?"

I sat up looking into his eyes across the table, I needed him to know I spoke the truth. Never have I ever wanted to strangle my idiot brother more than now. "You have my word."

He nodded. "Well then, you have my blessing. But most importantly, may the Heavenly Father bless your union."

11

KING OF THE SAVAGES

"You know you're in love when you can't fall asleep because reality is finally better than your dreams."

— DR. SEUSS

EARTH

I sat downstairs behind the cash register in Larry's bookstore doodling on a piece of paper. What was I doodling you ask?

Hmmm...

Earth
&
The Talented Mr. Black
Forever

Yeah, I know that's kind of corny, but that's a mood. Y'all know I'm telling the truth. Black is everything a man should be, caring, kind and generous... He is such a gentleman, the kind of guy that opens doors and pulls out chairs. He does things like help me clean up after we eat and takes out the trash. Last night he ran a bath for me, and when I was done, he laid me on the bed and massaged my body butter into my skin.

Amaaaazzzzing!!!

By the time he was finished, I was a noodle in his capable hands. I lay in my bed nice and relaxed, watching as he stood and slowly took off his clothes, my body tingling in anticipation. Anticipation that only grew as his beautiful muscles flexed when he slowly lowered himself over me. It was then I realized how much his sleek, powerful movements reminded me of his pet.

That night I wanted him to show me how to please him the way he does me. Oh, and he did, with gentle touches and loving patience. His quiet deep voice coached me through it until I had it down. Watching his strong body crumble under my caress was.... Amaaaazzzzing!!!

Afterwards he made love to me and literally put me to sleep, I kid you not. I didn't remember anything after I shattered.

This morning after I made breakfast, I placed his and Rain's plates on the table in front of them. After saying a quick prayer Rain dug in. But Black had waited on me to finish what I was doing at the stove and join them before he started eating.

I had decided to cook the chunks of meat he'd bought for Abner, although he told me his pet would eat it raw. That just seemed gross to me, so I seasoned it and threw it in the oven. Of course, Abner wasn't complaining, he truly would eat anything.

The other morning Rain made a bowl of cereal for herself and him, and sure enough, he ate it. Anyway, like I was saying,

Black waited till I finished giving Abner his food and sat down at the table with my plate to start eating.

He did little stuff like that, stuff Mitch would never think to do.

"Ahhh... You wear the look of a satisfied woman." Betty said interrupting my pleasant thoughts as she placed a kale, carrot and apple smoothie she'd just blended for me on the counter in front of me.

"Thank you." I told her trying to erase the smile from my face, but I couldn't.

I was in love...

She took a seat in the chair next to me and looked at me expectantly. With that grin still on my face I picked up my smoothie and took a sip pretending I didn't see her over there fidgeting for information.

"Come on, girl, spill it! Is he as good in bed as he looks? And don't try to tell me y'all didn't do anything, 'cause you got the look of a woman that has had multiple orgasms."

I laughed before taking another sip. Instead of talking I just lifted an eyebrow at her, telling her with my glance to mind her own business.

"Alright, Earth! Don't make me snatch you! Spill!"

"Okay! Okay!" I cried, as eager to tell her how great Black is as she was to hear it. But when I opened my mouth the only thing that came out was...

"Bettttttyyyyy!" Which was more of a moan than a word any day.

Lifting my hand, I caressed my neck that was still tender from his kisses. In fact, there were several parts of my body that were deliciously sore from being thoroughly loved by him. Black is the kind of man that gets it and lets you know he got it... A shiver went through me just thinking about how he takes it.

I groaned... "Bettttttyyyy! I'm so far gone!"

She was practically vibrating in her seat. "Ohhhh! I knew it! I said the other night, that man gon' turn my little Earth out! I knew it...damn you lucky girl!"

"He has a way of touching me and kissing me, and when he —" I stopped myself. Betty didn't need to know everything.

"And he's so good with Rain, she loves him." I said instead, redirecting the conversation.

"This is getting serious, huh?"

I turned to look at her nodding with a slight frown on my face. "It is, and it scares the crap out me."

She took my hand. "Shush! Black ain't his brother. He's a real man, everybody can see that. I don't want you to let your fears get in the way of your happiness. Good thing Black came along and wouldn't take no for an answer or you would have let your fears push him away earlier on."

"Did you forget I kidnapped the man?"

She thought for a minute. "About that...He's been here two weeks. Where does he belong? Why hasn't he left?"

I too had been wondering the same thing. "I asked him the other night, and he said he really needed a vacation from his life. He said it is demanding and draining and he just wanted to not have to worry about it for a while."

"But when is he going back? And when he does, what's going to happen to you guys?"

I shrugged. "He's assured me that I don't have anything to worry about with the custody issue. He says that he won't allow his family to take Rain from me."

Betty nodded. "That's good. I believe him."

"I believe him too."

I don't know how the younger brother ended up with so much authority, but there was no doubt in my mind he had it. His kind of persona can't be faked. And from what I've seen of him, he's not a liar, unlike his brother. If he says it, he means it. I think that's what I liked most about him.

Mitch and my relationship started off with a lie, and it just continued that way. He lied about pretty much everything. The successful record label he owned was just one of the many get rich quick schemes he was attempting at the time. It fell through just like everything else he'd tried to do.

Mitch was indecisive and easily swayed. Of course he faked at being an alpha male in the beginning of our relationship. He pretended to be the toughest guy in his crew, when in fact, his buddies were only using him until he had nothing left, and then they left. One had only to be around him and his crew for a little while to observe that Mitch was not the alpha at all. The real alpha was some dope boy who thought Mitch was going to be able to get his rapping career off the ground.

It was the same dope boy that tried to convince me to be with him and not Mitch. He was also the one who first told me when my husband started cheating on me. What a fool Mitch was. He would have those guys over, thinking they were his friends, while the real leader of their crew was trying to get at me behind his back. And of course when I tried to tell him, he didn't believe me.

Black on the other hand didn't try to fake at being a tough guy, or what Larry would call a rude boy. No, my Black is a gentleman and he doesn't care who knows it. I mean don't get me wrong, he is very alpha… But unlike Mitch, Black is the kind of guy that operates honestly. With him, what you see is what you get, he's a stand-up kind of guy.

"Who is that?" Betty asked gesturing toward the door.

I frowned taking in the Native-American man that was approaching. "I don't know."

"He looks like trouble."

She wasn't lying. Although dressed in a suit, the handsome man had bad news written all over him. He wore his long straight black hair pulled back in a ponytail. In his ear was an elongated earring that had a few feathers hanging at the tip. What made him look dangerous was the fact that underneath that expensive suit, he was covered in tattoos. Although there were none on his face, his neck was loaded. When he reached to ring the doorbell, I could see tattoos on his wrist and even a few on his hands.

Goodness!

"What should I do?" I asked Betty when he rang the doorbell again and neither of us reached for the buzzer.

And then his eyes met mine through the glass, and a shiver went through me.

Killer!

The Bible says the eyes are the window to a man's soul. This man looked at me with the eyes of a killer. He smiled, lifting his big hand to wave at me.

"I guess you have to open the door now that he sees us." She muttered taking him in. "It looks like his suit cost more than this store is worth, so at least we don't have to worry about him robbing us. Maybe he's just looking for a book that he can't find at Barnes & Nobles."

She had a point. He wasn't hurting for money. The only thing we had to worry about was people trying to rob us. Besides that, nobody was interested in us…we sold books! I hesitated for only a moment, something deep inside me telling me that this man was getting ready to bring change with him. Up until this point, change had not been kind to me.

The first time I felt it was the night my mother told me my daddy wasn't coming back. It's the kind of change that can't be stopped, the kind of change that's going to happen whether you welcome it or not.

However, I'll be lying if I said I wasn't a little curious as to why a Native-American man was in the hood. In all my life, I had only known two Native-American men, my late husband and Mike. Although I knew it was impossible, I couldn't help but wonder if this man had something to do with them.

I buzzed the door.

"Good afternoon, ladies."

Both Betty and I inhaled at the sound of his deep voice. The man sounded like jazz. Now I know it was impossible for someone to sound like jazz, but he did. His voice was deep and smooth... melodic. And then he hit us with a smile that I was sure caused many a pair of panties to melt away. Right off I could tell he was something of a lady's man.

However, lady's man or not, now that he was in, I couldn't shake the feeling that he was dangerous. Although extremely handsome, his eyes still said killer. I forced a smile to my face.

"How can we help you?"

I knew that Betty felt the same way I did. Now that she was a free woman, she flirted outrageously with every handsome man that crossed her path, but not this guy. This guy caused her to sit next to me and not utter a word. She just watched him, like one would watch an animal of prey on the move. I was so glad Rain had just gone next door to take a nap on the cot Betty kept for her in the kitchen.

Damn, I wish Black was down here with me.

"I really hope you can help me, young lady." He cooed with that smile still on his face as he came to a stop in front of the counter looking down at us with his deadly gaze.

I don't know if it was self-preservation or what, but I stood needing to appear bigger. It did no good, he wasn't as tall as Black, but he was way taller than me.

I cleared my throat. "Are you looking for a book?"

His gaze took its time raking over my body before it settled on my face.

"Now I understand." He muttered.

The little small hairs on my arms and neck rose. Betty clutched the back of my shirt; I don't think she was aware of what she was doing. That's how dangerous this guy felt. I was kicking myself for opening the door. *Larry, please come over here!*

"Are you looking for a book?" I repeated.

"No, beautiful, I'm not looking for a book."

"Then what are you looking for?"

He leaned a little closer as if he was going to tell me a secret. "The King of the Savages."

I frowned confused. "I don't understand."

He exhaled throwing one of his hands up as he stepped back away from the counter. "At first, I didn't understand either."

Okay, now I was really confused. What kind of mind game was this guy playing? He was talking in riddles.

"Understand what?" I asked playing along for the time being.

"I couldn't understand how it was that this place was still standing and not burned down to the ground."

Betty inhaled sharply. I reached back to squeeze her hand that was still clutching my shirt, willing her to stay quiet. We were in danger, there was no more doubt about it.

I chuckled, trying to sound like I was still in control of the situation, but it only proved how nervous I was.

"Sorry, I'm still confused."

That smile grew on his face, but with it the savagery in his eyes. All pretense of him being civil evaporated like morning dew. He reminded me of the Joker.

"Excuse me, sweetheart, please allow me to be clearer." Even his voice had changed. Now it was a killer voice to match those killer eyes. He reached into his jacket and came out with a gun. Betty cried out clutching my shirt so hard it pulled tight on the front.

"My boss came up missing two weeks ago. Imagine my

surprise when I found out a little pretty thing like you kidnapped him." The smile left his face as he pointed the gun at me. "Where the f*** is he!"

I held up my hands shaking in fear. I had never had a gun pointed at me. Tears welled up in my eyes so good it blinded me temporarily.

"Wh-…" My voice quivered so badly my words were barely legible. "Who is your boss?"

"Melech!" He growled.

"Who?"

I don't know if it was the shock of having a gun pointed at me or hearing my late husband's older brother's name come from his lips, but the gears in my brain weren't clicking fast enough for me.

Melech…

Of course, this dangerous man worked for him. Mitch had told me so much about his older brother. Without a shadow of a doubt he was dangerous. So dangerous that he made this man in front of me pale in comparison.

He opened his mouth to say something else, but right then the door that connected the juice bar to the bookstore burst open and Larry was thrown through it to crash hard into the book shelf causing books to rain down on him.

The next couple of seconds seemed like hours…

A giant Native-American man in a suit stormed in after him grabbing poor Larry up off the floor lifting him straight up in the air before slamming him back on the ground hard, so hard that Larry's body twitched violently from the shock of it.

"Larry!" Betty cried as she flew off her stool. I wrapped my arms around her stopping her as the giant came from inside his suit coat with a sawed-off double barrel shotgun. He cocked it and held it against Larry's temple.

"You better stop f****** with me, Jamaican piece of sh**!

Where the f*** is Melech! Speak now or I will blow your f****** brains all over this f***** up floor!" He roared.

Larry was stuttering so badly in his fear even I couldn't understand his patwah. Another giant came out of the kitchen, this one black; his big bald head seeming to glow in the bookstore light. I opened my mouth to scream, but right then Betty and I was grabbed roughly from behind and duct tape was over our mouths before I could utter a sound.

I couldn't see who'd grabbed me, but I knew it was two of them. They moved like smoke. We didn't hear or see them come behind us. The black giant hurried toward us and he and the mystery men quickly wrapped Betty and my hands with the duct tape, so tight I felt the blood leaving my fingers. Then we were roughly sat back in our chairs.

I was able to see then that the two men that had snuck up on us were really just boys. They both appeared to be just out of high school, maybe eighteen or nineteen, but in incredible shape. It was clear they were athletic, like I said, they came up behind us without us even noticing.

Also, they had to be brothers because they favored each other. I believed they were mixed as well. They were not dark like Black and the giant, but neither were they as light skinned as the guy with the tattoos and the giant that held the gun to Larry's head, who I was positive was full blooded Native-American.

However, my thoughts were cut off and my heart began to pound violently in my chest when another handsome man who like the boys, seemed to be mixed with Native-American and African-American walked through the door holding Rain in his arms.

"Hey look, I think this is Mitch's kid."

I shot out of my chair, but one of the boys put their hand on my shoulder and slammed me back down. Yeah, they were really strong.

I began yelling at them through the duct tape, pleading with them to let us go. They had made a mistake! Their boss wasn't here!

"Mommy!" Rain cried trying to push out of the man's arms. My desperate gaze went to tattoo man. I pleaded with him to let me talk. He put his hand on the giant's arm that held the gun to Larry's head.

"Hold on, Crush, it looks like the little lady is ready to talk." With tears streaming from my eyes I nodded desperately as he walked towards me.

"If I pull this tape off your mouth and you scream, I will blow this b**** head off." He said pressing his gun against Betty's temple. Squeezing her eyes shut tight, she began to weep behind her tape.

I nodded letting him know that I agreed. Bracing myself I waited for him to snatch the tape off. Surprisingly, he eased it off.

"Please! Please! Let them go! They didn't do anything! It was me!" I was crying so badly I could barely see him.

"You tell me where Melech is and I will let them all go."

I was shaking my head before he could even finish speaking. "There has been a mistake. I didn't kidnap Melech…I kidnapped Michael!"

For a moment he seemed stunned, before he turned his head to look at the black giant that stood to his right, then to the man that held Rain. When his gaze landed back to me there was laughter in his eyes. Seconds later that laughter made its way to his lips. Shockingly they all began to laugh at me.

All except Crush, who'd not taken his gaze from Larry.

My mouth snapped shut.

What the hell?!

"What's so funny?" I spat from between clenched teeth.

I didn't appreciate being laughed at when my friends and my daughter were in danger. My gaze went to Larry who still lay perfectly still on the floor not daring to move, because there was an angry giant holding a sawed-off shotgun to his head.

There was something wrong with Crush, it was clear he wanted to shoot Larry. He wanted to shoot Larry so badly he shook with anger. He was focused completely on my friend, his jaws clenched and un-clenched as if it was taking all his strength not to pull the trigger.

The Joker leaned uncomfortably closer, so close I heard him inhale as he smelled my hair.

"Mmm...you smell so sweet. Now I understand." He said so low that only I heard.

Anger at his action ripped through me so fierce it took my breath. "Then explain it to me! Help me understand!" I yelled.

He stood slowly, not batting an eye at my anger. Instead, that Joker smile grew on his handsome face.

"It's you who've made the mistake, my Queen. You didn't kidnap Michael. You kidnapped Melech Black, the King of Savages himself."

MELECH BLACK

I couldn't remember the last time I sat down and did something simple, like watch a football game with a cold beer. I took a swig. Damn this felt good. I've never had normal. My life has always been full of expensive responsibilities. There was never a quiet moment, never a still moment. Over these last two weeks with Earth, I've gotten more sleep than I ever had.

On any given night, I've slept maybe an hour or two. My world never stopped, there was always something to come up that demanded my attention. If not at the casinos, then definitely at Seminole Territory, which is what our reservation is called in the Appalachian Mountains.

Seminole Territory had been a very chaotic, unstable place until the Wheeler-Howard Act was passed by Congress in 1934, which reaffirmed the right for each Native tribe living on a reservation to establish a system of self-government. Many of the Seminole people held a healthy distrust of the American Government and didn't see any reason to reconsider how things had been ran up until that point.

Not Chief Holata.

Holata was my stepfather Frank's grandfather. At the time, Seminole Territory was being ruled by Holata, who was more of a figure head, while the council, which is generally a board of elders, held most of the decision-making power. The council still exists in our territory today, but thanks to Holata and the Wheeler-Howard Act, on our reservation, they don't hold as much power as they used to.

Holata means alligator. It was said that when he was born, his father could see his temperament and knew that like the alligator, his son would rule their people in a most savage way. And he had.

You see, Holata's theory was that the world was being ruled by savages and in order to play the game, one must become a savage. Seminole Territory, like other Indian reservations in America were very poor and the people were suffering from poverty. Holata made it his mission to reverse that and bring more jobs to his people.

He opened up his first casino and hotel on a small reservation in Florida our people also owned. The Seminole that lived there were majority black Seminole. Because back then, it was an insignificant piece of land. Holata's father and the council had stashed their blacks there, leaving my great grandfather on my father's side Isaiah Black to look over them and keep order.

The black Seminole didn't have a problem with that. Because they are descendants of a very small number of Africans who escaped slavery. They never lost their language or belief system, and being left to themselves practically forgotten, was able to practice it with no problem.

However, that was not to last. Holata, seeing as to how the small piece of land could be turned into a tourist attraction, forced all the black Seminole to relocate to South Carolina to the Seminole Territory in the Appalachians.

And because most people feared Holata, nobody put up a fuss. For whatever reason, he didn't harbor the disdain for the black Seminole that his father had, so he'd section off a small portion of the mountain and gave it to them, leaving my grandfather on my father's side Hosea Black in charge. Over that portion of the mountain, only Holata held more power than him, nobody else. And he took it one step further by putting my grandfather on the council with the other elders, so that my grandfather who at the time wasn't old enough to be considered an elder, could be assured of the black Seminoles' security there in the Appalachians, shocking the hell out of the system.

But hey, that was Holata for you. Anyway, his little tourist area took off and so did Seminole Territory. Because of Holata, the people had good paying jobs and could now afford better homes and businesses.

It wasn't long before he was able to add another casino and a few more hotels, then restaurants and homes, property he charged a fortune to obtain. He bought more property on that strip and now it's one of the biggest tourist sites in Tampa, ran primarily by our people, which it remains to this very day.

However, Holata wasn't satisfied with that and soon turned his eye to Vegas. He died during the building of the first Vegas Casino, and his son Paytah, who was even more vicious than his father took over.

Before Holata died he managed to accomplish several things. He managed to secure his hold on Seminole Territory. Through wealth and intimidations, he mauled most of the power out of the council's hands and secured it in his own. The people not only feared him but reverenced him. He'd turned them from an impoverished people to a very rich people.

He put several of his own people in the Bureau of Indian Affairs as well as other top branches of government, thus insuring his voice would be heard when he spoke. He'd successfully convinced the families that lived on Seminole Territory that he was the answer to all their woes.

And like his name says, he did it in such a way that garnered him the name Savage, a name he claimed boldly. He was known to get off on the fact his people had been called savages for simply living and breathing on their own land. Now he was going to show the world what a true savage looked like, because he was going to play the white man's game, but play it better than them.

He said the white man was the true savage. But he, Holata was going to become the King of Savages, and so the name was born. After Holata, only the most savage could be King. It had been Paytah behind Holata and Frank behind Paytah. I'm more than positive that Hawk, Frank's oldest son thought the bag was secured in his favor because he was quite vicious.

But then I was born across the river. Unlike the rest of the kids on our reservation, I had no fear of Hawk. If he said something to me that I didn't like, I kicked his ass. If he even looked at me the wrong way, I kicked his ass. Of course, my grandfather and mother begged me to stop, fearing that I was going to get myself killed.

"I rather die than let that coward rule over me!" I yelled at them both.

It's the way I felt about everybody. Some of the Native Seminole were known for treating the Black Seminole horribly. They believed we weren't true Seminole because we descended from African slaves and some of our ways weren't like theirs. Like the white man, they treated us like second class citizens. And because the Black Seminole on our reservation didn't want to rock the boat or create any ripples, they took it, thanking their masters for the mistreatment.

Not me, I treated people how they treated me. You said something to me I didn't like, I struck back. You hit me, I tried to destroy you. My grandfather said I had been born with a spirit different from the rest of our people, he said my generation was the beginning of a new day. I didn't know if that was true or not, but for the life of me, I couldn't grasp ahold of the idea that someone's skin color made them better than someone else.

The old crazed lady Longo, who lived across the river from us called me a little nigga one day when Horse and I were out playing ball, and in trying to catch the ball he'd thrown to me, I crashed into her gate.

I stood steaming mad as a million thoughts went through my head. What right did she have to call me names when she was bat sh*t crazy? She couldn't tell the difference between a cat and a dog. She was always yelling for me to get my dog off her property, talking about Abner.

If anybody needed to be called names it was her crazy ass. But had I ever called her crazy to her face? No! So, standing there holding my ball in my hand, I decided to teach her a lesson in manners. I threw it with all my might into her front window, getting a satisfied feeling when the glass shattered everywhere. If felt so good that I began to pick up rocks and break out the rest of them.

My best friend and cousin on my mother's side Horse, who was full blood Native picked up rocks and helped me. We got picked up by Frank's police and thrown into jail. My mother and my grandfather pleaded with Frank's sheriff to let us go. He said he would if my grandfather agreed to pay for the damages and I apologized.

I refused.

"She called me a little nigga, she had it coming! I ain't apologizing!"

Somehow that incident had caught Frank's attention and he and his bodyguards showed up at the jail a few hours later. I was surprised to see him. Frank was king. He was every little boy's hero. Everybody wanted to be him, in our eyes, he was like the Godfather.

"You the one burst out Old Lady Longo's windows?" He asked, walking to stand in front of my cell.

Now I got a little nervous. When I said I didn't put up with nobody's sh*t, that didn't mean Frank. Frank was a ruthless killer, and everybody knew it.

"Yeah." I muttered.

"Why you do that?"

I felt my anger coming back. *"Because she called me a nigga!"*

I didn't mean to yell it at him, but at the point, I was ready to die. If Frank demanded I apologize I was going to refuse. I ain't apologizing to that evil lady, no matter what nobody says.

Frank studied me for a minute before he nodded his head once with a smile on his face.

"Let them go." He told his sheriff, who unlocked our cell instantly.

After that, Frank started crossing the river more and more to watch me play or go through my manhood training. My grandfather hated it, but Frank, who held the power on our reservation would not be put off. Hawk got wind that his father was studying me and tried to kill me many times. It was because of Hawk I discovered my ability to set things on fire.

He had four of his friends hold me down while he hit me with a bat. The coward knew I would kick his ass one on one. I don't know what happened, one minute I was lying there helpless. He had already broken my leg with the bat and made me spit up blood. With a look of death in his eyes he aimed the bat at my head and swung it with all his might.

The pain was horrible. I felt myself beginning to black out. But right then, something else hit me hard in the chest and entered my body. I could feel it moving inside my veins. I yelled at the top of my lungs because it felt like fire.

"What the f***?" One of the boys said as I began to thrash around on the ground trying to get the fire out of me.

With the fire came rage. I had always been a little angry, but nothing like how that fire made me feel.

Rage!

I yelled again, not because of the fire, but of the rage. Chills went through my body as it rolled through me.

The next thing I knew, the boys that were touching me went up in flames as if they had been doused in gasoline. Both Hawk and I watched them burn with wide horrified eyes. They burned quickly, this fire was like nothing I had ever seen. In minutes all the flesh was gone off their bones. Even the bones began to disintegrate. The flames burned so hot the tips of them were purple.

When I turned to look at Hawk for help, all I saw was ass and elbows, he was wisely getting away from me as fast as he could.

Afraid I got up, surprised when my leg no longer felt broken. I took off at a full sprint, needing to get to my grandfather. I ran full speed through the woods towards our side for about five minutes before I came to a skidding halt.

Sitting on a crate in my path was a homeless man with no shoes. My whole body shook uncontrollably as I looked at him. I who never cried was on the verge of tears. My heart and my thoughts were racing trying to outrun the other.

The man opened his mouth and uttered seven words that caused my knees to give out.

"Everything is going to be alright, boy."

That day I sat there on my knees at his feet as he told me I'd been called to be a vessel for the Ancient of Days, whether I'll be chosen had yet to be seen. He said I was just a boy and I needed to grow to be a man. He said that I had been given five shekels and that when the Master returned, I would be judged on what I've done with them.

He told me to close my eyes and hold out my hands with my palms to the sky and pray that the Ancient of Days gave me the strength to overcome the temptation that was coming my way. He said to those who are given much, much is expected. And since I was of the group that received five shekels, more was expected of me. My test will be harder. He told me to pray that I was found worthy to receive the helper.

Something that resembled pity came into his eyes. *"Gold is purified in the fire...and nothing but pure gold can enter into the Gates. All who enter must go through the fire first. Stand strong and make it through to the other side. Your reward awaits."*

After his words I closed my eyes and I prayed with everything I had in me. This was not the first time I'd heard of the Ancient of Days. My grandfather taught me of him. He taught me the old way, the way our people worshipped before the slave ships came to the West African shores. I knew of the Ancient One, I knew well how to pray to him. And I did.

I prayed that I was found worthy of receiving the helper. I prayed that he gave me strength. I asked him why he'd given me five shekels. I was always in trouble. Between my grandfather and my mother, I was always getting punished. The teacher had threatened to kick me out of class. Surely, I am not worthy of five shekels.

I didn't even know what the shekels were. I just knew the

man with no shoes told me more would be expected from me. And finally, I prayed about the fire.

The fire that was now pulsing through my veins. I felt it like I felt the breath flowing through my lungs. I prayed that he'd take it away from me. I didn't want to hurt anybody else.

When I was done, the man with no shoes was gone and the fire still pulsed in my body. The next day I stayed close to my grandfather and mother, nervously waiting for Frank's police to come and get me for those boy's death. However, it was not the police that showed up, but Frank. And to my grandfather's great disdain, he forced my mother to marry him that same day.

My father had died when I was a baby, but had he not, I was more than convinced Frank would have had him murdered so that he could become my legal father.

"You can call me dad now," he'd told me that night, the look in his eyes was that of a conqueror. *"I am going to raise you to take over after I die."*

I frowned confused, everything was happening so fast. My life no longer felt like mine.

"But what about Hawk?"

"Hawk is my oldest son and I love him. However, I need to make the right choice for my people. Hawk is weak and will not make a good leader. You will."

"Why?" *I muttered, on the verge of tears.*

If ever the devil smiled, it resembled the look Frank now wore on his face.

"Because you are the most savage, son. After I die, you will become King of the Savages."

12

MEET MELECH BLACK

MELECH BLACK

*A*bner suddenly lifted his head looking back toward Earth's bedroom. I eased the gun out of my back holster and was up and off the couch, gun aimed toward the bedroom before my little brother stepped one foot out the bedroom. The chump had snuck through the window.

When he noticed me he threw up his hands. "Damn, how do you do that?!"

Shaking my head at his slowness, I slid my gun back in its holster flipping my shirt over it as I sat back on the couch picking up my beer. All these years he's still doesn't realize it's impossible to sneak up on me with Abner around. I should have known this brat would show up shortly after my pet, I'm surprised it took him so long. But I must admit to not being that happy to see him. Him showing up meant my vacation was over.

I had planned on telling Earth who I am this weekend. I wanted to ease her into her new reality, prepared to beg her not to leave me if I had to. If Michael was here, my men weren't far behind. There would be no easing her into it now because there was nothing easy about my crew.

"So, this is where you've been hiding." He said coming into the living room flopping down on the couch next to me.

"How did you find me?" I muttered without looking away from the game, my voice laced with my irritation.

"Bro, you act like you're not happy to see me, I've come to rescue you from your horrible kidnappers." He held his head high as if he was some kind of corny ass action hero. And just like that, my irritation with him faded. My little brother's goofiness always kept me from being angry with him for too long.

I wrapped my hand around his neck and pulled him close in a headlock hug.

"Miss you, man!" He said hugging me back.

"Miss you too. So, how did you find me?" I asked when I let him go.

The superhero look came back to his face. "You know I'm an amazing tracker. The medicine man told me so when I was only a boy."

The medicine man he spoke of was my grandfather Hosea. They called him the medicine man because the Great Spirit spoke to him. However, he had never told Michael he was a good tracker, in fact, he told him the complete opposite. When Michael went through his buck training, he was so horrible my grandfather told him to go to school and get a good education, because brains was all he had going for him.

Poor Michael, it was true. He made a horrible warrior. But like my grandfather said, he was highly intelligent. I'd paid for him to go to the best schools. He had just finished his last year at Harvard Law, he wanted to be a lawyer and one day a judge. He will be a great commodity for our people.

I exhaled. "How did you *really* find me?"

He chuckled. "Well, you didn't make it easy, did you? At first, we thought you weren't answering Horse or my calls because you had actually listened to me and took a damn vacation. But after one week passed, we realized something was wrong." He held up his hands.

"For the record, Horse knew something was wrong after day one. He said you would never leave town or anything and not let him know. I actually had to convince him to relax, assuring him you needed the time to yourself."

He chuckled. "I thought Horse was going to try and kill me after week's end and still there was no word from you, especially when we had Danny pull his security footage of the restaurant parking lot which showed two girls follow you to your car. Unfortunately, the spot you parked in was just outside of the camera's reach, so we couldn't see if they'd gotten in the car with you or not. We saw one of the girls leave and get in a little piece of sh*t car, but the other girl didn't go with her, so we assumed she was with you."

"I had a buddy of mine who works at Tampa City Hall pull a few strings and get me access to the city's camera feed. Once we logged your license plate number in it, it gave us footage of every street light that read your plate that day. Before our meeting at Danny's place, we saw footage of you driving your car. After our meeting there was only footage of Mitch's wife driving your car."

Hearing him call Earth Mitch's wife sent unimaginable rage through me.

"She is *not* Mitch's wife!" I growled cutting him off mid-sentence. He stalled for just a moment staring at me as he rubbed Abner's head.

"Well, that explains why this place is still standing. Of course she's not Mitch's wife now, he's dead. Have you fallen in love with her?"

I exhaled turning to look back at the television, picking up the remote I flipped to the other game I had been watching. I didn't know how to answer his question. Did I love Earth?

I don't know… but that was beside the point. I planned on keeping her anyway.

"She's mine."

He nodded. "Well, you had better get downstairs, those savages you call bodyguards are introducing themselves to her."

I put the remote on the table as ice raced down my spine. "What?" This is not how I wanted this to happen. This was not good!

"Who's all down there?" I asked this question for a very important reason.

"Horse, Big Troy, Crus-"

I didn't wait for him to finish that name before I was off the couch racing out the door. My fear had become a reality. Crush was a bonified psychopath. He will kill everybody down there if he thought they had hurt me, including Rain.

My heart dropped when I got to the bottom of the stairs and saw that the kitchen was trashed. Had Larry not played loud reggae music twenty-four seven, I would have heard this. This was definitely Crush's work. I ran from the Juice Bar into the bookstore and came to a halt at what I was seeing.

Rain was in Tocho's arms trying to get out. Earth and Betty sat with tears in their eyes with their hands tied behind their backs, Shappa and Shiloh standing over them. In front of Earth leaning over the counter speaking to her was Horse. Big Troy stood next to Crush who held a sawed-off shotgun to Larry's head.

"Crush!" I growled bringing everybody's attention to me.

"Daddy! Help me!" Rain cried reaching for me. Without taking my eyes off Crush, I took her out of Big Tocho's arms. She wrapped her little arms around my neck squeezing me tight. She was so afraid her little body was shaking with her tears.

Damn, this is all my fault.

"Shhh, Hobbit, don't cry, baby. Everything is okay. Daddy won't let anybody hurt you, ever. These are my men. They're good guys. They will always keep you safe." I didn't even notice she had called me daddy and I'd said it back to her. My only thoughts were on calming her and Crush.

"Crush." I said again, but the giant never looked up at me.

"Wassup, Boss?" He said still without looking away from Larry. The bloodlust in his eyes was there. He wanted to kill Larry.

"What you are doing, buddy?" I held out my hand speaking easy to him.

Crush is a special case. His mind wasn't all right in his head. He had violent thoughts and very violent tendencies, but it wasn't his fault. His father had beaten his mother while she was pregnant with him, forcing her into early labor, the result of which caused minor brain damage in Crush.

Growing up the kids at the reservation picked on him and called him a retard, never in my hearing though. If I heard somebody picking on him, I would try to hurt them badly. I didn't know what it was about him, but like Horse, Big Troy and Michael, Crush was my own.

When we were nineteen, I caught his father beating him with a tire iron, calling him a retard. Horse and Big Troy tried to tell me to be calm, but it was no use. In a matter of seconds, Crush's father went up in flames. By the time the fire department got there to put him out, there was nothing but ash left.

I didn't worry about going to jail. At Seminole Territory I am the law. After that day, Crush had been loyal to me to the death. I had killed the only dragon he feared. Now he would kill anybody that he even thought was trying to hurt me.

"Going to blow his f***ing brains out." He growled.

"Yeah, but I don't want you to do that. Larry is my friend."

Crush looked up at me then. When he saw I was standing in front of him healthy and whole he exhaled.

"He's your friend?"

I nodded. "Yeah."

He smiled standing up straight, and as calmly as if he was walking his dog, put his gun back in the holster inside his coat. Then he reached down and snatched poor Larry off the floor with one hand, dusting some of the flour or whatever the powdery white substance was that was on him off with the other.

"Relax, buddy, we cool." He told Larry as if they were old friends. Poor Larry nodded staring at him with wide eyes.

"Yeah mon, we cool."

"Melech, what the f***?!" Horse said turning to face me. "You just disappear on us without telling us! No call, no letter…no f***ing carrier pigeon…nothing!"

I smiled at my cousin. He, Big Troy and I have all been best friends since we were very young. Horse is my mother's sister's son. She died of cancer when he was six and he came to live with us. He and I have been inseparable ever since.

"Because I needed a vacation from your whiny voice."

He chuckled before his gaze went back to Earth. "Yeah, I bet that's why."

My gaze followed his to Earth. She was shooting daggers at me. If looks could kill, I would be a dead mutha f**** right now. This was a strange feeling. Never in my life have I cared whether a woman was angry with me. If any woman I was dealing with showed even a small bit of attitude, she was history. Period.

But here I stood in a place I didn't want to be, Earth's anger. I found myself wanting to erase that look off her face and do something I couldn't remember ever doing with a woman that wasn't my mother, explain myself.

"You okay, Minx?" I asked.

Her eyes narrowed. "Don't Minx me, you bastard! Is it true?"

See what I mean? She was pissed!

"Is what true, sweetheart?"

I felt all my mens' heads whip around to stare at me as if I'd suddenly turned into the abominable f***ing snowman. Rightly so, I don't think they ever saw me do gentle. Hell, before I met Earth, I didn't even think I had that setting.

"Are you Michael?"

"That would be me, beautiful." Michael said as he and Abner moseyed into the bookstore as if it was just another day in the park and I was not facing my enraged woman. My eyes cut to him, I didn't appreciate him calling her beautiful. He and I will have a talk about that, after I convinced Earth not to leave me.

"So, you lied to me?"

I held up my hand. "I didn't lie to you. It was *you* who was convinced I was Michael. I just didn't bother to correct you."

Big fresh tears welled up in her eyes. "I thought you were different." She said through her sexy quivering lips.

Damn, her heart is broken and it's eating me up. I wish so badly she would just let me hold her and convince her that everything was going to be alright.

Damn!

"I *am* different."

"I thought you were a gentleman."

This caused my whole crew to erupt in laughter, including Crush. These mutha f*****! Now was not the time for this. I gave them a look that caused them all to fall silent.

"Baby, I *am* a gentleman." My gaze shot to Horse, who was the ring leader, daring him to get started, I swear I will barbeque his ass. He held up his hands.

"If you say you're gentle, you're gentle. You won't get no argument from me."

Ignoring him, I signaled for Shiloh and Shappa to untie the

women. Judging by Earth's body language when Shiloh untied her, I could see she was not going to be willing to hear anything I had to say right now. She had made up her mind to leave me.

As if to confirm that, the first thing she did was cross the floor and take Rain out my arms.

"Come here, baby. Come to mama." She cooed before she quickly put as much space as she could between us.

That sh*t hurt. Seeing her withdrawing from me was worse than anything I'd felt in a long time. I exhaled as I felt the man I'd become over the last two weeks melt away. It's true, I had lied to her about something. I am not a gentle man. I sliced with a hammer.

And... Unfortunately for Earth, I was not prepared to let her go, now or ever.

EARTH

He was a liar!

Melech!

Oh God, I can't believe I slept with Melech!

Mitch told me his older brother was a murderer. He said he could and would kill at the drop of a dime. All of their people feared him. It was why Mitch's father made Melech Chief of their people. He knew that if he didn't, Melech would kill him.

Mitch believed Melech got power from Satan. The first time he told me that, I'd laughed thinking he was joking. But he didn't laugh back. He truly believed his brother was some kind of demon who received powers from his master.

After getting to know him over the last couple of weeks, I could say that may be a bit over the top, but one thing I knew for sure was that he was a liar. All this time he'd let me believe he was his younger brother. He must have had a great laugh at my expense.

Now it all made sense.

The authority he wore like a second skin. His assurance that nothing would happen to Rain---

"Wait!" I said turning to face him. "Is this some kind of game?"

He frowned. "Is *what* a game?"

"You sending your lawyers to court to take my daughter from me and not saying anything when I thought you were your brother. Letting me fall—" I stopped myself, I would never admit that I'd almost been stupid enough to love him.

"Earth, I swear I didn't know anything about this. Until you told me, I didn't even know Mitch had a daughter."

"It's true." Mike supplied. "We just found out ourselves a few days ago. Mitch never told us."

My gaze fell on the baby brother and I couldn't help the humorless laugh that escaped my lips. He looks like Mitch and Black, his features were like Black's, but his skin color was like Mitch's.

And guess what. He looked like their baby brother. His speech was more polished than Black's, like maybe he was highly educated… Wait… I'd seen him before. He was one of the men who joined Black at the table the day I'd drugged him.

Damn, I am so stupid. Leave it to me to have the right brother under my nose and still grab the wrong one, even though Bre and I both observed the authority he wore naturally. He's the oldest and the most dangerous of the lot.

"Why should I believe you?" I hissed at Mike. "You're probably a liar like-"

"Watch it, Minx!" Black growled cutting me off. "I don't deal well with disrespect." I could see his men start to get restless. They were sending concerned looks to each other.

Were they worried because Black was now clearly getting angry with me? I almost laughed at that, because I didn't give a damn about his anger. He'd made a fool of me. All this time he'd just been using me, the stupid ghetto girl, good for nothing but an easy lay.

He exhaled. "Look, just calm down, alright? We're going to figure this out." He turned to look at Mike.

"Call a meeting for tomorrow morning. I want the council, Kevin, Julie, you and my attorney to meet with me at High Stakes. I don't care what they have going on, tell them to drop it and be there." He turned to look at me.

"Pack a bag for yourself and Rain. We're going to get to the bottom of this."

I turned my nose up at him. "Yeah right, I ain't going nowhere with you, rude boy."

He took a step toward me and I took several back. For a second pain flashed in his eyes before his gaze hardened.

"Earth, try to be reasonable." There was a slight tinge of desperation in his voice and for just a moment, it moved something on the inside of me. I couldn't stand to hear him plead. But then I got myself together.

Y'all see what I mean? Stupid!

"The only three people that have the power to operate and do something like this in my name," Black continued. "Is Mike, his aunt Julie and uncle Kevin. As you can see, Mike doesn't know anything about it. I'm calling a meeting so that we can get to the bottom of this situation and discuss the next move to make. And…" He paused for a moment. "Technically, I have custody of Rain, which means you're going to want to stop acting like a little girl and come to this meeting."

I narrowed my gaze at him. Did he just threaten me?

"But you promised you wouldn't take her from me." I meant for my words to come out tough, but they were barely over a whisper. Tears came to my eyes as I realized he had probably lied about that too.

"I won't take her from you, but we still need to find out what happened, why it happened and where we go from here." His voice had gentled. "You're going to want to be at that meeting."

I exhaled. Yeah, he was right, I needed to be at that meeting to make sure me and Rain had a say in the *'where we go from here,'* part. But then I thought about it.

"Isn't High Stakes a casino?"

He nodded. "Yes, hotel and casino, it's one of the ones we own in Tampa. Whenever I'm in town I do business from there."

"Will it be alright if I bring Rain?"

"Of course, people bring their children all the time. We have an excellent activity area for children. She just can't go on the gaming floor."

I nodded before I looked away from him. "Will you help me upstairs?" I asked Betty.

"Of course, sweetheart." She wrapped her arm around me and together we left the bookstore. It took everything within me to keep it together, but as soon as I closed the door to my apartment, I put Rain down and collapsed crying in Betty's arms.

"Shhh!" she told me as she rubbed my hair.

"I can't believe I was so stupid!"

"Mommy what's wrong?!" Rain asked squeezing my hand.

Betty began to lead us towards the couch. "Come on now, sit down for a second, let's figure this thing out. I'm sure it seems worse than it really is."

Rain sat down as close to me as she could get. Wrapping my arm around her I pulled her close, feeling bad that I was making her worry about me.

"What do you mean is seems worse than it really is?" I asked Betty, not sure I had heard her correctly.

"I mean, I know with your emotions all muddled up from being ducted taped and what not, your situation seems worse than it really is."

Okay, so I hadn't heard incorrectly.

"Betty, I had the wrong brother, it was really Melech this whole time!" I didn't mean to raise my voice at her, but she was insinuating I was overreacting.

Did she forget that some maniac just had a gun to her head and an even bigger maniac had one to Larry's?

And guess what. Those maniacs worked for a man all his people thought was the damn devil!

Betty sucked her teeth. "Just because you had his name wrong doesn't mean it was a different man. So, what his name is Melech? He's the same man that just had you downstairs writing love letters. The same man that made love to you so good you've been glowing. The same man that made you feel like a woman." She grabbed my hand.

"What difference if his name ain't what you thought it was?"

I snatched my hand away from her coming to my feet.

"Are you crazy? Did you forget the man with all the tattoos held a gun to your head and Larry just had a double barrel sawed-off shotgun held to his?"

She waved her hand. "Girl please, we from Jamaica. That's not the first time Larry had a gun held to his head."

My mouth dropped. I couldn't believe she was ready to forgive and forget just like that. Well, not me! She didn't know what I knew about him. I began to pace.

"You don't understand."

She threw up her hands. "What don't I understand?"

Her tone of voice insinuated she still thought I was overreacting, and that just pissed me off more. I stopped pacing.

"Rain baby, go in your room and start packing your bag. Mommy will be in there to help you finish." Rain nodded, but instead of walking to her room she came to me and wrapped her little arms around my waist.

"Don't be mad at Uncle Black, mommy. He didn't mean to hurt your feelings." I hugged her tightly.

"Okay, baby. Mommy's not mad anymore. Go ahead and start packing." She nodded and after hugging Betty made her way to her room. As soon as her door shut, I went in.

"He's dangerous. He's a murderer. All the Seminole people who live on their reservation think he's the devil. He hurts people." I was one step away from saying he eats children, really needing to sell this. But I reined myself in in time. I didn't have to lie to prove Melech was a bad man. His reputation preceded him.

Betty folded her arms. "And how do you know all this about him?"

I folded my arms to match her stance. "Mitch told me."

One of her eyebrows went up in the air. "And haven't we established that your late husband is something of a liar?"

"Yeah, about where he was last night or what he did with money that should have gone to pay the rent. But something like that he wouldn't lie about."

"Reaaallly? And how do you know?"

Ohhh… her attitude was getting on my nerves. "I know because— because…"

I couldn't think how I knew. Mitch was a liar. And in all truthfulness, I didn't know him long enough to know when he was lying and when he wasn't.

"You getting ready to let your fear cause you to walk away from a good thing."

I held out both of my hands. "Are you serious, Betty?!"

"I'm dead serious. That mon is hot, and rich, and strong…he's good with Rain. And he knows how to love your body in such a way that you glow all the next day. Girl, don't be no fool. You ain't never gon' to find another mon like that!"

She got up and went into my room to get a brush and comb.

"Sit down here and let me put two braids in your hair while you calm down a bit so that you can think clearly."

Sulking like Rain I sat down on the floor between her legs. My hair was a mess. After the tussle downstairs most of it had escaped my ponytail. Betty was tripping. She didn't see the look in Mitch's eye when he warned me about his brother.

Yeah he's a liar, and yeah I didn't know him well enough to separate his truths from his lies, but I knew fear. And when he warned me about his brother, there was real fear in his eyes.

"Now, this is what you're going to do." She told me as she began to braid my hair. "You're going to go to that meeting. Make sure our little Rain is squared away, and then you're going to talk to him and tell him you didn't appreciate him lying to you. Although whether he lied or not is up for debate."

"Lying by omission is still lying." I volunteered.

She sucked her teeth again, this time longer than the last. "Yeah whatever. Then you're going to let him lay you down in the bed and make you forget all about your worries in that special way that he can."

I shook my head; the only thing Betty could think about was sex. Many women put up with a lot of drama for a man that is good in bed. I couldn't afford to do that, I knew better than to get sexually involved with him and I did it anyway.

Not only that, I was starting to fall in love with him. Hell… who was I kidding? I am in love with him. And this whole time he had been making a fool of me, this whole time…

"Betty, I hear what you're saying and I appreciate what you're trying to do. But I've already been through a horrible situation. Mitch and my marriage was started on a lie." I shook my head.

"I can't go through that again no matter how good the sex is."

"Yeah, but Melech ain't Mitch."

I sighed. "I know, he's his wiser, stronger, older brother. If anything, that makes him more dangerous than Mitch."

13

UNWORTHY

"When I dare to be powerful, to use my strength in the service of my vision, then it becomes less and less important whether I am afraid."

— AUDRE LORDE

EARTH

I clutched Rain's hand as we rode up the elevator of High Stakes. The Casino was massive and breathtakingly grand. My heart was beating faster and faster as the reality of what I did consumed me.

I had the owner of this grand establishment tied up inside my little ghetto apartment, feeding him what he must have thought was scraps from my little refrigerator, sitting at my little broken-down table and sleeping in my pieced together bed for two weeks.

The farther up the elevator went, the closer I came to having a full fledged panic attack. I was so far out of my element I felt lost a sea. These halls were being perused by some of the wealthiest people in the world. Rain and I didn't belong here.

Closing my eyes, I took comfort in Earth's Cry that I had wisely placed in its case and strapped to my back. Although I haven't played the violin in years it still gave me immense comfort, just like it had the day my mother left me, and the day Mitch died leaving me a single mother.

I was so afraid right now. These people were too powerful. Standing in court fighting their lawyers had been intimidating. Riding up an elevator in the heart of their territory was petrifying.

I just wanted to get this meeting over with and take Rain home back to Crazy Larry and Betty, Bre-Bre, Sis. Dinah and Bro. Abraham, the bookstore, and kale and apple smoothies.

When the elevator dinged on the top floor, I nearly jumped out of my skin, just to show you how frayed my nerves were. Luckily, by the time I came downstairs from my apartment, Black was gone and I didn't have to see his handsome face again. Waiting on us was the giant called Big Troy.

Surprisingly for a giant, he was quite gentle. He even had a really gentle, soothing voice.

"You all set, Ms. Earth? I'm going to take you to the hotel and get you and the hobbit squared away." He'd said as he took Rain and my bag from me.

"Earth is fine. You don't have to call me Ms." He nodded as he led the way to his car.

I looked back longingly at Betty and Larry as they waved bye to me. Larry told me the fellas had stayed long enough to help him clean his place back up, and Black had wrote him a check big enough for him to do a full remodel on both the juice bar and the bookstore.

Like Betty, he encouraged me to let my emotions die down before I made any rash decisions. Neither of them understood.

Betty was only thinking about the amazing sex and Larry about the fact that Black was his new best friend, thanks to him, his property was getting ready to get a new fresh look that would attract more business.

Neither of them knew what it took to pull myself out of the dark place I was thrown after losing Mitch and having to take care of a baby on my own. Neither of them knew how it felt to be completely rejected by Mitch's family and made to feel unworthy. Neither of them understood that it was exactly how I felt the night my mother left me, unworthy.

His family said I was unworthy to come to his funeral and unworthy to grieve with the rest of them. Like my mother, they just put me outside of their love. And then when they finally found out about Rain, they said I was unworthy of being her mom. And now I found myself tangled with the very head of that family, and my friends wanted me to put myself out there so that he could hurt me worse than anybody ever did.

I can't, I'm not that brave.

I know that when Black realizes I'm not worthy and he leaves me like everybody else, it will kill me. Somehow, I survived Mitch's abandonment. And somehow, I survived my father's abandonment. It took me a long time to get over my mother's abandonment, I nearly didn't make it.

But HalleluYah, I did.

Black is different. In a very short time he got inside, and it felt like he was the other half of my soul. To lose that would be too much.'

I am not that strong!

Sis. Dinah used to tell me that the Heavenly Father never put us through more than we can handle. And I wondered if maybe for the first time, he'd made a mistake. I am the girl without. Rain and Earth's Cry are all I ever had. Why did he continue to take from me? Why did I always find myself in these highly stressful situations?

Folks say karma is a monster, but it should only be a monster for bad people, right? If what you reap you sow, then good things should happen to good people, right?

I'm not a bad person. Rain and I go down to volunteer at the soup kitchen several times a month. I try to instill in her to always give back. We may be poor and not have a lot, but of what we do have, we give. Sometimes people come in the bookstore hurt and searching and I try to give them a positive word, reminding them that the Most High has not forgotten them.

I don't rob anybody, or lie, or steal. I just don't understand why stuff like this keeps happening to me.

"The best room in the house." Big Troy said bringing me out my thoughts.

He flashed a key card in front of a lock to a massive golden door opening it and Rain and I followed him in.

"Ohhh! Mommy, there's a golden water fountain in our room!" She yelled as she ran ahead of us farther into the luxurious suite to get a better look.

"Rain, be careful, don't lean over it, you might fall in!" I looked around stunned at the glamour.

My gaze went to Big Troy. "Whaa!" Was all I was able to get out.

Smiling at my shock he nodded. "Only the best for the best."

"This is too much. A simple room would have sufficed."

He shrugged setting our bags down just inside what must be the bedroom door. "Hey, my job is to follow orders." Then he turned to head for the door. "If you get hungry just pick up the phone and dial zero, room service will bring you anything you want, all you have to do is ask. Someone will come and get you for the meeting tomorrow morning. The boss doesn't like for anybody to be late. Feel free to explore, I'm sure there are tons of activities for you guys to do. We have the best spa in the Tampa Bay area, feel free to indulge. Have a good night, Earth."

Still stunned to silence, I watched as he quietly closed the golden door behind him.

"Mommy, it's so pretty!" Rain yelled as she pressed her little face against the huge window that had an amazing view of the Tampa strip. I'm surprised that she was not afraid of being up so high.

I eased down on the couch feeling even more out of my element. Why would he put us in the best suite in the hotel? This was the room movie stars and politicians stayed in when they came to gamble, the room rap videos are shot in.

"I'm hungry, mommy." Rain said crawling up on the couch next to me. I thought about calling room service, but I didn't want to be in anymore debt to Black. I know that sounds petty, but the more he did for me, the more I felt like I owed him. I didn't want him to have that kind of control over me.

I just wanted this to all be over so that I could get back to my life. I picked up the room key that Big Troy left on the table and after grabbing my wallet took Rain's hand and headed for the door. There were tons of restaurants downstairs.

"You want to go to one of the restaurants downstairs?"

Her face brightened and she did a little dance. "Yeaaaahhh!" I smiled despite myself. Rain's joy had that effect on me.

When we left out the room I exhaled. It was a very luxurious suite, but it felt like a silken cage. Being here in this hotel was almost suffocating.

Rain hurried to the elevator to push the down button, it came almost instantly. When we stepped on, I pushed the two, that was the level where I saw the majority of the restaurants. Before the door could close, a huge hand came in to stop it. Crush stepped on the elevator.

My heart dropped when he smiled at me as if bumping into

him on the elevator was just coincidental. This giant Native-American man scared the hell out of me, and Rain must have felt the same way, because together we both stepped back away from him until our backs were pressed against the mirrored wall.

Please push a level! Please push a level!

When he never did, my suspicions were confirmed. *He was following us.*

The elevator opened a few floors down, but the giant never moved from in front of the doors to let the people on.

"Get the next one." He grumbled before he pushed the close button.

Oh God! The only thing I could think about was him throwing Larry through the door and holding that cruel looking gun to his head. He wanted to kill Larry.

"Sweet baby Moses!" I hissed pulling Rain back against my leg when he suddenly moved squatting down in front of us.

"I'm sorry I scared you, Hobbit." He spoke staring at the floor and for the first time, he appeared almost childlike. "But I got something for you." He reached inside his coat where I knew he kept that monster of a gun and pulled out a tiny book.

Rain's eyes lit up. "What is it?" She asked taking the small book from him.

"It was my favorite story when I was little. It's called, *Broken Flute*."

"Why is it so small?" She whispered, holding her head closer to the giant's as they both looked down at it.

He grinned at her. "It's hobbit size." He whispered back. And of course, that made her erupt in giggles. Then she did something that surprised us both. She threw her arms arounds his big neck and hugged him.

"Thank you, Crush." Slowly he turned and looked up in her eyes.

"You're welcome, Hobbit."

He stood, but he didn't look me in my eyes, instead he stared at the floor in front of us.

"I know you don't like me, but I'm sorry I scared you." He spoke low, as if he wasn't sure of himself. Then he reached inside his coat and came out with a beautiful daisy. It looked as if he plucked it from somewhere. The gift was so child like it pulled at my heart instantly.

Crush was a special adult. I took the flower from him smiling.

"That's not true. I *do* like you. But you did scare me." I spoke gently. During my time in college I did volunteer work at a school for people like Crush. Before Mitch died, I was going to school to get my degree in early childhood development; I'd wanted to be a teacher.

We had to complete so many hours of volunteer work in the field and I chose to complete mine at the Noble Institute of Learning, which is a school that caters to the needs of students with special needs.

Crush had a very mild case. You wouldn't know he was special unless you talked to him.

He nodded. "I thought the Jamaican had hurt Black." He continued still not looking into my eyes. I had only seen him look into Melech's eyes and now Rain's, which meant he trusted Black and loved him.

"Is Black your friend?"

He nodded. "He's my best friend. He saved my life."

I gently touched his arm. "From who?"

"The dragon." He whispered, before the door opened and his mask of fierce protector fell back into place. He silently followed Rain and I around the restaurant area. He was not close enough that he invaded our privacy, but he was close enough that he caused folks to give us a good space as they stared wondering who we were to garner such a fierce looking bodyguard.

Rain chose to eat at a beautiful restaurant that had somehow managed to get the Tampa Bay Beach feel indoors. There were sand and palm trees and coming from a speaker somewhere overhead was the sound of birds soaring over the ocean.

As we were led to a table that gave one the feel of eating outdoors, I feared I wasn't going to be able to afford anything on the menu. I had just gotten my check from Larry, but after paying my bills, I didn't have much left.

I inhaled when I opened the menu. "Damn."

The cheapest thing on the menu was fifty-two dollars.

"Hi, Ms. Earth, welcome to Baja Beach Café. Please feel free to order anything you want, your bill has already been taken care of. My name is Mandy and I will be honored to serve you." A beautiful bubbly waitress said smiling down at us.

Surprised that Mandy knew my name, my gaze went to Crush, who was leaning against one of the palm trees that were a good distance away, he was watching us closely. As soon as our gaze met, he lowered his eyes.

"I want the fish sticks." Rain said pointing to the item on the little kiddie menu she had.

My eyes nearly bulged out my head when I saw the price of the fish sticks. *What the hell?* The waitress jotted it down on her little pad.

"And for you, ma'am?" At my hesitation she continued speaking. "May I suggest the salmon? It is so good. We have the best chef in all of Tampa in our kitchen, and he prepares the salmon in such away that it's light and buttery, with the perfect charbroil on the outside giving it just enough crunch." By the time she finished my stomach let out a long loud growl.

I nodded. "That's sounds great, thank you."

"And to drink?" she asked.

"Water will be just fine." My goodness, who knows how much that salmon costs? I had already spent more than I ever had in a restaurant. I didn't care that my bill was already taken care of. I wasn't used to that kind of spending. Asking for a drink just felt greedy.

After assuring us that she'll have our food right out, she left. As Rain and I waited we colored a picture that was on her kiddie menu.

"Excuse me, Ms. Earth." Mandy said drawing our attention a few minutes later.

"Just Earth, you don't have to call me Ms."

She nodded. "Okay, excuse me, Earth."

In her hands she held two big tropical, delicious looking drinks. They were loaded down with pineapples and cherries.

"This is our house special. The Baja Pina Coladas." She put one in front of me. "And the virgin." She said placing the other glass in front of Rain. These drinks looked very expensive.

"But I didn't order these, Mandy."

She giggled as she gestured across the building. "The boss did, madame."

Frowning I followed her hand and my breath stalled in my throat as if I was sucker punched in the stomach. Standing there on the third level across the building from us was Black. He watched us through the glass. I almost didn't recognize him. This was not the man I had gotten to know over the last two weeks.

Gone were the jeans, t-shirts, and funny island shirts. He stood dressed in a pair of expensive black slacks and a black buttoned up shirt that fell on his muscled chest and shoulders as if it had been tailored especially for him. In stark contrast to the black shirt, he wore a pair of blood red suspenders.

The orange glow of a cigar seemed to wink at me as he took a pull. He looked at me with the eyes of a predator. It was the same look I had caught on his face the night he first awakened me as a woman. The same look I caught on his face the night he'd first made love to me.

And now it dawned on me… that is his normal look. The kind, caring eyes I'd gotten used to was the stranger. Those predatory eyes that stared back at me now is the man Melech Black.

And even though he scared me to death, I nearly groaned because he looked so damn good, way better than he had in any of Larry's clothes.

He looked good and powerful.

So very powerful.

This is his territory. He is King here.

MELECH BLACK

It was killing me to stay away from her. I wanted to pull her in my lap and kiss her until she felt safe with me again. I wanted to make her body feel good, so that she'll know I will always make it so. I wanted to taste her to assure myself that she was still mine and will always remain so.

"You've got to stop smoking those things."

I didn't need to look away from Earth to know who that deep voice belonged to or try and figure out how he'd gotten into my office without using the door. Granted, the last time I heard that voice I'd been a boy of twelve, and he'd been teaching me how to control the fire that lived inside of me.

I grinned. "Preacher."

"How have you been, son?"

I turned to look at him then. He was looking across the building at Earth and Rain. I was not surprised that it didn't look as if he'd aged a day. He still wore that cowboy hat on top of his long hair that he wore in cornrows down his back. The smell of his leather duster filled my nose over the smell of the cigar.

My grandfather said that he'd been the only one in his family since the days of Chief Abraham who ever saw the Preacher and it had only been once. It was because of that visit that my grandfather had become the medicine man of our tribe.

I never told anyone that the Preacher had come and visited me for a week straight as he taught me how to control my emotions so that I could control the fire. If our people knew, they would put me up on an even bigger pedestal than what they had because of the fire. At first, I hated that they did that, but Frank taught me to love it. He said my people should have a healthy love and fear of me.

Anyway, the legend our people brought with them from the African shores was that the Preacher was the father of our family. Nobody knows how old he is or when he was born. Only that he has walked the earth for a long time, following his lineage. Watching them grow from the shadows. To be visited by him is a great honor.

"To what do I owe the honor of your visit, Great Father?"

He exhaled. "What did I tell you about calling me that? No one is great except for *One*, the Ancient of Days. We... we are just men."

I nodded. Amongst our people he is known as the Great Father. However, my grandfather said that the one time he'd talked to the Preacher he admonished him for calling him that. He admonished me for doing the same when I was twelve. I won't forget again.

"What does it mean that my grandfather has seen you, and now I...twice?" Sightings of the Preacher are something of legend. Before Abraham the great war chief, who fought alongside the Seminole and helped our people retain their freedom, the last sighting of him had been documented during our peoples' stay in Timbuktu.

According to Abraham, the Preacher had come to visit him the night the fort that they had built at Prospect Bluff in Florida was attacked in 1818. Had not the Preacher warned him, he would have not survived. He said it was the Preacher who led him to Suwannee River Town in Florida and told him to continue to fight against Andrew Jackson's men alongside the Seminole.

Abraham became known as the *"Sauanaffe Tustunnagee,"* Suwannee Warrior. Because he played such a major role in the Seminole obtaining their victory over the United States Army, he was adopted as a member of the Seminole Nation. He became the Prime Minister of the Cowkeeper Dynasty and a chief adviser to Micanopy, principle chief of the Alachua Seminole, thus beginning our family's beginnings with the Seminole.

And that was all because of the Preacher. It was no wonder our people placed him on a pedestal. However, the great war chief Abraham claimed to had seen him in 1818. The last sighting of the Preacher by our family before that had been in Timbuktu Africa in 1492.

So the fact that he has come to us three times in just a fifty-year span meant something. He turned to look at me then. I could see that he was impressed with my question. With his hands claps behind his back he walked away from the window.

"We are reaching the end of a four-hundred-year prophecy." He finally spoke.

I made eye contact with Crush. *Protect my girls.* He nodded as if he heard me. This was why Crush was one of my own. I didn't have to verbally express things to him all the time for him to know what I needed done. I knew he probably scared the hell out of Earth, but I needed her protected by my best. And Crush was definitely the best warrior I had.

Knowing that she was in good hands, I turned away from the window and sat in my chair behind my desk. The Preacher stood in front of the fireplace with his hands still clasped behind his back staring at the sword he'd given me after teaching me how to harness the fire all those years ago.

I'll never forget that day. Imagine being handed something so beautiful from the Father of our people.

"This is for you, son." He'd said handing it to me.

"Wooow!!" *The sword was so heavy it took two hands to hold it. I leaned it against the tree and got down on my knees to get a closer look at it.*

I had never seen anything like it. The metal of the blade seemed to flash blue in the sunlight. I ran my hand over the funny looking markings on it.

He squatted down next to me. "Careful, don't touch the edge, it is very sharp. This sword will never go dull, it sharpens itself."

"I don't know how to use this." *I told him.*

"When the time is right, I will teach you."

When I became Chief of Seminole Territory, I'd brought it here and hung it over the fire place, because this is Holata's office. In my mind there was no better place for it. This was the beginning of our empire. It all began in this room.

"What four-hundred-year prophecy?" I asked when he didn't say anything further.

"For it was written," He began to speak without turning away from the sword. *"And He said unto Abram, "Know for certain that your seed are to be sojourners in a land that is not theirs, and shall serve them, and they shall afflict them four hundred years. Genesis 15:13."*

"Yes, I've heard of it. I remember my grandfather telling me of it when I was a little boy."

He swiftly turned, taking me in with those deep, dark ancient eyes of his. "Tell me, son, when was the last time you prayed?" Slowly he began to approach me.

I searched my brain trying to remember the last time I prayed. I was ashamed to admit that it had been the night the fire came into me and I spoke with the man with no shoes. After that night, Frank came into my life and began raising me to take his place.

"It's been a while." I paused for just a moment trying to study his body language. But I don't know why I bothered. Trying to read him was the same as a blind man trying to read a book without Braille.

"Why do you ask?"

As he walked back towards my office window that looked out over the casino, his duster opened enough for me to see the handle of his sword. He didn't respond, he just stared at Earth. I turned my chair so that I could see her too. Rain had said something that made her smile.

It felt good to see that. The look of betrayal she'd worn earlier when she looked at me was tearing me apart.

"Preacher?" I asked.

"Hmmmm..."

"She's a daughter of Sarah, isn't she?"

Without looking away from her he nodded. "She is."

"Is she mine?"

He nodded again. "She is."

Wondering at it was one thing, knowing it to be true was another. So, my fears were correct. The Ancient of Days had come for me, just like the man with no shoes said he would.

"My time is up, isn't it?"

"Yes, son." His words were barely over a whisper.

I knew this day would come, the day I would have to choose between this lifestyle that I've come to love and the lifestyle I'd been called to serve. I took another pull of my cigar. How can I change who I've become? This life is a part of me.

I have become a child of the night, my hands were covered in blood.

Why would the Ancient of Days still desire me?

As if he could hear my thoughts, the Preacher began to speak.

"Your thoughts are only carnal. You worry about appeasing things that will sooth your flesh. However, if Earth is to survive, you must learn to deny your flesh."

I stubbed the cigar out in the ash tray. He had my full attention.

"What do you mean if Earth is to survive? Is she in danger?"

"Not now…but she will be. An enemy is coming and the only way you're going to be able to save her is if you can make fire come from that sword." Without looking away from Earth, he pointed at the sword behind his back on the wall.

I got up from desk and took the heavy sword off the wall. I could make fire come from anything. If that's all it took to keep her safe, then so be it. Holding the cold metal in my hand I saw it on fire. Seeing it was the first part, after seeing, it should go up in flames.

Nothing

"In order for your sword training to begin, you must first awaken it." The Preacher's quiet words seemed to encompass me as I focused on the sword.

Frowning, I stared down at the sword, concentrating harder. Burn!

Nothing

What the—

"There are some beings that your fire is not strong enough to burn. Because you are carnal and cannot see past the flesh, your fire will only consume the flesh." He began to slowly circle me as he studied me.

I ran my hand over the markings that I'd later found out was ancient Paleo Hebrew writing. The delicate script ran gracefully down the whole length of the blue steel. My grandfather knew how to read ancient Paleo fluently, but this script he could not. When I got a bit older, I hired a famous linguist who was known for his studies on ancient script to come and take a look, and even he could not decipher it.

He said that this form of paleo had not been used since the Antediluvian time period. At best the scholars of this day can try to guess what it said, but in reality, that form of language had been lost to us. And then he had tried to buy the sword from me.

Hmmm… I wondered if the writings had something to do with the sword not catching fire?

I inhaled and tried to focus harder. I could see the sword burning in my mind. I could see…yet.

Nothing

It continued to sit cold and unchanged in my hands.

"There are some beings who are not of the flesh. They are of the spirit. In order to kill such a one, you will need to use that sword. That sword without the Rauch is useless. When the fire first came to you, it was your call. When you can make the fire come from that sword, you have been chosen."

I didn't understand why the sword was not burning. This has never happened to me. Anything that I saw burning in my mind burned. Period!

"I don't get it, what have I been chosen to do? It all sounds like riddles!" I was trying not to lose my temper. To do so could result in the Preacher killing me. However, I didn't have time to try and figure out riddles when Earth's life was in danger.

I inhaled, willing myself to keep my cool. "If Earth's life is in danger, I need to know how to protect her! No more riddles!"

The Preacher stood and studied me for a moment before he spoke. "You have been chosen to protect the Earth's Cryer."

I frowned, "Isn't that the name of Earth's violin?"

"Yes. But Earth is the Cryer."

I was confused.

"In order to destroy what's coming after her, you will need to learn how make the sword burn. When you learn this, you will be ready to begin your training."

"What!? Preacher, I don't understand!"

He walked to me and put his hand on my shoulder. "Tell her to play the violin for you, and then you will see." His words were so low I barely heard him.

Tell her to play the violin for me. How in the world was I going to get her to do that? She didn't even like talking about that violin, let alone playing it. Hell, she didn't even want to talk to me. I ran my hand down my face frustrated. I didn't like not having control over a situation, and this whole thing seemed to be spiraling out of control.

"How am I supposed to do that? How am I going to get her to play the violin?" If anybody knew a way, it was him.

"Preacher?" I asked looking around when I didn't get an answer.

"Wonderful!" As quietly as he'd come, he'd left, leaving me to try and figure out the puzzle by myself.

Damn!

I needed to get to my grandfather, he will be able to help. But first, I had to get this meeting over with and secure Earth to my side.

14

THE MEETING

EARTH

Mitch had been right! Black was a monster!
A monster that could control fire!

"Help me!" I yelled through the gag that had been shoved in my mouth.

I'm being kidnapped!

"Help me!" I continued to yell although I knew I was wasting my breath.

Crush was carrying me over his shoulder to a helicopter that was waiting for us on the roof of High Stakes. Even if someone could hear me over the roar of the chopper blades, they would not be able to hear me over the deafening blare of the fire alarm. But even still, who would come up against what I'd just witnessed?

Who would come up against Melech?

Who would come up against the fire?

I should have known by how afraid everybody was of him. I

should have known there was more to the peoples' uneasiness around him than him just being a casino boss and a tribal chief.

Oh y'all…I messed up!

I messed up so badly and now I didn't know what was to become of me and Rain.

Rain…

I had no idea where my baby was right now. I had no idea where they were taking me. Yesterday, Black told me he didn't take well to being disrespected.

Oh, God…why didn't I listen to him?

Let me tell you guys what happened…Please!

I need to tell you guys what happened…

It all began with the babysitter that showed up to Rain and my room this morning before the meeting. I should have known something was going on, but I had been so nervous and anxious to get it all over with I didn't stop to really think about it.

Now granted, when the beautiful dark skinned Native-American girl named Tonya first showed up to my room, I was a little leery because I didn't know her and didn't know what her credentials were. However, she'd surprised me by pulling references out of her bag.

"I was prepared for this." She'd said as she handed me the references.

Impressed, I looked over the material she'd given me to see she came highly recommended by several families she babysat for. And for a young girl of only fifteen, she was very well spoken and super intelligent. I could imagine having a classroom full of pupils like her.

When I still continued to be a little leery, Big Troy told me that the meeting would probably last for a couple of hours, which would be torture for Rain.

Of course, that was true. I had a hard time trying to get my daughter to sit still for a couple of minutes, let alone hours. So yeah, I agreed to let Tonya babysit for me. She took Rain to the play area and told me they would be there waiting on me when I got back.

Alright, nothing too strange about that, right?

Right...

Except she said something that threw me for a loop before we parted ways on the elevator.

"I hope I make you proud so that you will let me be Rain's babysitter permanently."

Hmmm...What was she going to do, drive an hour each time I need her to my house? But I didn't want to hurt her feelings, she was looking so hopeful, so I'd nodded.

"I'm sure you will do just fine."

She wrapped her arm around mine in typical teenager fashion. *"You mean that? Ohhh! All of my friends are going to be so jealous. Little Tonya, babysitting the King's children. My mom and dad will be very proud of me too!"*

I opened my mouth to tell her Rain wasn't Melech's child, but right then the elevator doors opened on the third floor, and I was being led off by an impatient Crush. Apparently, I'd taken too much time getting to know Tonya and was now running late for the meeting.

"He doesn't like for people to be late!" Crushed muttered, clearly agitated.

What did they expect, for me to just leave my baby with someone without asking any questions?

So, after telling Rain to behave and to listen to Tonya, I left them with Big Troy, who assured me he would watch out for them and make sure nothing happened to them while practically pushing me off the elevator.

"Please Earth, you need to hurry. You don't want to make him angry."

"Alright already, I'm going." I huffed following Crush off the elevator.

Geesh! I had heard of wanting to please the boss, but this was just ridiculous. Now good and irritated myself, I followed Crush down the massive halls that led to the boardroom where the meeting was being held. It looked as if the third floor was the casino's business center, here all the executive offices could be found.

When Crush and I walked into the meeting it was well underway. There was a huge oval table where about twenty people sat. At the head of the table looking extremely powerful in a tailor-made charcoal suit was Melech, he held a file that he was going over in his hands. Behind him lying on top of a desk, looking as regal as I ever saw him was Abner. His big tail swished through the air as if he owned the place.

When we entered, Black looked down at his watch, the only sign to show his displeasure was a slight frown on his face and the lift of an eyebrow. The people who sat at the table all looked very nervous, and I wondered if it had anything to do with the frown that was on Black's face.

Well, all except for Mike, who grinned and gave me a little wave when I entered the room. I waved back as I slid in the chair Crush was holding out for me at the head of the table opposite Black's. I was a little uneasy sitting at the head of the table, but I did it anyway, telling myself just to go ahead and get it over with.

The table sat quiet while Black continued to read through the papers he was holding. I took the time to study the people who were in the room. The man with the tattoos, whose name I found out was Horse, stood off to the side reading a newspaper. The two strong boys, who had grabbed Betty and me, stood on either side of the doors. The man who had carried Rain out the kitchen yesterday, I think I heard Black call him Tocho, stood against the far wall. Crush walked to stand against the opposite wall from him. These men were clearly Black's bodyguards or something.

At the time I wondered if maybe they were the reason most of the occupants at the table with me looked nervous.

Ha! That was before I found out what Melech really was. Anyway, I'm getting ahead of myself. Like I was saying, I took in the people that sat at the table with me.

Mike sat in a chair next to his brother's, scrolling through his phone. He was the only one at the table that seemed relaxed. However, across from him sat a Native-American man and woman, they looked really nervous. Really nervous and rich.

The woman was perfectly beautiful, but she looked like she'd paid millions of dollars to get that way. Both she and the handsome man kept shooting curious glances down the table at me before their eyes would creep back to Black, and then down at whatever papers they had in front of them.

There was a brown-skinned man in a suit, who had attorney written all over him. He was looking through papers and sliding some of them in front of Black. This was making the Native-American man and woman even more nervous.

Also joining us at the table was a group of older folks. Some of them were Native, some of them African-American...I wondered if that was the council Black spoke of yesterday. Finally, I let my gaze settle on Black and almost cried out when I found him studying me over the papers he was reading.

Goodness gracious!

The impact that gaze of his had on my nervous system was a damn shame. I had to force myself not to fidget under the intense look.

"Good morning, Minx." His deep voice floated down the table and gently caressed the back of my neck. It seemed as if the whole table was now watching me.

Swallowing I tried to smile, but my lips quivered so badly I failed miserably. I cleared my throat.

"*Good morning.*" I addressed the room as a whole, not wanting this to seem personal. I wanted this to remain as professional as possible.

Several people nodded their greeting and several others uttered theirs. It was as if they were afraid to speak. Black's lips lifted in a slight grin. He was very aware of what I was attempting to do.

"*How did you sleep?*" He continued.

Nobody had to tell me I was beet red. I already knew it. I didn't know if he was intentionally trying to embarrass me, or if he just didn't care that the boardroom was no place for such personal questions.

"Great, how about you?"

It was a lie. After sleeping in the bed with him for the last two weeks, I'd grown accustomed to having his big warm body next to mine, to the feel of his strong arms wrapped around me, holding me close. Last night was horrible. Not only was I in a strange bed, but he wasn't there to make it familiar.

"*I'm glad you slept well.*" He responded. "*I on the other hand had a miserable night. I found myself tossing and turning. Something... or shall I say, someone... was missing.*"

OMG! I couldn't believe he just said that in front of all these people.

"So, ummm...have you found out what happened with Rain?" I said trying to cover up the fact that I was blushing like crazy.

He didn't seem fazed a bit. He still looked across the table with a slight grin on his face.

"*I did.*" His gaze settled on the Native-American man and woman. "*Why don't I let Isabel here explain.*"

The woman's mouth dropped open. "*You want me to explain to her?*"

The way she said her, as if I was unworthy of an explanation, let me know right off that this was the person responsible for the custody battle.

Black's expression didn't change. *"Oh yes. You will explain to her. You might want to get used to it. In fact, allow me to introduce you all to Earth."*

At his statement several people looked down the table at me, now studying me with new eyes. What the hell did he mean, *she might want to get used to it?* That's when the first inkling that something was wrong started to tickle the back of my neck.

He gestured to his right. *"Michael, you know."* I nodded.

He gestured to the man and woman who sat on his left. *"This is Michael's Aunt and Uncle, Isabel and her husband Paul. They pretty much oversee the day to day operations of all seven of our casinos. The two of them make my job indisputably easier."*

Using both his hands he gestured to the group of elders who sat on both sides of the table.

"This is our elders board, they oversee the day to day operations of Seminole Territory. I don't know where I would be without them. In my absence, they make sure law and order abide in our small town. The only one missing is my grandfather Hosea. He's a bit eccentric and doesn't like to travel too far from the reservation. I put up with his insubordination because he's my grandfather and the tribe's Medicine Man."

Michael chuckled. *"You put up with insubordination because you don't want to hear his excessive nagging about how you're wasting your life in these dens of sin."*

Black grinned. *"That and the fact that he pretty much raised me after my father died."* There was love and respect in his voice when he spoke of his grandfather. I wondered what kind of man could garner such respect from a man like Black.

However, I didn't get a chance to ponder on it long because Black's gaze fell on me.

"Everybody, this is my Earth." The way he said my caused that little alarm that had been going off in my head, signaling something was wrong to get just a bit louder.

I waved to the room. "Pleased to meet you all."

Black nodded, pleased with my statement. "Now that introductions are out the way and everyone is aware of who Earth is, I'll expect you all to act accordingly." His gaze settled on the woman that had turned noticeably paler since the introductions.

"Isabel, will you please explain to Earth what happened?"

Isabel cleared her throat. "We had no idea Mitch was a father. Quite naturally when we found out we did what we needed to do, which was to make sure the child was safe and secure."

Ohhh! That pissed me right off. How dare this woman assume the best place for my child would be with them?

"You felt that taking her away from her mother was the best option?" I hissed. Telling myself to keep my cool and don't let the ghetto me reign freely.

Isabel swallowed. "Rain comes from a wealthy family. Her uncle is the chief of our tribe. Of course, it is better for her to be with this side of her family, where she can be better supported financially."

"You filed a custody suit in my name." Black interjected. "Tell me, how was I going to raise her if I knew nothing about her?"

Good damn question! I mean mugged Mrs. *Have-The-Answers-To-Everything* to see how she was going to respond to that.

"Of course, we didn't expect our Great Leader to be bothered with such a trivial matter of raising your brother's child. We'd made arrangements with one of the tribal mothers to do it for you."

This b****! I opened my mouth to tell her off, but Mike beat me to it.

"Come on Isabel, who are you kidding? You can give a flying f*** about Rain and her wellbeing. You filed for custody so that when Earth *realized she held a diamond mine in her hands, she couldn't get one red cent. Let's be honest."*

Isabel didn't try to deny it, in fact she shrugged. *"Are you going to fault me for doing my job? It's my duty to make sure our Chief and people are protected from any outside interest. Without a father, the Chief is the child's next of kin, he should have custody of her. It's our peoples' way."*

When she said *outside interest,* her gaze shot down the table to me. That's me the outsider. Her words hurt, but I'll be damned if I let her know that.

"All you had to do was come and talk to me, and I would have let you know that I don't want any of your family's money. I've been taking care of Rain on my own, and I will continue to take care of Rain on my own. As a matter of fact, none of you have to ever worry about seeing us again. Just reverse what you've done and me and my daughter will be on our way!"

Yep! The ghetto me slipped on through. *"And for your information, I am Rain's next of kin...You know, her mother! Your chief does not have a right to my child!"*

The man that sat next to Isabel turned to look at Black who was watching me through narrowed eyes.

"Chief, do you want us to undo the custody papers and sign the child back over to her mother?"

*Don't do it, Earth! Don't curse these mutha f***** out! That's what the devil wants you to do!*

"Rain!" I hissed, not able to tolerate one more person calling her *the child. "The child has a name, it's Rain!"*

Black smiled then, and it sent chills up my spine. It was not a nice smile, it was wicked, very wicked.

"She is correct, from now on, you will address the hobbit as Rain. And Isabel..." When he called the woman's name she inhaled as if she was waiting for a death sentence to be handed down to her.

"I am not upset with you. It is your job to protect the tribe." Isabel

exhaled, clearly relieved. My angry gaze shot down the table to Black as those alarm bells began to blare in my head. The powerful man that sat across from me was not the man that I'd lived with for the last two weeks.

This man was cold and ruthless. How could he congratulate that she-bat for taking away my child? It was a heartless thing to do. Just because I was not rich didn't mean I should lose my baby. But I tell you what I'm getting ready to lose…my temper. I was getting ready to show all these people my ass as I tell the bunch of them off.

Mitch had called his family vampires. He told me they were cold and would do anything for money. Hadn't he warned me that they chewed people like Rain and I up? He was right! I should have listened to my husband.

"As you know, I had a little trouble sleeping, so I decided to look over all the paper work for this case." Melech began to address the table. "And thanks to Isabel for sight, it looks as I'm now the guardian of a very smart and beautiful little lady."

Isabel now sat preening like a dog whose master had just patted her head. I wanted to rip all her hair out. How could they be so heartless?

Black's intimidating gaze settled on me. "The question is, where do we go from here?"

The fact that he said that only angered me more. What did he mean, where do we go from here? Where Rain and I went from here was none of his damn business. The only thing he needed to do was sign the papers giving me back custody. Period!

"You promised you would not take her from me." I shot back, not caring what the other people at the table thought about me speaking to their *Great Leader* this way.

He lifted an eyebrow at the insolent tone in my voice. "And I won't. I'm a man of my word, which is why I had my attorney draw up a new agreement." The man in the suit, who I'd pegged for an attorney earlier stood and began to pass a document out to everyone at the table.

"I brought the council here to bear witness and place their seal on said agreement. All are present but one, my grandfather, but I will get his seal when we return to Seminole Territory." Black told the table as a whole.

Frowning at his words I began to read the paper that was placed in front of me. The lawyer began to go over it out loud, but his voice faded to the recesses of my mind. I couldn't believe what I was reading. The document basically said Black would turn guardianship of Rain back over to me, if I agreed to marry him.

Completely shocked, I looked up at him stunned. I didn't know what issue to address first, the fact that he'd lied to me, or the fact that he was trying to use extortion to get his way. There was no way in hell I was marrying back into this cold, loveless family. No way!

"And if I say no?" My words must have shocked the room, because there was a collective gasp before everybody turned to look at me with startled eyes, including Crush.

Black continued to look at me with that ruthless gaze of his. That gaze that said he would have his way, whether I liked it or not. I'll be damned!

"Why would you say no?" His voice was casual as if he was asking about the weather.

"Because I don't like the idea of being blackmailed into marriage?"

"It's not blackmail, it's me keeping my promises."

I felt my temper slip through my grasp and before I could catch it, I'd found myself shooting to my feet staring hostilely down the table at him.

"To hell it is! You told me that you will not let anybody take Rain from me!" As I spoke, I pointed down the table at him. "You said I *could trust your word! Forgive me if I'm not surprised, you're just a filthy liar!"*

The look that came across his face should have been enough to make me apologize and ease on back down in my seat. He'd told me yesterday he didn't tolerate disrespect. The inhabitants of the room visibly began to fidget in their chairs looking longingly towards the door. Horse put down his paper as he and the other bodyguards shared worried glances with each other.

Side note: Now looking back on the situation, I could confidently say this is the point I should have *shut my mouth*. This is where I should have maybe tried a more gentle approach. But I didn't…and well, this happened.

"I am a man of my word. Yes, I promised I will not let anybody take Rain from you. But I also promised myself I will not let anybody take you from me. And like I said, I'm a man of my word." He'd growled those words, a good warning for anybody with even a little bit of sense, but quite obviously, I didn't have good sense.

"Ha!" I yelled across the table. *"I wish I would marry you. I should have listened to Mitch when he warned me about you. My hus—"* I never got the rest of that out.

A flame suddenly leaped to life inside his irises. My mouth dropped open as my mind tried to make sense of what I was seeing. In a full rage he came to his feet, slamming both fist down on the table, causing everyone at the table to jump. The flame that was burning in his eyes grew bigger with anger, until no more of his pupils could be seen…it was all flame.

He looked at me through burning eyes!

"Mitch, is not your husband!" He roared. *"Don't you ever call him that again!"*

As he spoke those words, a wave of fire rolled across the ceiling, casting the room in its hot glow. It framed him, making him look like an avenging angel from little children's nightmares.

The only thing that missing were two powerful black wings opening from his sides.

My scream got lost in the sudden blare of the fire alarm. Seconds later the overhead sprinkler system came on, but no water fell. That purple flamed fire that burned on the ceiling evaporated it instantly, frying the system as well as the paint.

Feeling like I was in the twilight zone, I looked around confused as to why the people in this room were not running for their lives. They all just sat cowering in their chairs, shaking in fear, staring at Black and the burning ceiling with frightened eyes. Like me, they were all drenched in sweat from the heat. Everyone was sweating but Black. It looked as if Mike and Horse wanted to try and talk to him but didn't think now was a good time.

Nobody wanted to draw his attention. The problem was, his attention was on me. With a fierce scowl on his face, he stared at me through eyes of fire. Opening and closing his fists as if he was trying to calm himself, he began to approach me.

I don't know what the hell was wrong with these people, but I was getting out of here. Petrified, I turned to flee out the door, more than positive he was going to kill me, but before I could get to it, the door burst into flames...flames that ate away at the wood as if it was acid.

My feet came to a screeching halt, staring at the burning door horrified, I began to back away from it. However, when my back came in contact with warm muscles, I cried out. Black's arm shot around my waist holding me to him.

"Where you going, baby, this meeting is not over yet."

"Don't hurt me!" I yelled snatching away from him. Turning to face him I took a step back for every step he took forward. My eyes filled with tears.

He was the devil! Mitch had been right! There was fire

burning in his eyes. He had caused fire to wash across the ceiling. The door still burned.

I continued to back away from him till my back made contact with the wall. Through wide eyes I watched as he closed the distance between us, his big body blocking out the other occupants of the room.

He studied me with that burning gaze, and even though I was afraid, I couldn't help but be amazed at the hunger I saw in his eyes. His fiery gaze took in the way my blouse clung to my sweat drenched breasts, revealing my pink bra underneath, it slowly slid up my neck, I swallowed in fear. For just a moment, it settled on my lips that quivered, when his eyes finally connected with mine, a whimper escaped my throat as I got an up-close look at the flames that burned in his gaze.

Slowly he lifted his hand and gently wiped away a tear that rolled down my cheek. He was standing so close the heat from his body drowned out the heat from the burning ceiling. Amazingly, I could smell his expensive cologne.

"You broke a few promises too, you know?" His words were so low only I could hear them.

"Wh-.." I swallowed. *"What promises?"*

Still studying my face through the flames, he lifted his other hand and wiped away the tears on my other check.

"You promised that when you found out who I was, you wouldn't want to leave me." He brought the same hand in back of my neck to gently palm it.

"You promised you would never look at me this way."

"What way?" My voice quivered so badly I didn't even think my words were coherent.

"Like I'm a monster." He whispered before he slowly brought his head down to mine. I had time to turn my face away. The hand he held behind my neck was not applying enough pressure for me to say he forced me to kiss him.

No...there was even a point, if I was being honest with myself, where I could say I raised my mouth for him.

But when our lips touched, everything else in the world faded to black. It was just him and I, his soft warm lips caressing mine. And then I felt him in my mouth, and like a drug, I was lost. Even though I was afraid, this man had the power to make me feel highly aroused.

When he deepened the kiss, I moaned remembering how much I missed him last night, remembering how much I missed his touch and feeling his fullness inside of me. My center seemed to come to life at the thought. I had to press my legs together to give it a little relief.

Damnit, Earth! What are you doing? My inner voice yelled so loudly it caused me to stiffen.

What the hell was I doing? Black was the enemy, and he was kissing me in a room full of people. Not to mention the fact that he may or may not be the devil. I pulled away from him, touching my lips that were still wet from his kiss with fingertips that shook.

The first thing I realized was that the room was noticeably cooler. The fire was gone from the ceiling, the door and his eyes. Breathing heavily he stared at my lips, and I could tell by his hungry gaze he wanted to kiss me again. The ceiling was toast, as well as the door, smoke lingered around their charcoal remands.

"*Marry me, Minx?*" He pleaded, still speaking so only I could hear him.

I shook my head as my eyes filled with tears. Now that he was no longer kissing me, I could think clearly. He'd just asked me to marry him, but I wasn't sure if he was even human. How could he ask such a thing of me after what I'd just seen?

"*I'm sorry, I can't marry you.*"

His demeaner changed right before my eyes. It a split second he went from being a begging man, to a man that was ready to take what he wanted.

That deadly grin came back to his face as he took several steps back. *"Then you leave me no other choice."*

That didn't sound good.

"No other choice but to do what?" I asked, already knowing I didn't really want to hear the answer.

He bared his teeth at me, reminding me of the animal that still sat on the desk watching us as if our only job was to entertain him.

"You leave me no other choice but to show you the correct way to execute a kidnapping." Without looking away from me he spoke to his men.

"Tie her up and take her to her new home. Tell the tribe to prepare for a wedding. Their King has found his Queen."

Before I could scream, Horse was behind me shoving something in my mouth. I went to swing on him, but Crush grabbed my arms tying my wrists together with his belt.

My panicked gaze went to Black's to plead with him not to do this, but right then something covered my head, throwing my world into complete darkness.

15

NOBODY MESSES WITH THE MEDICINE MAN

EARTH

When the pillow case was finally removed from over my head the helicopter was landing on a beautiful green lawn. Crush and Horse were in the helicopter with me.

"Where is my daughter?!" I cried as soon as Crush removed the gag from my mouth.

Horse held up his hands. "Calm down, she's already inside waiting for you." He pointed out the window to my right. I turned to see what he was pointing at and my mouth dropped open.

"Wow!" The word gushed out my mouth in a startled breath. The chopper had just landed in front of a mansion log cabin. I had never in my life seen anything like it. It had to be at least five stories high and as wide as a football field.

"This is your new home, it's amazing, isn't it?" Horse asked and I could hear the pride in his voice.

"It's beautiful." I could not deny it. It was breathtakingly beautiful, something you would see in a Disney cartoon. However, this was not my new home. My home was over Larry's bookstore and juice bar. And as soon as I found out where I was, I was going to find Rain and make my way back there.

"Chief Holata had it built nearly sixty-years ago."

I turned to look at Horse. "Who is Chief Holata?"

He smiled. "The very first King of Savages."

"What does that mean? King of Savages? Isn't that kind of offensive to the Native, and African-American people of your tribe?" He'd called Black that back at the bookstore. I wondered if it had anything to do with the fact that Melech was some kind of demon that could control fire and make the flame appear in his eyes.

"Here… let's walk and talk. I'm sure little Rain is as anxious to see you as you are to see her." Horse said as he untied the belt from around my wrists, handing it back to Crush.

"Aren't you worried I'll try and run away?"

He shook his head. "Our reservation is surrounded on all sides by miles and miles of woods. If you make it pass our gates, you wouldn't get far before you ran into your first wolf pack. If by some miracle you survived their attack, I assure you, you won't survive the next."

My eyes widened. "Seriously?" *I'm a city girl, I didn't know nothing about no woods.*

He held his head back and laughed at my stricken expression as Crush opened the door jumping out the chopper. Then he turned and helped me out.

"Is he serious?" I asked Crush "Is this place surrounded by wolves?"

He grunted. "You don't want to be there when it gets dark."

Crush I believed. People like him didn't do much lying. However, they needed not worry about me trying to escape on foot. I wasn't crazy about dogs, let alone wolves. That being said, if I happened to find a ride or a car...all beats were off.

As we walked toward the beautiful log palace that Horse said was my new home, he began to tell me the tale of Chief Holata who had been responsible for bringing great wealth to his people here. Horse said it was because of him their reservation wasn't impoverished like many other Native-American reservations.

He said Holata embraced the American way, which he felt meant the survival of the fittest. And in his opinion from what he had observed, the fittest in America were the criminals. Holata felt that savages ran the world and if he was going to compete, he would need to become King of Savages.

Horse said Holata lied, stole and killed to pave a way for his tribe. Because of it, he'd become something of a god amongst his people. So much so, they continued to honor the spirit of the King of Savages and agreed to be subjected to anyone who held that title, which was now Melech.

"But is Black a descendent of Holata?" I asked as we continued to cross the massive lawn.

"Technically no. Frank, Holata's grandson, married Black's mother just so he could become Black's father."

I frowned. "Why would he do that? Didn't he have children of his own?"

Horse nodded. "By that time, he'd already had a son, Hawk. But as King of Savages, his duty was to make sure his successor was the strongest and the most ruthless amongst our people. Holata believed that was the only way we could survive and continue to be on top. Hawk was not the most ruthless. The most ruthless had been born across the river to a Native Seminole woman and an African Seminole man. Frank did what he had to do to make sure Black ruled in his stead."

"But what about Black's father?"

"He died of alcohol poisoning when Black was a baby."

"Mommy!" Rain's cry cut me off just as I was about to ask another question. We'd just walked through a side door that led into a massive kitchen. Rain was sitting at the counter with a plate of cookies and a cup of milk in front of her. When she saw me, she jumped off her stool to run towards me.

"Hey, baby!" I cried opening my arms needing to feel her in them.

"Where was you, mommy? I was so scared. Tonya and me rode in a helicopter!" Her sentences were rushed together as she excitedly told me all her news.

"Ms. Lily says this is our new house. Is this our new house, mommy? It's so big! Ms. Lily made me some cookies!"

I looked over her head to a beautiful heavy-set Native woman who looked to be in her late fifties, early sixties. She was very short. In fact, she wasn't that much taller than Rain. When our eyes connected, she smiled warmly at me.

"You must be the new Misses." She said holding her little pudgy hand out for me to shake.

"Earth, you can call me Earth." I took her hand amazed at how soft it was. "And you must be Ms. Lily."

With the warm smile still on her face she nodded. "I am. I'm the housekeeper here. I've been taking care of this old place for well over thirty years. My mother took care of it before me, and my grandmother took care of Chief Holata himself." Her voice was laced with pride.

I looked around the beautiful kitchen, and I could see their presence everywhere. "It is very beautiful here."

"Thank you. Come, let me show you around."

I turned to look back at Horse and Crush, but they had already helped themselves to the cookies and milk and weren't paying any attention to me. Ms. Lily made her way over to where Crush sat on a stool and poured a big glass of milk for him before taking a paper towel and stuffing it inside his collar. I smiled at the way she automatically babied him. Crush mumbled his thanks as he shoved a whole cookie in his mouth.

Something was cooking on the stove that smelt simply delicious. The smell must have attracted Horse, with a cookie in his mouth and one in his hand, he made his way to the stove and was reaching for the lid of the pot.

However, Ms. Lily was having none of that. Moving with a speed that shocked me for one so short and chubby, she picked up a spoon and popped his fingers before he could even reach the lid.

"Now you know better than to come in off the street looking in my pots without washing your hands!"

I couldn't help the laugh that escaped my lips, Ms. Lily didn't play.

"Ouch! Ms. Lily! You don't ever say anything to Black when he does it." Horse said pulling his injured limb back out the way.

At the mention of Black's name, the housekeeper got a most satisfying look on her face.

"That's because my Melech is a good boy. His hands are never dirty."

Horse's mouth fell open. "Do you really believe that?"

She smiled. "Yes, I do."

Shaking his head, he turned to look at me. "To Ms. Lily, Black can do no wrong, even if he does it right in front of her face. She's always spoiled him rotten. Just wait, you'll see what I'm talking about."

She hit him in the chest with her spoon. "Don't you go poisoning the Misses' ears with all that gobbledy-goop. Speaking of Black, where is my boy?"

Horse looked at me and rolled his eyes. As if to say, *see what I mean?*

"Your boy has made a mess at the casino and need to see about getting it cleaned up. He'll be here when he's finished."

She put her hand on her lips. "He didn't—" Before she could finish Horse was nodding his head.

"He did, and now he needs to deal with the fire chief."

Ms. Lily inhaled as she patted her hands down her dress as if to straighten it. The news of what happened at the Casino had clearly troubled her.

"Well, let's just hope that will be the last time we see that side of him."

Horse snorted as he picked up another cookie. "Yeah, right!"

Ignoring him, the kind little woman turned to face me. She forced the smile back to her face.

"Ready for that tour?"

I nodded, not sure what I was supposed to do here. Did Black really expect Rain and I to stay here with him? Did he really think I was going to marry him? The man was nuts. As soon as I found a way I was gone. However, I would bide my time. Ms. Lily obviously didn't know I was here against my will, I would let her show me around, but I would use this as an opportunity to get some info.

The first thing I needed to know is where the heck we were.

I took Rain's hand. "Come on, baby, Ms. Lily is going to show us around."

"Remember what I said about those wolves." Horse called after us as we left the kitchen.

The first room Ms. Lily showed us was the huge living area. Just think of any logged cabin living room you'd ever seen, now magnify it by fifty. That's what I was standing here looking at. The fireplace was so big one could walk in it without bending over. I could only imagine what it would look like lit on a cold snowy night.

The view from the two giant arch shaped windows nearly

brought tears to my eyes. As I walked toward them, I couldn't help but marvel at their artistry. The windows went from floor to ceiling and the ceiling in this room went all the way up to the fifth level. Hanging from said ceiling was a beautiful crystal chandler that must have taken a team of people to install. I wondered if it was real crystal.

"That is real crystal." Ms. Lily supplied as if she could hear my thoughts.

"It's amazing." It must have cost a furtune.

"Come look at the view from here." She stood by the window beckoning us to join her. Transfixed, I looked at the beauty that was before me. As far as the eye could see, there was green.

"Are we on a hill?" I asked when I noticed that the trees were going down on a slope.

"No, sweetheart, we are on a mountain, the Appalachians."

Startled my head whipped to face her. "The Appalachians? You mean we're not in Florida anymore?"

"Ouch! Mommy, you're hurting my hand!" Rain cried out.

"Sorry, baby!" I loosened my grip that I hadn't been aware of tightening. Goodness! I had not expected to hear that. We were hundreds of miles from home. How was I going to get back now?

Ms. Lily chuckled. "Of course not, silly, we're in South Carolina."

Oh! Wow! *Don't panic, Earth... Don't Panic!* As if she could sense my inner turmoil Rain slid her hand out of mine so there would be no more accidents.

Smart girl that Rain.

Black had screwed me big time. I had no idea how I was going to get us back to Florida. Heck, I've never even traveled outside of Florida.

I continued to follow Ms. Lily from one fantastic room to another only half listening to the things she was saying. Finding out we were in South Carolina had made the gravity of this situation settle in on me. The feeling that I was completely and utterly at his mercy was suffocating. He said he was going to show me how a kidnapping was done, and I guess he did.

"It sure is going to be good having a Misses around this old place again. Ever since the last Misses died this house just hasn't been the same. Maybe now the sounds of little feet running the halls will breathe life back into these walls."

Her words got my attention. "Was the last Misses Black's mom?"

She nodded. "Her name was Tracy. Such a beautiful girl. Many people thought she was full Native, but she wasn't. Her mother was a Black Seminole from a tribe in Wyoming. One of the Native Seminoles from our tribe met her at an art fair in Florida and brought her back here to Seminole Territory and married her. Nine months later Tracy was born. She was so light, she passed all her life as a full-blooded Native."

"People here always looked at her funny 'cause she chose to live across the river with the Black Seminoles, not realizing she simply chose to live with her own people. Personally, I think she just felt more comfortable living with her father in law, after her husband died leaving her the mother of a very mischievous little boy that was more than a handful for any single mother."

Ms. Lily was a wealth of information and was not shy about sharing it. However something she said bothered me.

"Is this reservation segregated?"

She chuckled without any humor. "Not as much as it used to be. Ever since Black has come into power, he's done a good job at bringing the people together. But before him, it was very segregated. The Natives stayed on one side of the river and the Black Seminole on the other side. And well...there is Hosea, his grandfather. He's the Medicine Man...no matter what color, everybody goes to see the Medicine Man at some point in their lives."

That amazed me. I never would have imagined that to be the case. Seeing as to how the African slaves and the Native-Americans suffered at the hands of the same system, you would think that would be something to bring them together.

I wanted to ask Ms. Lily more about it, but I didn't want to offend her, seeing as to how she's a Native. So instead I changed the subject.

"How did Tracy die?"

Real grief crossed her face. "In a horrible car accident. She and Frank were returning home from the airport when they were run off a cliff by a drunk driver that didn't even have the decency to stop. Nobody knew what happened to them until some hiker found their car overturned many days later. Their bodies had already begun to decay."

"That must have been so hard on Black and his little brothers."

She nodded. "Yes, it was. Poor Melech had to stand tall and accept the weight of the tribe and the casinos on his shoulders. He had been so young, and it didn't help that his wayward brother Mitch--" Her words came to a halt as if she'd just realized what she was about to say.

"I'm so sorry, Earth, I didn't mean to speak ill of your late husband." I took her hand in mine.

"You are simply speaking the truth. I'm not upset. He was quite wayward."

She smiled. "Even still, I shouldn't speak ill of him. Come, let me show you to your bedroom, so that you can rest up before dinner. We can finish the tour and our talk a little later."

I nodded. "That would be great."

I could use a moment to think. It all was a bit much, and I'm not just talking about the house. We had only made it to the second level in the *tour* and still had not covered half of it. I was relieved to find out she didn't clean this museum of a house by herself. She in fact oversaw the team of people that cleaned the house during the day.

Rain and I followed her up to the third level. "The bedrooms are on this floor." She told me as she headed towards the second door to the right.

"This will be little Rain's room. When the King told me she was coming yesterday, I got a team of people in here to prepare her room for her."

"Wait…he told you we were coming yesterday?" That bastard!

She nodded as she opened the door. As soon as Rain got a peek into the room she screeched at the top of her longs.

"Moooommmmmyyyy!" she screamed as she ran into the room.

"Rain, wait…" I cried, but she wasn't listening. The room had been prepared for a princess. Pink, purple and glittered items were everywhere. Sitting in the corner was a pink motorized toy jeep. Rain asked me to buy her one of those little cars every time we'd go to Walmart, but of course, I'd always had to tell her no, because who had five-hundred dollars to spend on a toy car?

She jumped in the car and Ms. Lily helped her start it up.

"Look, mommy, I'm driving!"

I looked at the housekeeper that seemed to be having just as much fun as Rain. "This is too much!"

She waved her hand. "Oh, this is nothing, wait till you see the master suite."

"Master suite? As in Black's room?"

She nodded. "Yes, silly, where else did you think you were sleeping?"

Things were happening too fast for my brain to process. He told her we were coming yesterday? When? Had this been a set up all along? Did he get me to come to that catastrophe of a meeting knowing he was going to kidnap me if I said no? And what the hell did she mean, *where else did I think I was going to be sleeping?*

I had to get out of here! It was too much...I felt like my control was being ripped away from me.

"Ohhh mommy, look at my bed!" Rain yelled as she jumped out her car that was still moving to race across the room to a---

Dear God! The full-sized, four poster, pink canopy bed was draped in pink mosquito netting. It hung from the ceiling like pink smoke to drape the bed. Rain jumped into it with both her arms and legs flat out to her sides like she was an airplane.

"While she get's comfortable in her room, I will show you yours." Ms. Lily said as she sailed passed me out the door.

I wanted to grab Rain's hand and drag her out this room, but I couldn't. I don't think I'd ever seen her so happy. She was literally vibrating with happiness. Holding my head down, I followed Ms. Lily to the double doors at the end of the hall.

Even though we couldn't stay, I could let her have her fun for now. She was going to hate me enough when I told her we had to go. Thanks, Black! Now I was going to have to be the wicked wit—

My thoughts scrambled when I finally got a look at the master suite.

"Oh my G---"

This wasn't a room. It was a photoshoot for a magazine. Like the living room, there were no floors over this room. The ceiling went up all five stories. This room was set up Japanese style. It was heaven on earth, and against everything I was feeling right now, I loved it.

The huge windows were Japanese bamboo shutters. Never in my life did I think I would ever see anything like this. Slowly as if in a trance, I walked towards silk screens that opened to a private Japanese garden that was equipped with several waterfalls that sent the soothing sound of trickling water through the air, and Japanese style man-sized towers.

Just beyond the garden wall was a perfect view of a rushing river. Because the house was built into the side of the mountain, the garden sloped down, so from this view you could see both the beautiful garden and the river as well.

I turned to face Ms. Lily. She was looking at me expectantly. "It's the most beautiful thing I've ever seen."

Clapping her hands together she did a little dance that reminded me of Rain. "I knew you would like it. The King had the room redone when he took over. He has such amazing taste."

Her king was quite the puzzle. Over the last two weeks he had slept in my little matchbox bedroom, on my little broke down bed and never once complained. If this awaited me, I would have had a fit.

The king-sized bed was a fluffy mattress that sat up on an elevated dais. It would give one the feeling of sleeping on the floor but raised up, so that you had to walk up two steps to get into it. It was made neatly in a set of black silk sheets that looked extremely soft to the touch.

I could smell Melech in this room. There were faint undertones of his expensive cologne.

"When they brought Rain, they brought your belongings as well." She gestured toward the closet. "I put them away in the closet for you."

Needing to lay eyes on Earth's Cry, I walked into the massive closet, not surprised that it was the size of my apartment. Hanging on a rack that looked as if it was remotely operated were many suits. They had been arranged by color. A shoe shelf had been built into another wall, and Black's shoes and boots were stacked neatly on it. Surprisingly, he had several pairs of brand new gym shoes.

Funny, I didn't take him for the type that wore sneakers. My gaze landed on my bag that had been placed on the other side of the closet. This side was empty of all but my bag and Earth's Cry. Needing to feel its comfort, I picked it up and put the strap around my shoulders so that the violin rested against my back.

When I exited the closet, it was to find Ms. Lily gone and Rain climbing up the stairs to get into Black's big bed.

"You're just having the time of your life, aren't you?" I asked climbing the stairs to join her.

With a huge smile on her face she nodded. But then her gaze fell to Earth's Cry on my back.

"Can you play something for me?"

I gave her a sad smile. Rain asked me to play for her nearly every day, and every day I told her the same thing.

"I wish I could, baby."

"You forgot how to play?"

I shook my head. "I don't think I will ever forget how to play it."

"Then why won't you play anything?"

How can I explain to her that her mother was a coward? I wanted to play so badly my fingers twitched from muscle memory. I just--

"Look, mommy, there is a little old man out there."

Frowning, I turned to see where she was pointing. And sure enough, sitting on a little bench that had a great view of the yard and the rushing river beyond it was a little dark-skinned old man with a head full of snow white hair. He leaned heavily on the crude looking staff he held in his hands.

"Should we go say hi?" I asked Rain.

With a goofy grin on her face she nodded.

I held out my hand to her. "Come on then, down you go."

Clutching my hand, she leaped down the stairs and half dragged me through the screen doors and into the garden. The smell of jasmine heightened my senses and made me feel comforted.

"Hi." Rain called when we got a little closer to the man. He was dressed in a traditional Native-American buck skin outfit. It was well worn as if he'd had it for a while. Hanging from the corner of his shirt were two long tassels that had been interwoven with a cord of blue material. I wondered if he had two more on the other side.

Rain came to a stop directly in front of the man. I wanted to reach out and pull her back some, because she was straight up invading his space. But he didn't seem bothered, in fact, he smiled kindly at her.

I narrowed my eyes on his face. He looked very familiar. In fact, he looked like an older version of Melech.

"You're Hosea aren't you?" I blurted out.

He grinned. "I am, and who do we have here?"

"Rain. And this is my mommy, Earth."

His gaze came up to me and a feeling shot through me that was a little strange. I felt grounded. It was as if he could see straight through me to all my secrets. His irises had begun to turn white around the edges with age, but that didn't take away from the wisdom that was there in his gaze.

"Earth and Rain...You don't say." His voice reminded me of the wind. I wanted to be closer to him.

As if he understood he patted the bench next to him. "Well now, take a seat. Old man can't be looking way up there. My neck ain't as nimble as it used to be."

I chuckled as I sat down on the bench next to him. Rain, with the attention span of broom, walked away to get a better look at the water fountain a few paces away.

I inhaled deeply. I liked Hosea's scent. He smelt like frankincense and myrrh.

"So, you're the young lady that's gotten my grandson's attention?"

That made the smile disappear from my face. Instead of answering, I just looked out at the water. He seemed like a nice old man, and I really didn't want to hurt his feelings.

"What's this? You're upset with him?"

I still didn't answer.

"He's an ass, isn't he?"

That got my attention. I turned to look at him with a smile on my face. "Yes, he is."

He shook his head. "What he do now?"

The way he asked that made me hold back my head and laugh. He reminded me of this little old guy that used to come to the house and visit Bro. Abraham sometimes. He was always up for hearing the latest gossip.

"He lied to me and then he kidnapped me."

His mouth opened in shock. "He kidnapped you!?"

I nodded. "Sure did. And he lied to me!"

"That bastard! What he lie about?"

I didn't even think about whether I was going to tell him what happened. I just started talking. I needed somebody to talk to and he was a really good listener. Hadn't Ms. Lily said everybody eventually went to see the Medicine Man? Today was my lucky day, he came to see *me*.

I told him everything, including the fact I'd kidnap his grandson and why I'd done it. I told him how I felt foolish, because now I know Black could have gotten free anytime he wanted. I even told him I'd started falling in love with Melech. I don't know why I poured my heart out to this man, but once I started, I couldn't seem to stop.

"I know he's your grandson, but I don't think he's human. Or if he is, he's called on the dark arts. He can control fire. Did you know that?"

He nodded. "Yes, I know what he's capable of. The sad thing is, he's capable of so much more. However, his power does not come from the devil. His power comes from the Great Spirit."

I blinked at him confused. "Great Spirit?"

He chuckled. "Come now, surely you believe in the Great Spirit, the Ancient of Days? Yahuah?"

I nodded. "Yes, I believe in the Heavenly Father, I just didn't believe what I saw Black do came from him."

"Tell me this, do you believe in the Bible?"

"Absolutely."

"So, when the book said one man had the strength of a thousand, did you believe it?"

"Yep."

"And when it said one teenage boy slew a giant with a rock, did you believe it?"

I nodded without hesitation. "Sure did."

He smiled. "How do you think it was possible for those warriors to perform such miracles?"

Hmmm…that was a good question. Everybody has read a story or two out the Good Book, but I don't think many people actually stopped to imagine what they were reading actually looked like in real time. What the people must have seen the day David slew Goliath?

"Power came down from on High." I told Hosea.

He nodded. "The same Power has called on my ass of a grandson. The same Power has given him a gift that if he doesn't soon learn how to harness, he will lose." When he said that, his face saddened.

"Curse the day Frank came into his life, bringing the temptation of unlimited wealth."

I touched his arm, concerned at the rage I felt going through his body that was thin with age.

"What do you mean?"

"The adversary is busy. At the same time the Great Spirit gifted Melech the power to rain down fire, the devil came and gifted him with the wicked power ultimate wealth brings, in hopes that he could draw him away from what the Great Spirit has called him to do."

He looked at me, and for a second, it looked as if his eyes teared up. "I lost Melech that day. All the training, all my teachings gone. He walked away from all he knows to be right and never looked back."

Could what he was saying be true? Could God have given Melech the same power he gave King David and Samson? Was The Heavenly Father still granting men the power to perform miracles?

It made sense that he was, it's just that one rarely saw it with their own eyes. The closest thing we got to *seeing a miracle from God* was from the minister that performed tricks on TV for a little bit of your hard-earned cash.

I didn't know how to take the information Hosea was giving me. If it was true that Melech was meant to be like King David and Samson, a Warrior of God, what was The Heavenly Father calling him to do? Whatever it was, It must be very important, if like Hosea said the Devil offered him great wealth to distract him.

I wondered if I asked Hosea about it, would he think I was being nosy. He had offered me enough information for me to be curious, so maybe not. I inhaled, here goes nothing.

"Why has he been gifted with such power?"

Hosea turned to look at me, studying me with those eyes that had began to whiten with age.

"He's been called to protect you, child."

I put my hand on my chest. "Me?"

Oh wow! This poor man was delusional. There was nothing special about me.

He smiled at my surprise. "Yes, you."

I opened my mouth to correct him and tell him he was mistaken, but he suddenly stood, causing my mouth to snap shut with the shock at seeing how agile he was for a man so old.

"Now, it's not nice that he tricked you, lied to you, and then kidnapped you, is it?"

The subject change kind of threw me, but I rebounded. "No, it wasn't very nice."

"We can't let him get away with that, can we?"

"How can we stop him? He has power from on High, remember? Who can stand against it?"

He whacked my leg with his staff.

"Ouch!" I cried rubbing it. He didn't pop me hard enough to leave a bruise, but he hit me hard enough to get my attention.

"You sound like a wimp! How in the world are you going to get respect from my grandson if you don't demand respect?"

Damn it! He didn't know me at all. I was nobody's rug.

"I demand respect!" I growled from between clenched teeth.

He leaned against his staff smiling down at me, and right then, I saw that Melech's grandfather was a bit of a rascal.

"So, are you going to be here waiting for him like a good little kidnapping victim?"

I straightened my shoulders as he continued to spark the anger inside me.

"I ain't nobody's victim, old man!"

The grin grew on his face "What are you going to do about it?"

"I'm going to leave!"

He nodded. "That's the spirit. Where you going to go?"

I stood from the bench. "Home!"

The smile suddenly left his face, and all the wind he'd built up in my cells deflated.

"What's the matter?" I asked.

He shook his head. "I can't help you leave the reservation, Melech's men will be on us before we took three steps outside the gate."

My shoulders slumped. Even if they didn't catch us, the wolves would. This old fella obviously didn't have a car.

"But I can help you leave here and maintain custody of your daughter."

My head popped up as the flame of life was rekindled in my chest. "You can?"

"I can…I will be honest with you. Outside of these walls the white man's laws stand, there is nothing I can do for you. But inside of these walls we do not honor documents drafted in the white man's court. Those unjust custody paper can be used to wipe somebody's ass as far as I'm concerned."

The more he spoke, the more excited I got. I nodded, "Yeah, toilet paper."

"I can take you across the river. Black can't touch you there. That is my territory. Once you're under my protection, I can guarantee your safety from the tyranny of the rich."

I nearly clapped in my excitement. "You can?"

He gave a look that said, *hang with me and I'll show you the ropes.* "Didn't you know? Across the river, *nobody messes with the Medicine Man.*"

16

THE OUTSTANDING MIND OF THE MEDICINE MAN

EARTH

"You know what, Pop?! I have put up with a lot of your shenanigans with the patience of a saint. But this time, you've gone too far!" Black growled from where he stood surrounded by his men in front of the porch.

Hosea folded his arms as he looked down at his grandson. "Sorry, son, your frowns and scowls don't work here. You forget I used to change your bedsheets when you pissed in the bed, so your mama wouldn't find them and tan your hide."

Black's mouth opened a bit, as if he couldn't believe his grandfather had just said that. I put my hand over my face to hide my laughter. However, Black's men and the many children, who clung to Hosea like glue laughed openly. The children stood surrounding Black and his men.

Oh my goodness, y'all, Hosea is a trip. Black had called him eccentric, but that didn't even begin to sum up his grandfather.

When I tell you he is full of mischief, please believe me. But thanks to him, I didn't feel as if the ground was falling out from under me anymore. With him, there was no time to feel sorry for myself. I would soon discover that Hosea was the heart and soul of this reservation.

Ms. Lily said it was Black who brought all the people together, but I dare to disagree. It was his *grandfather*. Because of Hosea, the next seven days of my life would prove to be the best I'd ever had. I couldn't remember the last time I had so much fun. Pull up a chair and let me fill you in on the outstanding mind of the Medicine Man.

He'd snuck Rain and I away from what I now know is the big house and brought us back to his cabin, that was located a good distance away from the big house. Hosea said they called it the big house because it sat smack dab in the middle of great divide, which is the river; in fact, the river ran underneath it.

He said Holata built it there to show the people he was ruler of both sides, the Black Seminole and the Native. Their reservation was huge; Hosea said it was a little over two-thousand acres. It took us about an hour and a half to get to his place on foot.

After talking to Ms. Lily earlier today about how Seminole Territory used to be segregated, I'd expected to see a ghetto that made my hood look like Beverly Hills when we crossed the river. However, I was pleasantly surprised to find beautiful log cabins and brick homes on sparkling clean streets. This area actually made Beverly Hills look like the ghetto. I'd asked Hosea how it was so that the African-Americans here could be segregated and yet still have so much?

He chuckled and told me never to compare the Native Seminole to the system of the oppressors. Although the Natives stayed to themselves and the Black Seminole stayed to themselves, because of Holata, the Black Seminole here had all the opportunities the Natives did.

Holata did not allow discrimination. Segregation he didn't mind, discrimination he didn't tolerate. So, like the Natives, the Black Seminole were able to get good jobs in Holata's casinos and tourist areas. Many of them even had their own businesses in said areas.

Wow! Holata sounded like a very complexed man. On one hand, he prided himself at being King of Criminals, robbing, stealing and killing to get what he wanted in life. But on the other hand, he'd managed to create a system that worked for all men under his rulership, a feat our supposedly advanced nation still has not managed to do.

I was even more pleasantly surprised to discover quite a few Natives with homes here across the river. Hosea said it was because they worshipped the Ancient of Days in Spirit and in Truth and wanted to be closer to his servant. Then he waggled his bushy eyebrows at me and caused me to erupt in laughter.

He reminded me of the Black I'd come to know over the last two weeks, the playful, intuitive Black. I exhaled. That man was gone, and a cold, calculating, gansta took his place.

Anyway, I digress. I was telling you guys how I ended up in one kooky adventure after another because of Hosea.

When we finally made it to his cabin, it was to find it overrun with children, Native and Black. There were so many children it looked like a school. I couldn't help the laugh that escaped me when they swarmed us.

"Scram...get now! Can't a man come home to peace and quiet every now and again?" He said trying to shoo them away, but they didn't go anywhere.

They all ran to him and hugged him. You could see in their faces that they loved him. And I realized then, it was something about Hosea that drew a certain kind of people, especially children. Like Black, Rain had taken to him instantly. She'd walked this whole way holding his hand, chattering on about everything she could think of. And Hosea with the patience of Job, entertained all her ideas.

When he finally got the children out the way enough so that we could get inside, he placed his staff against the wall then told me he would show Rain and I where we would be sleeping. Surprisingly, there were a group of teens in his kitchen. One of the teens I recognized, Tonya...She stood at his stove cooking something.

"Whatever you're making, make enough for us." Hosea called out to her. When she saw me, she ran to me wringing her hands.

"You're not mad at me, are you Misses?"

"Earth." I told her with laughter in my voice. You couldn't help but be joyous around this group. "Call me Earth."

"Earth, I swear I didn't know what they had planned. I cried and told them it wasn't right to steal your baby. But then that bully Shiloh threatened to tie me up and gag me." She slammed her little fist in her hand. "He better be lucky my brother wasn't there. Bruce would have mopped the floor with his head."

"Speaking of Bruce," Hosea interjected. "Run along and fetch him, tell him I need to see him ASAP." She nodded and after taking her food off the stove ran out the house.

"I've got an idea on how to pay my grandson back for being the world's biggest asshole. My grandson Bruce is going to help us out." He told me as he led the way upstairs, dodging children.

So, Tonya was Hosea's granddaughter and Black's cousin. I wondered how many grandchildren Hosea had here. Biting my lip to keep from grinning, I observed how he was so used to having little ones underfoot that he artfully maneuvered past a pair of Native look-a-likes coloring in a coloring book without even looking down at them.

Hosea's cabin wasn't as big as the big house, but it wasn't all that small either. There were several bedrooms located on the second level.

"Shalawam, Pop." A young brown skinned man called from the first bedroom we passed. He sat at the foot of the bed playing the PlayStation. Behind him stretched out in the bed was a very pregnant young lady. Hosea stopped to look in at him.

"Did you go down to the college and enroll in those mechanic classes?" Without looking away from the game, the young man nodded.

"I sure did, and I painted the back deck too."

Hosea looked surprised for a minute before his eyes narrowed. "Did you paint the whole deck?"

The young man paused the game and looked up then. There was a confused look on his handsome face. "You wanted me to paint the whole deck?"

Hosea threw up his hands. "Sweet Master, give me strength." He muttered before his gaze settled on the young woman.

"How you feeling, Kelly? Still not able to hold anything down?"

She shook her head. "I threw up three times today and I'm so hungry."

Hosea nodded. "Just hold on a little longer, the nausea will pass. I'll make you some tea in a little while that should sooth your stomach."

"Okay." She groaned, her voice laced with her misery.

"Young people, we have houseguests. This is Earth and her little baby girl, Rain. These," He said gesturing at the young couple. "Are my only tenants. You may find that hard to believe with all the people underfoot. This is Dan and his wife Kelly."

"Wow! They're married?" I didn't mean to blurt that out. But I was surprised. They were young…they had to be eighteen, maybe nineteen.

Hosea nodded. "Dan is one of my many grandchildren. As you can see, it was a shotgun wedding. After getting her pregnant, Kelly's father threatened to disembowel Dan if he didn't do the right thing and marry his daughter. Meanwhile, Dan's parents were good and fed up with his trifling ways…"

"Ah! Come on, Pop! You ain't got to tell her all that." The youth muttered as he went back to playing his game.

Hosea scoffed. "Well, it's true." He focused back on me. "They kicked him out and sent him my way…" He threw up his hands.

"He becomes my responsibility. I'm a bit of a stray magnet."

"I can see that." I laughed. What was even more funny was the fact that Rain and I was now here in this house of strays. So, what did that make us?

After the introduction, we continued down the hall and he opened the next door we came to. "This is the upstairs bathroom, trying to get those two kids to keep it clean is like trying to pull teeth with a blade of grass, so may the Great Spirit be with you in that endeavor."

"Now, this is where our little Rain will sleep." He opened a door and had to shoo several children off the twin sized bed from where they sat also playing the PlayStation.

"Black brought those damned game boxes here, now I can't get any of them to do anything else." He grumbled as he placed Rain's bag up on the shelf.

"You want to play?" A beautiful little African-American Seminole girl who was about Rain's age asked as she handed her the control.

Rain looked up at me. "Can I play, Mommy?"

"Sure, sweetheart."

And that was all she wrote. Rain was in little children heaven. She was happier now than she had been back in her room at the big house. And secretly, that did my heart good to see. I didn't want her going goo-goo for material things. It is more to life then what money could buy.

Hosea showed me to the room I was going to be sleeping in next. It had clearly been a boy's room. Although there were no sheets on the twin sized bed, the curtains that hung over the sliding door that led to a small balcony, had basketballs on them. There were even a few basketball rewards hanging on the wall.

"You don't have to worry about the kids coming in here."

"Why not?" I asked.

He chuckled. "There is no game box."

"Ahhh! Got you." I said putting my bag down and taking Earth's Cry from off my back, setting it against the wall.

"That's a very special instrument you have there. I pray one day soon you will play it for us."

My gaze flew up to his. Did he know about Earth's Cry? Did he know what it had shown me? I studied his face searching for any sign that he did.

"Umm...I don't play anymore." I knew he would find it odd that I traveled with a musical instrument I no longer played.

Now it was he who studied me. He watched me so long I started to fidget under his gaze.

"It's a shame you and my grandson can't work things out... you two would have made a great couple."

I tilted my head to the side. "Why do you say that?"

"You are both attempting a useless expedition."

"Oh yeah? What's that?"

He smiled sadly. "You are both trying to out run your destinies." He headed for the door. "Get some rest, you're going to need it.

"For what?" I called after him.

"Melech will be home after while, and he ain't going to be happy you're not there waiting on him."

Melech Black

. . .

"WHAT THE HELL you mean they're gone?!" I sat on my kitchen stool breaking bread with my personal security detail. They all sat around the island looking like lumps on a damn log as Ms. Lily spooned food on our plates.

It had been a long day and I was ravenous. Although food was not really what I was hungry for, I dug in. I'd just been informed that the true object of my hunger was gone. I wasn't worried that she'd escaped the reservation, the men at the gate had my instructions, had they let her slip past, they wouldn't be the only ones to suffer my wrath, Crush and Horse would as well.

Horse threw up his hands. "Hey, man, don't fry the messenger. Your grandfather took them."

Damn it! I forked some of Ms. Lily's meatloaf into my mouth to keep from shredding into my best friend. I was not in the mood for this sh*t. I'd just paid Tampa's f***ing fire marshal an arm and a f***ing leg to pretend they didn't have to come to my casino to see why the alarm had gone off. The bastard walked in with a huge grin on his face because he knew today was his payday.

I didn't mean to lose my cool like that earlier. Hearing her throw Mitch in my face and spouting some of his nonsense pissed me off, but then when she started to say she should have listened to him, like she's his…that sh*t tipped me over.

And now, after finally getting everything straightened out and Mike back on a plane to school, I was prepared to come back here and do whatever it took to get that smile back on her face, so that I could sink into her softness, only to find out my grandfather that didn't know how to mind his business had taken her across the damn river.

"Why the hell didn't you stop him?" Horse and Crush looked at me like I'd gone mad.

"So I can wake up tomorrow covered in boils or some sh*t?" Horse shook his head. "No thank you! Last person messed with your grandfather got attacked with all fifty plagues that hit Egypt."

I exhaled. "It was *ten* plagues, heathen."

Horse shrugged. "Yep! And he got hit with all ten of them mutha f*****."

"Why do I even have a security crew if they can't stop a little old man from stealing my family from under my roof?"

Big Troy and Tocho chuckled. Horse grunted. "Old man my ass. You need me to pay a visit to an asshole that owes one of the casinos money…no problem. You need me to break a few ankles of some big shots who didn't know who they were dealing with…I'm your man. Hell! You need me to murk somebody who crossed the line…look no further." He stood from his stool with his empty plate in his hand.

"You need somebody to go and tell Hosea *no*, or stop him from doing something he's gotten his mind set on…you're on your own."

"I'm telling you, Hosea was responsible for that fly infestation that hit that old racist sheriff's office over there in Pinkerton." Big Troy said as he held out his plate for another helping of meatloaf.

I frowned. "What happened in Pinkerton?"

Pinkerton was the next town over from ours. They were always trying to give the people at Seminole Territory a hard time. Their racism ran deep, some of the people in that town has always hated living so close to what they called a filthy Indian reservation.

The fact that said Indian reservation had some of the richest houses they'd ever seen only rubbed salt in the wound. So, some of the time when our kids passed through Pinkerton on the way here, the sheriff gave them a hard time.

"They'd arrested Bruce on some bogus charges. Said he'd supposedly vandalized Charlie's gas station."

I lowered the fork from my mouth. "What? Why didn't anyone tell me?"

Bruce was my little cousin. I loved him like a son. Frank had even noticed him before he died. Bruce's nature was very much like my own, he didn't put up with crap from anybody. But he wasn't a bad kid and didn't go looking for fights. He wouldn't vandalize Charlie's place without being provoked.

"By the time we found out, your grandfather had already handled it. They say as soon as he walked into the sheriff station, folks there got really nervous. None of them expected you or Hosea to come yourselves. Said the old sheriff could not apologize enough for the mix up." Troy shook his head.

"It did no good, word is, as soon as Hosea and your little cousin walked out the door, the first fly flew in. An hour later, the station was covered in them, inside and out. Said the flies was biting them and sh*t. Man, that joint was so wild it ended up on YouTube. And get this, they called pest control and they couldn't do nothing for 'em. Old sheriff had to come over here with his tail tucked between his legs and beg Hosea to call off the flies."

"Of course, your grandfather acted like he didn't know what he was talking about, but told him he would pray for him and see if The Great Spirit would show mercy on them. And sure enough, by the time the sheriff returned to the station, the flies were gone."

Horse hit the counter. "You see that?! And you want me to try and stop him." He shook his head. "Nobody's that stupid, not even Sheriff KKK."

The rest of the fellas nodded their heads in agreement as they finished off their dinner.

"Fine, you coward bastards, I'll go and take care of this myself. Pull my truck around front."

* * *

WE PULLED up three trucks deep in front of my grandfather's and were swarmed by children instantly. It had been about six months since I was last at the reservation. And nothing had changed. My grandfather's house still attracted all the reservation's children. Although, a good amount of them were his grands and great grands. Folks here never paid a babysitter, they just told their kids to go down the road to the Medicine Man's house.

They knew their children would be safe and well fed. I should know, I paid a grip to feed them. As soon as Abner and I stepped out the truck, the many little arms that wrapped around my waist nearly took me off my feet.

"Hey, King!"

"Daddy!"

"King, we ain't seen you in a looooonggg time!"

"Daddy!"

"King, look at my new bracelet!"

"We missed you!"

"I missed y'all too!" I told them chuckling at their enthusiasm. No matter how tired I was, I took the time to show my people love. It was one of the things Frank had drilled into me. He said, without the people, there would be no us. Always show love to your people, no matter what is going on.

"Daddy, it's me!" That little voice finally rose loud enough over the others for me to hear.

"Rain, baby...where are you?" I struggled to identify her through the crowd of children that swarmed me.

"Alright now, give the man some room so that he can get out of the truck!" Horse said as he and the other fellas began trying to unwrap their little arms from around my waist. It did no good, it was way too many of them.

However, I was able to get a hold of Rain and lifted her up into my arms. She wrapped her little arms around my neck and squeezed me tight.

"I missed you...where was you?" She said as she buried her face in my neck.

"Shhh baby, Daddy here now." Holding her in one arm, I took my time and hugged the rest of the children.

The bigger kids wanting to appear cooler than their younger siblings, stood off to the back pretending they weren't as anxious as the short legs. As soon as I opened my arm for them, they too swarmed me. I laughed when my little cousin Bruce embraced me in a bear hug and actually lifted me off my feet with Rain in my arms.

"Damn, cuz!" I said when he put us down. "Step back so that I can get a good look at you." Bruce was a mammoth of a boy. He was captain of the football team, basketball team, and the wrestling team. He looked so much like me that outsiders mistook him for my son.

Hell, if none of my future sons were able to compete with him, I will make him my heir in a heartbeat. As soon as he finished school, I was going to move him in the big house and start training him to be a part of my personal security team, that way, I'll have him close to start his training to take over should something happen to me.

After I hugged all the youths and a good number of their parents while still holding my Rain, I made my way to my grandfather's porch, needing to feel Rain's mother in my arms. Damn, I've missed her soft touch and her smell... Hell, I was feening for her taste.

However, I came up short at the sight of my grandfather standing in front of the door, staff in hand and dressed in his full Medicine Man get-up, from the elaborate feathered headdress that flowed down his back to touch the ground behind him, to the buckskin tunic and breeches.

The only time he put on this costume is when he was going to make some grand announcement or herald the Green Corn Festival. I turned around and took in the crowd that was gathered behind me and to the side of me. The fact that there were more people here than usual was another sign that my grandfather was about to piss me off.

"What the hell is he about now?" I growled.

Bruce grew really nervous. "Cuz, you know how Pop is. Just don't kill me... okay?"

"Wow, what the hell did we just walk into?" Horse muttered from beside me. Tearing my gaze away from Bruce, I scowled at my grandfather.

"Pop, I don't have time for your theatrics, where is Earth?"

He held up his head as if he was offended by my frankness. "Shalawam grandson, how are you this evening?"

"Shalawam, grandfather, tired. Where is Earth?"

I could feel the number of people growing behind me. The street was now jammed with cars as people made their way over to see why my grandfather was dressed up in such a way.

"Earth, can you please join me on the porch." He said without looking away from me.

When my lady stepped out, I inhaled. Although it had only been hours since last I touched her, it felt like days. I wasn't lying when I told her I slept like sh*t without her. I lay in my bed and tossed and turned, missing the feel of her soft warm body next to mine.

Something was up with her though. She was going out of her way to avoid looking at me. I growled in my throat not liking that sh*t and took a step towards her, but my grandfather held his staff out in front of me stopping me. My first instinct was to grab it and crack it across my knee. The only thing that kept me from doing it was that fact that Horse and Big Troy was right, the Ancient of Days was with my grandfather, and he punished all those who did anything ill against him.

"Why are you attempting to approach this woman that is under my protection?"

I chuckled. "Your protection? What nonsense is this? She's my betrothal, she's under *my* protection."

Earth nervously picked at the hem of her white blouse, the same blouse that earlier gave me a clear view of her beautiful breasts incased in that little pink bra that made me want to rip it off with my teeth.

My grandfather leaned on his staff, the grin that came to his face made me uneasy. "This woman has refused your offer. She's not impressed with your prowess."

EARTH

I…could…not…believe…he…just…said…that!

Something told me I was going to regret agreeing to go along with Hosea's antics.

As soon as the three black Range Rovers pulled up outside of his house, my heart started beating so fast, I had to clutch my chest to prevent myself from having a heart attack. Once word got out that Black was expected to make an appearance at his grandfather's house, folks started showing up in droves.

Quite naturally with him being the leader here, he was something of a superstar, but this was ridiculous. It was so many people here I felt like I was standing on stage at a concert. And it didn't help that Black's grandfather was crazy. As he was walking toward the door to greet his grandson, he'd told me to trust him, and let him do all the talking, to just nod my head and agree with whatever he said.

"Wait, what are you going to say?!" I called after him, feeling myself about to panic.

He stopped before he went out to the porch. "You and me are partners now."

"Partners? For what!?" Every alarm in my body was going off. Something told me that Hosea was getting ready to get me in even hotter water than I was already in.

"Together, me and you." He brought his finger up to indicate him and I. "We're going to get my grandson back focused on what's important."

I held up my hand stopping him. "I don't think I signed up for this."

He smiled then. "Sure you did…when you agreed to come under my protection." And then he stepped out on the porch.

Like a coward, I had stood in the living room and watched as Black and Abner stepped out his truck. The little children surrounded him instantly. When Rain saw that it was Black her little friends hurried to greet, she'd joined them before I could stop her.

He lifted her in his arms instantly and still held her. When I heard Hosea ask me to come out to the porch, I started to refuse. But I didn't want all these people to see just how big of a coward I was, so with false bravado, I stepped out.

"I assure you, old man, she's quite satisfied with my prowess."

My face was on fire. I could not believe they were discussing me this way in front of all these people. I was beginning to get angry.

"Maybe she was, but she's not anymore. In fact, another has come forth to ask for her hand in marriage. So, by the authority inves—"

"Wait! What?" Black interrupted him. "First of all, you have no authority! And what the hell do you mean another has come forth to ask for her hand?"

"You're wrong, son. I have all the authority on this side of the river. There was an unwritten treaty between my father and Holata. It is still honored to this day. What happens on this side of the river has nothing to do with you."

Black held up his hand toward Hosea. "Let's pretend this *treaty* you speak of really exist, and is not something you just made up. Even still, I would have everything to do with what happens on this side of the river because I'm your heir as well, or have you forgotten?"

Hosea's eyes lit up. "My forgetfulness is not on trial here. However, yours is. You have been called to be my heir, whether you'll be chosen has yet to be seen."

Black lifted his hand rubbing the spot between his eyes trying to relieve the pressure there. "Pop, just move to the side so that Earth can come to me and let these good people go home and get some rest. I'm sure like myself, they've had a long hard day."

Hosea stood up straighter, squaring his shoulders. "Shema, people of Seminole Territory. The Ancient of Day's created life in six days and on the seventh he rested. Today, I announce the opening of the Green Ear Festival. For six days, two men will compete for this woman's hand. On the seventh, we will rest."

He gestured back towards me. I had to bite down on my lip to keep from protesting. I trusted Hosea, but I didn't know what he was doing.

"Whichever one of these two great warriors prove to be the strongest, fastest and most skilled, as well as convince her to marry him by the end of the sixth day, shall rule the Black Seminole in my stead. And that warrior will become this beautiful woman's husband."

The crowed erupted in a loud cheer, excited that Hosea had called on the opening of the Green Ear Festival, and that this year, it will go on for six days, where it generally went on for three.

Black however, was so angry the muscle ticked furiously in

his cheek. His men began to shift on their feet sharing looks with the other, much like they'd done earlier today. As if she could sense the anger in his body, Rain wrapped her little arms around his neck and buried her face just under his chin.

I moved to take her away from him, but Hosea held out his hand stopping me.

"Who is this other man that is laying claim to Earth?" Black growled from between clenched teeth. The tone in his voice sobered the crowd, they were all aware of the danger that came when their leader was upset.

Hosea smiled at him, the only one that was not intimidated by the change that was coming over his grandson.

With a grand sweeping movement, he gestured towards Bruce. "May I present your opponent, my grandson, Bruce Black."

The flame leaped to life in Melech's eyes as his head whipped towards his little cousin. For a big boy, Bruce was very stealth as he held out his hands and began to dance around as if he was trying to dodge bullets.

"Cuz, don't cook me. Please!" He cried out, causing the crowd to erupt in laughter.

"Damn it, boy, stop dancing around and stand like a man!" Hosea yelled at him.

Ignoring his grandfather, Bruce didn't look away from Black or stop moving until he was assured that his cousin was not going to fry him. Slowly, with the flame still burning in his gaze, Black turned to look at his grandfather.

"You know what, Pop?! I have put up with a lot of your shenanigans with the patience of a saint. But this time, you've gone too far!"

17

PRE-GAME JITTERS

EARTH

"Hosea, what are you doing?" I hissed at his back.

He'd just announced to all these people that Black and his little cousin, Bruce will be competing for my hand in marriage. This was madness! I didn't want to marry either of them. First of all, I'm pretty sure Bruce was still in high school, and although Seminole Territory probably didn't honor the statutory rape law, I was not in the cradle robbing business.

And the whole reason I'd agreed to come with him in the first place was to escape Black. Now it looked like he was trying to serve me to him on a silver platter.

"Remember we discussed you trusting me earlier?" He said out the side of his mouth.

"Yeah, that was before you offered to marry me off to a child."

He held up his hands. "What do you mean? Bruce is eighteen."

I rolled my eyes. "Eighteen is still very much a child in my book. And what happened to you saving me from Black? It looks to me that you trying to serve me up to him."

Seeing the discrepancy between Hosea and I caused the flame to fade from Black's eyes. He eased Rain to her feet. She instantly wrapped her arms around his leg as if she feared he would try and leave her. However, he was not interested in leaving her, he was interested in the fact that I was unhappy with Hosea.

With a smug grin on his face, he pulled a cigar out his suit jacket and lit it as he shamelessly listened in to Hosea and my conversation.

Hosea gestured to Black. "Look at him. Do you honestly think he can compete with this fine strapping lad? He smokes, he's out of shape, and he has a beer belly. He's forgotten the ways of his people and now lives like the heathen. Worry not, daughter, he'll faint from exhaustion on the first day."

"None of that is true." Black interrupted him sounding bored. "I may smoke, but I'm not out of shape. And I do not have a beer belly. Make no mistake about it, my little cousin may be a spectacular young man in the making, but I will hand him his ass on a platter." He said the last so matter of fact his men chuckled as they high-fived each other.

Black's gaze went to Bruce's. "No offense, lil cuz." Bruce shook his head as if to say none taken. It was clear Black was his hero.

Not impressed, Hosea turned to look at me. "He does have a beer belly. And no matter what his mouth says, he's not going to be able to compete with Bruce. The rules of the match say that the winner has to also convince you to marry him. If he doesn't, oh well, you and Bruce can go your separate ways, no harm, no foul. But what you definitely won't have to do is marry the loser." He gestured toward Black and lifted his eyebrow, willing me to understand what he was saying.

And you know what? I believe I knew what he was

attempting to do. Bruce was basically my champion and would be competing with Black to release his hold on me. The youth didn't look at me with the slightest bit of attraction. He was doing this because his grandfather was making him. That was comforting, I didn't want to have to go through the trouble of telling him that there was never going to be anything between us.

"So basically, if Bruce wins, then Black will no longer have a claim on me?"

Smiling Hosea nodded. "Now you understand what I'm saying."

"Except there is only one problem." Black interjected, taking a pull off his cigar. "Bruce is just a kid, I'm a man. There is no way he can defeat me. I'm bigger, stronger, and faster…and no matter what my grandfather thinks, I don't have a beer belly." He leaned a little closer, as if he was going to tell me a secret.

"We'll be married by Sunday." His statement caused his men to go into another round of laughter and high-fiving at my expense.

His cockiness was so irritating I now found myself getting into the spirit of things. My gaze went to Bruce. Yeah, Black was his hero and he probably wanted to be just like him. But his body was younger, and if not stronger than most, definitely faster than Black's. It will be fun watching him get defeated by his little cousin after talking so much smack.

Hosea lifted his hands in the air garnering everyone's attention. "And so it is settled. Bruce and Melech will pick their teams. The two teams will compete in various war games over the next six days. The team with the most points at the end of six days wins. The winner will then ask for Earth's hand in marriage, if she says yes, we will have a feast to celebrate their union on the seventh day. Do both men agree with these terms?"

"I agree." Bruce's voice rang out.

"I agree." Black's deep voice followed.

"Choose your teams." Hosea told them.

As if prepared, several young strapping men stepped out of the crowd to come and stand next to Bruce. He slapped hands with each of them. It was clear they were all very close. And like Bruce, they were all young, well-muscled, and bright-eyed with the prospect of competing against the famous Melech Black.

With an eyebrow raised Melech took in the youths. Laughter escaped my lips when he turned to look at his own men and realized the group of them looked like geriatrics compared to the kids. When they stepped up beside him all proud like, hitting their chests to show their superiority, it was too much, I held my head back and laughed till tears came out my eyes.

"What's so funny, baby?" Black asked with a smug grin on his face. "I'll have you know we're the same group, minus Shappa and Shiloh, who won these same games twenty years ago."

Hosea shook his head as Horse held up his arms making muscles and kissed both biceps. Tocho and Big Troy both wore smug looks on their faces to match their boss. And of course, Shappa and Shiloh wasn't worried, although, they were older than Bruce and his crew, they still had enough youthful spring in their steps to compete for real.

The only one that showed doubt on his face was Crush and that was simply because he wasn't the lying type.

Hosea held his staff in the air gaining attention of the crowd. "By the power invested in me, I now announce the opening of the Green Ear Festival. Let the games begin!"

A loud cheer went up into the air as music began to play from somewhere. A full-fledged celebration broke out in minutes. If I didn't know any better, I would have thought this whole thing had already been planned.

Kegs of beer appeared out of nowhere, as well as a DJ and a

food truck. Let me tell you one thing about these Seminoles here on Seminole Territory Reservation, they knew how to celebrate.

The first competition between Black and Bruce started immediately. Someone placed a cup of beer in both of their hands and standing facing each other, they began to chug down the beer as the crowd cheered them on.

Concerned that the young man was being pressured into drinking, I turned to question Hosea about it. He was shaking his head at them with a disapproving look on his face.

"Isn't Bruce a little too young to be drinking?"

He humphed. "I'd like to say he is. But the truth of the matter is most of these boys turn to the bottle shortly after leaving their mama's breasts." He shook his head. "Leave it to these knuckle-heads to get drunk off their asses the night before an intense competition."

And get drunk they did. Cup after cup was shoved in their hands. It wasn't long before the beer turned into shots of whiskey. Both Bruce and Black were funny drunks, at some point they got into a wrestling match that was being refereed by Horse, but they were too drunk to do anything but cause the crowd to fall over with laughter.

I too found myself laughing at them. Although they were competitors, you could see the love between them. Black treated Bruce like a younger brother. He wrestled and fought with him, but you could tell he did it in a way as not to hurt him.

While this was going on, I found myself surrounded by some of the tribe's women. They asked me tons of questions, curious about the woman their leader had brought home. I was surprised to discover they knew about Rain, and that I'd been married to Mitch. I guess news traveled fast around these parts.

This whole situation was so crazy that if I wasn't standing here actually living it, would never had believed if someone else told me it happened to them. Yesterday, I was living a simple life over an Afrocentric bookstore. Today I am amongst a group of people that made their own rules, whose ways are so different from everything I was used to, I couldn't help but be excited.

Tonya in taking her nanny job to Rain seriously, kept up with her so that I could do a little mixing and mingling, her words. Honestly, I didn't know how much mingling I wanted to do. I didn't want to risk being cornered by Black. I didn't quite know what to say to him.

On one hand after talking to Hosea, I had a better perspective on what I'd witnessed at the casino earlier today. But on the other, the fact remains that he'd lied to me, praised that she-bat for taking my baby, and was now trying to force me to marry him. The thought of that meeting made me see red all over again.

The fact that Black could ever think I would marry him after that is laughable. Just like it's going to be laughable to watch him and his old men try to compete in a young man's competition. I wasn't going to feel sorry for him either. Not only was he trying to force me to make another mistake like the one I'd made in rushing into marriage with his younger brother, but he was doing it in such a way that he was making me choose between being with him or losing custody of my baby.

How low can you go?

No, I wasn't ready to talk to him just yet. If I did, the result would be much like it had been earlier, me yelling and cursing at him, and him setting sh*t on fire.

However, I needed not worried because the tribe's men kept him busy pouring drinks down his throat, but several times I'd looked up and caught him watching me with that hungry gaze of his. I knew he was just waiting for the right time to break away from the merry making, so he could confront me for not waiting at his house for him, another conversation I was not looking forward to.

When I saw Hosea slip inside the house, I retrieved Rain and followed. She was a little fussy because she wanted to stay at the party, but she was so sleepy she couldn't articulate that. Yeah, clear sign it was time for her to call it an evening.

After I cleaned up the bathroom, I bathed Rain and got her to bed. Because I'd packed enough clothes for a day, we were all out of clean items to wear, which meant I needed to find a washing machine.

The house was pretty much quiet except for the low hum of the television coming out of the young couple's room. Right then poor Kelly ran out headed toward the bathroom holding her mouth. I went in after her and held her braids out the way as she dry heaved in the toilet.

"I don't even have anything on my stomach, I'm just throwing up air!" She whined as I helped her back to her room. Dan must be out drinking with the fellas because there was no one in the room but Kelly.

"You know what helped me when I was pregnant with Rain?" I told her as I helped her climb back in the bed.

"What?"

"Early morning before I got out of the bed, I would have a light breakfast. And then I would eat before I got hungry. Hunger pains is what make you nauseas."

She groaned. "Food is not my friend."

Chuckling I gently moved her braids back off her face. "Trust me, I understand. That's exactly what I said when Crazy Larry was shoving dry toast down my throat at 6 AM but you know what? It actually worked."

She smiled. "Who is Crazy Larry?"

"A very crazy Jamaican."

I went on to tell her a few Larry stories that had her laughing so good she momentarily forgot about her misery. When I was done, I asked her about a washer and dryer so that I could wash some clothes for Rain and me.

"We have one, but it makes a noise so loud it'll raise the dead."

"Why won't Hosea get another one?"

"He's old-fashion. He believes that the last great things were built in the sixties. The washer and the dryer were his parents', and he refuses to get new ones. Black has been trying to buy him one forever, but he refuses. If those things break down, he grabs his old tool belt. Rumor has it, the washer started making the noise back in the eighties. They fixed it and it got louder. Hosea swears the noise mean it's still running strong."

By the time she finished I was in tears. Just as I figured, Hosea was quite the character. In the end she let me borrow a few items that she could no longer fit due to pregnancy. At first, I was a little leery, Kelly is a tiny girl. However, she was more than convinced I could fit her clothes. She even gave me a few things for Rain from the many clothes items left here by the random children that inhabited the place.

When I left her resting in bed, I checked in on Rain one more time and placed the clothes beside her bed so that she could see them in the morning. Not being able to resist how peaceful and beautiful she is while sleeping, I leaned down and kissed her little head.

Today, she had a wonderful time with her father's people. It was as if she was getting a dose of something that she'd been missing, something that I haven't been able to give her till now. Foolishly, I'd thought that I would be able to fulfil all her needs, but it wasn't true. She was half Seminole and quite naturally, she would have question I couldn't answer.

Maybe it wouldn't hurt if we stayed around for a few days. Larry wouldn't give away my place or job, so I wasn't worried about that. I will have to call Bria, Sis Dinah, and Bro. Abraham and let them know where we are and that we're okay.

My stay might not be too bad if I could avoid being cornered by Black. I know hiding behind Hosea was a cowardly thing to do, but you guys just don't know the pull that man has on me. Even now, with all he's done to hurt me, the only thing I can think about is the way he makes love to my body. The way he possesses me so completely that the only thing I can think of is remembering to breathe after my body shatters for him.

Needing a cold shower, I eased out of Rain's room and gently pulled the door up. Hosea's room wasn't up here, I think it was somewhere downstairs around the kitchen area. Either way I was careful to be as quiet as I could as I made my way to the bathroom.

Kelly had been kind enough to let me borrow a pair of pajamas. After I got out of the shower and used my mixed fruit body butter to moisturize my skin, I stood holding the pajamas up eyeballing them.

Bless her heart, she'd really believed I could fit all these thighs and butt into these little bottoms. Shrugging, I put them on anyway. For now, it was all I had. Nobody would see me anyway.

Just as I figured, the bottoms fit like second skin, they were long enough, but they hugged my butt scandalously. I slid the cami-like top over my head and had to force it down over my braless breasts. My outfit left nothing to the imagination.

I peeked my head out the bathroom door to make sure the hall was still empty, and then quickly made my way to the bedroom Hosea was letting me use. As I was shutting the door behind me, I noticed some activity by the slide door that led to the little balcony. Somebody had just climbed over the rail and landed on the surface without making a sound.

My heart lurched in fear and excitement that momentarily snatched my breath. I knew instantly who it was. Although he didn't make a sound when he landed, he was very unstable on his feet. Before I realized what I was doing, I'd crossed the floor and switched the latch to lock, just as he reached for the handle to slide it back.

"Ha! Sucka!" I cried as I snatched the curtain back so that he could see it was me who'd throttled his plans.

His gaze landed on my breasts that the shirt made appear as if they were being thrust out as an offering to him.

He licked his lips. "Minx, open the door. I just want to talk to you." His words were slurred, and his attention focused on all things carnal. If he just wanted to talk to me, my name was Judge Judy.

"What are you doing trying to break into my room?"

Finally, his eyes came up to meet mine and a sexy grin appeared on his face. "This is *my* room. Look around...all those plaques on the wall have my name on them."

Crap!

I turned to look at the nearest plaque and sure enough it read that Melech Black was receiving the award for being the team's MVP.

I held my head up a bit refusing to be embarrassed in front of a drunk man.

"So what, Hosea let me use it, you have no right to try and break in."

His gaze traveled down my body again. At this moment, he was being ruled by nothing but his lust. And I don't know if it was a need to regain the upper hand after finding out that this was his bedroom, or just a reckless streak I didn't know I had in me, but I arched my back a bit, causing my breasts and butt to push out even more.

I swear, the pupils in his eyes delighted as he stared down at me. By this point, he had both hands on the glass.

"Come on, baby, open the door..."

With a grin on my face, I shook my head. "Nope."

He looked up at me with pleading eyes. "Why not?"

"Because I'm mad at you."

"I know you are, and if you open the door, I can make you feel better…Don't you want me to make you feel better?"

I nearly groaned. *Stay strong, Earth!*

He licked his lips watching me with that hungry gaze. "Come on, baby, open the door."

"You need to go somewhere and sleep off that drunk."

He put his hand on his chest as if my words wounded him. "But I'm not drunk." As he said that, he swayed on his feet.

"Psst! You need to sing to her or start reciting poetry…like Romeo and f***ing Juliet." Those slurred words came from somewhere on the ground underneath the balcony before drunken laughter followed.

I stepped over and looked out the window to see who it was. Bruce, Horse, and Big Troy stood underneath the balcony. They were all so drunk they had to hold each other up to keep from falling. The ill advice came from Bruce.

Black hit his head with his palm. "That's right… girls do like for brothas to sing to them. Sorry 'bout that, not quite used to serenading the ladies."

At least I think that's what he said, he was so drunk his words were barely comprehendible. But none of that took away from how completely and utterly adorable he was preparing himself to sing to me. He cleared his throat…

The smile that I was trying hard not to show burst through when it became clear that he really was going to try and sing to me.

"Darlin' I… I can't explain, where did we lose our way… Girl, it's drivin' me insane… and I know I just need one more chance to prove my love to you…"

I held my head back and died laughing, he sounded terrible, so terrible a wolf's howl filled the night as if the animal was begging him to stop the torture.

Y'all, he wasn't trying to sing quietly either, he belted the lyrics out like R&B singing was what he did for a living. He was even trying to bust a move, but he was so drunk he was just swaying from side to side trying to keep from falling.

I looked out the side window and laughed harder when I saw that Bruce, Horse and Big Troy were now doubled over laughing at their chief. But he didn't seem to mind, still focused only on me, he kept on singing...

"If you come back to me, I'll guarantee that I'll never let you gooooo. Can we go back to the days our love was strooooong. Can you tell me how a perfect love goes wroooong. Can somebody tell me how you get things back the way it used to beeeee... Oh God give me the reason, I'm down on bended kneeeees..."

And then he went down to his knees in front of the glass, holding his hands up in a begging motion, his eyes pleading with me to open the door.

Oh Damn! I was going to do it...I was going to open the door. Apparently, Bruce was right. Even though I knew Black was drunk off his ass and sounded horrible, his serenading was working.

"Dammit, boy!" I heard right when I lowered my hand to the latch. It was Hosea's voice. Still laughing, Bruce, Horse and Big Troy ran away disappearing in the night.

"Why are you up there keeping up all that racket? I thought Armageddon was happening and the demons from hell had been loosed to torture mankind." Hosea continued flashing some kind of light up towards the balcony.

Black jumped to his feet, but he moved so quickly it threw his balance off and he tipped over, falling over the rail.

"Oh, sh*t!" I heard him yell as he went down.

"Melech!" I cried, opening the door racing to look over the railing. He lay flat on the ground not moving. I held my breath as Hosea peered down into his face.

Please don't be dead! Please don't be dead!

Abner appeared out of nowhere and began to nudge his face with his big head. When Melech still didn't move, he licked up his cheek. A frown appeared on Black's face before he swatted at his pet.

"Stop, Abner…What I tell you about that, man?" He muttered before he turned over on his side getting more comfortable.

Shaking his head Hosea looked up at me. "Go on back to bed, he'll be alright." He looked off into the direction the fellas had ran.

"Get over here and get this drunk fool off my lawn." And then he turned and made his way back into the house.

I didn't move until I saw that he was okay with my own eyes. Still laughing, his men came and woke him.

"Did it work?" He asked as they helped him to his feet.

"Did what work?" Horse asked him.

Black grinned doing something really goofy with his eyebrows. "My singing…Did it knock her off her feet?" He slurred.

Bruce shook his head. "No…but it sure as hell knocked you off yours." This caused his men to erupt in another fit of laughter.

18

SOMETHING ABOUT HER BRINGS OUT THE BEST IN ME

EARTH

DAY 1 OF THE GREEN EAR FESTIVAL

I came awake when I heard little voices coming from downstairs. One of those little voices was Rain. I picked up my watch off the nightstand. Goodness, it was six-thirty in the morning. Hosea warned me last night that the little ones would begin showing up at his place really early, but this was ridiculous.

Grudgingly I dragged myself out of the bed and performed my morning rituals. Leaving Rain alone with other tiny tots for too long was definitely not a good idea. We'd just got here, I didn't want Hosea putting us out so soon. Plus, now was a good time to make a light breakfast for Kelly.

Needing to refresh my Pocahontas braids as Betty calls them,

I took them down and redid them after moisturizing my hair really good. Then I put on the clothes Kelly let me borrow. Because I was taller than her, the jean skirt fit like a mini skirt, the t-shirt didn't fit any better, it was quite snug, hugging my breasts in a way that was sure to garner attention.

I was going to have to talk to Hosea about getting Rain and I more clothes. Maybe there was a Goodwill or something in town that I could go grab a few items from. What I really needed to do was convince Black to let us go home. It's not like we can't come back another time, a time that's planned and packed for.

I know that technically I didn't have any right to be upset that he'd kidnapped me, seeing as to how I kidnapped him first, the fact that I am is quite hypocritical. Through the eyes of cognitive dissonance and a healthy dose of vain reasoning, I've convinced myself that he kidnapping me is far worse than me kidnapping him, because he had the power to escape anytime he liked, whereas I didn't. He's taken away my power and now I'm at his complete mercy.

When finally I got downstairs, it was to find Rain with about eight more of her little friends all sitting on the couch watching Sesame Street. It looked as if they were all piled high on a pillow or something. Because the back of the couch faced the stairs and the kitchen, I couldn't quite see what it was they were sitting on. But whatever it was caused them to giggle amongst themselves as they leaned in close to whisper to each other.

Stretched out on the floor in front of the television was Abner. It was strange to see him without his master. Smiling at the little ones who burst out in another fit of giggles, I made my way into the kitchen and nearly tripped over a big body.

At first I thought it was Black, but as I got closer I was able to see it was Bruce.

"What the world?!"

He was sprawled flat on his back in the kitchen, knocked out cold.

I leaned down and poked him in the chest. "Bruce?"

He didn't budge, in fact, he opened his mouth and let out a loud snore. Shaking my head, I stepped over him and continued on in the kitchen. He must have stumbled in here and just passed out where he lay. Chuckling, I was now curious as to where Mr. Serenader ended up. No doubt he was somewhere sleeping his drunk off like his cousin.

"Who all wants breakfast?" I called into the living room. All the little hands flew into the air. Abner lifted his head off the floor and looked at me. "Gotcha, buddy."

I opened the fridge and was surprised to see everything in it was in bulk as well as in the cabinet. Hosea was definitely a Sam's Club shopper.

"Who all likes oatmeal?!"

All the little hands flew up again, Abner lifted his head waving his tail through the air. "Gotcha, buddy."

And so, after finding a pot big enough to make a vat of oatmeal, I got started. When I got it good and on the way, I took out a few loaves of bread for toast.

After I got everything cooking, I sat down at the table with a cup of tea. The children were now bouncing up and down on the couch and for some reason, that had them erupting in fits of giggles.

Abner came to his feet and looked toward the front door seconds before it opened. Hosea came shuffling in carrying a small animal in his hand. It looked like a fox or a big rabbit, it was hard to tell. He tossed it to Abner who caught it between his teeth. Then he held the door open as the big cat ran past him to enjoy his meal in the woods.

Okay, so I guess he found something better than my oatmeal.

When Hosea saw what the children were sitting on, he frowned down at them.

"Look at this." He grumbled. "Why are y'all sitting on the King? Melech, get up. Get yourself up, boy!" Suddenly the line of children toppled over in a mass of giggles as Black suddenly pushed up off the couch coming unsteadily to his feet.

I put my hand over my mouth to cover up my laugh. The kids had been sitting on Black that whole time.

"Ohh sh*t!" He said lifting his hands to clutch his head.

"Watch your mouth around these babies!" Hosea admonished as he made his way into the house.

Black looked around as if he was wondering how he'd gotten here. He frowned down at his wrinkled clothes. Then his blood shot eyes came to me. They took their time looking me over, starting from my Timberland clad feet, up my bare legs, the good portion of my thighs that showed, my breasts, to finally settle on my face.

He put his hand on his chest and grinned in a way that made me wonder if he was still a little tipsy. "Damn, Minx, I missed your sexy a—"

"Melech!" Hosea snapped cutting him off, gaining his attention. "Look at you, bet you can't even remember how you got here. Are you aware you fell off the damn balcony?"

I wonder if he remembered he'd fallen off the balcony too.

Black's grin grew as he rubbed his hand down his head. "It was a wild night." His deep voice sounded more gruff than usual.

Goodness, it was just a shame. Here this man stood clearly hung over, and he still looked simply adorable, disheveled as he was. At some point he'd lost his suit jacket and now only wore his pants that was good and wrinkled. His black button up shirt was also wrinkled and the top four buttons of his shirt were opened, causing it to hang off his massive shoulders really sexy like.

Hosea was wrong about what he said about him yesterday, Black in no way had a beer belly. If he wanted, he could easily be an underwear model. Even hung over, he still looked so very capable.

Hosea watched him get his bearings about him. Although he shook his head in disapproval, I could still see the pride in his eyes. Honestly, if Melech was my grandson, I would be proud too.

"You here sleeping your life away while this child and her baby girl don't have any clothes to wear. Get yourself upstairs and get cleaned up so that you can take them shopping."

I stood. "Oh no! Hosea, that's not necessary—"

"Hush up now!" He waved his hand at me dismissively. "It's his fault you're in this situation. The least he can do is make sure you and baby girl have all that you need."

As Black walked to the stairs, he grinned at me. "Yeah, hush up now." He said so low that only I could hear him, before he took the stairs up two at a time. I watched him go with narrowed eyes.

"Will you look at here?! I knew the cub couldn't have been far behind. Boy, get your tail off my kitchen floor!" Bruce sat straight up like Black had just done. Something about their grandfather's voice causes them to be alert instantly.

"If you don't get yourself off my floor, I'll get my gun and shoot you."

"Come on, Pop! Why you yelling this early in the morning?" Bruce groaned as he dragged himself off the floor and slid into one of the kitchen chairs. I went over to the stove and started spooning oatmeal into bowls so that it could cool for the little ones. While I did, Hosea laid into Bruce for not only underage drinking, but getting so drunk he ended up passed out on the kitchen floor.

Feeling sorry for him because it looked like he was really

suffering, I spooned some oatmeal in a bowl and gave him two pieces of buttered toast. With a grin on his handsome face, he looked up at me through blood shot eyes and winked. Goodness, this kid looked just like Black. I mean he could literally be his clone.

"Thank you, future wife." His grin was contagious. Because I knew he was in no way serious, I returned his smile. Like his big cousin, he's a very charming boy.

"You're welcomed, little brotha."

However, his grin didn't last, Hosea walked past him and smacked him hard on the head.

"Ouch! Pop! My head is already killing me!"

"You shouldn't have went out there and got drunk like a fool!" He told him as he sat down in the chair next to him. I slid a bowl of oatmeal and toast in front of him as well.

"Thank you, daughter."

A door closed over us before the sound of hurried footsteps could be heard.

"Watch this…" Hosea said, just as Dan came running down the stairs heading for the door.

"What up, cuz!" Bruce called.

"What's up, cuzo…" Dan returned without even looking back.

"Where you going, son?" Hosea asked with a grin on his face. Dan turned around to look at him, but he didn't stop walking toward the door.

"To finish painting the porch." Moments later he was gone.

Both Bruce and Hosea erupted in laughter. I frowned as I laid out newspaper on the floor to serve as temporary floor mats for the children.

"What did I miss?"

"You didn't see how fast that boy was moving?" Bruce asked before he stole one of the children's bowls of oatmeal and toast.

Damn! He'd eaten the food I'd given him so fast I hadn't even noticed it disappear.

"Yeah, I saw that. Why was he in such a rush?"

"Black!" They both said at the same time.

"If Black sees him laying around…" Bruce didn't even finish that statement, he just shook his head.

Bruce and Hosea watched as I gathered all the children and told them to pick a mat to sit on, then placed their bowls in front of them. I set out nine juice boxes and had to threaten to chop Bruce's fingers off if he stole one. Then I informed the little ones that once they were done and they'd cleaned up their bowls and floor mats, they could have a juice box.

"You're really good with them." Hosea said from where he still sat at the table observing me.

I grinned. "Thank you. I was going to school to become a teacher once upon a time."

"What happened? Why didn't you finish?" He asked.

"I got pregnant and had to focus on providing a roof over our heads. At first, I was able to still do both, but it was so draining, and I barely got to spend any time with Rain." I shrugged. "So, I had to make the tough call to quit school."

He tapped the table. "You should go down to the local college with Dan and enroll in some classes and finish getting your degree, so that you can come back here and open a school for these tiny-tots, and then maybe, I can have some peace and quiet."

I chuckled as I finished off the last of the breakfast dishes. "As amazing as that sounds, I'll be leaving to return to Florida soon…back to my life. Back to the bookstore."

Even though I wasn't looking at him I could feel Hosea staring at my back. "Why are you afraid of change, child?"

I placed the last dish in the drain tray. "Because it has never been a friend of mine."

After drying off my hands I spooned some oatmeal in a bowl for Kelly, placing two pieces of dried toast on the side. And without looking back at Hosea, because I didn't want him reading me and discovering my secrets, escaped the kitchen to take the food upstairs.

By the time I made it back downstairs, Black was ready to go. He looked simply amazing in a pair of black jeans and a brown sweater. On his feet were a pair of brown leather boots. He must have clothes upstairs in his old room or something.

Hmmm...something about that amazed me. It was obvious the Blacks were a close knit family, with their grandfather being the very center. All his grandchildren felt at home with him, including Black, the leader of this clan. It said a lot about him, that he so powerful, and so wealthy, kept changing clothes at his grandfather's house for the days he crashed here.

He walked towards me looking good enough to eat. I had to remind myself I was angry with him.

"You all set?"

Nodding, I held my hand out for Rain. Goodness! He even smelled good. "Come on, baby, we're getting ready to go."

She shook her head. "I don't want to go, Mommy."

"Come on, Rain, I'm not going to argue with you." There was no way I was going to be alone with this chocolate temptation on legs. However, Rain was not helping, she stood up from the couch with her head hanging so low you would have thought her dog died.

Hosea waved his hand from where he and Bruce still sat at the table watching us. "You might as well leave her here. It's not like I can get rid of these other children."

"It's true, my pop is like a magnet for kids, it's why I don't come over here that much, too many kids!" Bruce said as he walked to the fridge and took out a carton of orange juice. He didn't bother to get a glass, he just flipped it open and turned the whole thing up to his mouth.

Hosea shook his head as he watched his grandson drink the whole thing.

Black leaned closer to me, causing my senses to come to life with his scent. "You're not afraid to be alone with me, are you Minx?"

"Of course not!" I snapped. Both Hosea and Bruce grinned to themselves. Black lifted an eyebrow.

I cleared my throat. "It's just that if we are going to get clothes for Rain, don't you think it's a good idea if she's there to try them on?"

"Why, don't you know her size?"

"Yeah, I know her size. It's just that—um.."

"Ummm, what? You're scared."

I put my hand on my hip. "Ain't nobody scared of you."

"Then stop torturing her and let her stay with her friends." He looked up at little cousin. "Go get your sister, tell her she's on duty."

He lifted Rain by both of her arms and planted a loud kiss on her cheek before lowering her back to the floor.

"Be good, Hobbit."

"I will!" She yelled back as she excitedly ran out the door with her little group of friends. Great! She'd abandoned me. She didn't even give me a hug goodbye.

Black reached down and wrapped his big warm hand around mine, then gently began to pull me toward the door.

"Be a big girl and face this conversation that is long overdue."

Feeling my heart accelerate at the thought of being alone with him, I looked back towards Hosea. He and Bruce still wore those knowing grins.

"Don't worry about Rain, sweetheart. She will be waiting for you when you get back. Remember, son, the games start at one." He called after us.

Black lifted his finger without turning to look at his grandfather. "Indeed."

Face the conversation that was long overdue, he says. Be a big girl he says. Well... I aim to please. Desperately, I grabbed a hold of my anger. Anger was a safe emotion to feel around Melech. Anger I can do and do it well.

Last night there were three black Range Rovers parked out here. Today, there was only one. Black opened the passenger door for me.

"Thank you." I told him as I stepped up into the truck. All the anger I felt about him lying to me and about how that meeting went down was now bubbling just underneath my skin. I was ready for a fight.

"So, you want to talk about the meeting?" I asked him a soon as he got in the car and closed the door. He looked over at me for a moment studying me. I lifted an eyebrow, although I wasn't frowning, the look on my face said it was about to go down.

He chuckled as he started the truck. "Yeah, I want to talk about it, but not right at this moment, I need to replace my electrolytes. I can't think with my electrolyte level being so low." He clutched his head and groaned.

I opened my mouth to shred into him, but then closed it. Did he just say he needed to replace his electrolytes?

"O-kay... how are you going to do that?"

"I know this really nice restaurant. We can grab a bite to eat while I rejuvenate myself for our conversation and that ass whipping I got coming this afternoon."

I put my hand over my lips to hide my smile. "Are you saying you think Bruce is going to whoop your ass?"

He pulled away from the curb. "I know Bruce is going to whoop my ass. Have you seen that kid?"

"Then why are you doing it? Why did you agree? You should have just said no."

He didn't respond right away. In fact, he didn't say anything for so long I thought that maybe he wasn't going to respond.

"I'm doing it for you."

"For me? Why?"

He looked over at me as he drove. "Because… for you, I will take an ass whooping."

I quickly looked away so that he couldn't see the effect his words had on me. Why did it feel like his words were sincere? Why after being lied to by him and betrayed, did my body still crave his? And if he kept saying things like that, there was no way I could hold on to my anger. And without my anger, I was good and conquered.

It took all my focus and replaying him telling that she-bat he wasn't mad at her for all she'd put me through to regain my rage. By the time we made it back to the Big House, I had gathered enough of it to still shred into him.

"We're going to take the helicopter so that we can make it back to the festival in time. The restaurant I was telling you about is in Greenville, and it's about an hour and a half drive away."

I nodded and allowed him to lift me into the loud machine. This time I was able to actually enjoy the ride compared to my first time. Surprisingly, the helicopter let us out on the roof of the restaurant. The maître d met us on the roof.

"Good morning, Mr. Black. So very good to see you again. How was your trip?"

The two shared small talk as he led us to our table.

"You ready to talk now?" I asked as soon as we were seated and the maître d walked away. The restaurant was really nice, it kind of reminded me of the one I'd first seen him at, the one where I'd put the poison in his water.

He held up one finger. "Almost, not yet though... my electrolytes are still pretty low."

I pressed my lips together to smother the smile that was trying to take over them. He was being a nut, acting like his electrolytes were keeping him from having this conversation. He was stalling point blank and period, but doing it in such an adorable way that it made me want to smile.

I could not smile at him, he's the enemy.

"Good morning, Mr. Black...it's very nice to see you again. Tell me, how can I be of service to you?" My gaze rose to take in the Native kitty cat that had just purred next to us. The waitress was practically undressing him with her eyes.

"Yeah." He said without looking up from the menu. "Can I have seven glasses of orange juice, two cups of water and a cup of tea?" His gaze came to me over his menu.

"You want something to drink, baby?"

When he called me baby, it forced Miss Thang to finally look over at me. She smiled, although it didn't reach her eyes. "Yes, can I get you something to drink?"

I gave her the fake smile back. "Tea, please."

Heffa!

Black stopped her before she left. "Can you bring French Vanilla cream with her tea."

Damn! She had completely taken me off my game. I had meant to ask for that cream. I watched her sashay away from the table before I turned to look at him.

"Regular here?"

He chuckled. "I own the place."

My eyes widened in surprise. "Wow! No wonder she was so friendly."

He looked confused. "Was she friendly? I hadn't noticed..."

I held my head back and laughed. He was too much. "Smart man..."

He leaned forward with a grin on his handsome face. "Let me tell you something, I ain't got this far being no dummy."

When she came back with our drinks, she took our orders, I'd made toast and oatmeal for the kids, but hadn't eaten anything myself, so I ordered a cheese and spinach omelet. Black ordered steak, potatoes and eggs.

"So, about that meeting—" I began when she left to put in our orders. Black held up his finger again cutting me off.

"Not yet, got to replace the lytes." He gestured to the seven glasses of orange juice, two cups of water, and the cup of tea in front of him.

I folded my arms. "There is no way you're going to drink all that."

He lifted a challenging eyebrow and at the same time, he picked up the first glass of juice, drinking it down with no problem. He then proceeded to do the same with the next six glasses of orange juice, the two glasses of water, and had the nerve to take his time and stir honey and lemon in his tea before looking up at me and saying, "Now, you were telling me what it was about the meeting you didn't like."

He said it so smoothly I could not hold my laughter, for some reason, he had chosen this moment to be silly and it was just too much.

He smiled sipping his tea as he watched me laugh.

I pointed at him. "You think you slick."

"Me? What did I do? I just simply replaced my electrolytes."

"Don't say electrolytes again?!" I screeched through my laughter. He was being so silly!

"Okay, let's get serious. Tell me what about the meeting upset you most?"

I folded my arms again as the smile left my face. "How could you tell that…that…she bat, that you weren't upset with her? She didn't even take the time to get to know me before she tried to take Rain from me. She thought that just because you guys were rich that Rain would be better off with y'all. But you know me..." I paused, that sounded way too intimate.

"I mean you've gotten to know me...right?"

He looked down at his tea cup as he stirred it. A smile came to his face. "I think I know you very well in every way."

The last of his statement had me blushing like crazy.

I cleared my throat. "And would you say I'm a bad mother?"

He looked up at me. "Absolutely not. You're an amazing mom, which is exactly why I want you to be the mother of my children."

Okay!!!! He was not making this easy for me. I inhaled. "Then why would you tell her you're not mad at her? How can you not be mad at her?"

He didn't answer right away. He just looked down at that tea while he stirred.

"How could I be mad at her? If she hadn't done what she did, I would have never gotten kidnapped by the person who makes my soul complete." He looked up at me.

"How can I do anything but thank her? Without her, I would have missed out on the best thing to ever happen to me."

19

BECAUSE YOU'RE MINE

"Love is like a friendship caught on fire. In the beginning a flame, very pretty, often hot and fierce, but still only light and flickering. As love grows older, our hearts mature, and our love becomes as coals, deep-burning and unquenchable."

— BRUCE LEE

EARTH

STILL DAY 1 OF THE GREEN EAR FESTIVAL

"Foul!" Big Troy yelled throwing his fifth bundle of corn to the ground to go after the kid he'd been racing. "You little cheating sh*t! Be still so I can catch you!"

The crowd erupted in laughter. In fact, that's all we've been doing since this debacle of a game began. The Green Ear Festival centered around the end of the year harvest, so not only were there games, there was also a huge farmers market.

There were pie and jam contests, chili judging competitions and even produce growing competitions. Folks brought their prized horses out to show off and even some cattle. However, the game portion always drew the biggest crowd.

According to Panda, only the boys transitioning into manhood participated in the games. It's sort of like a rite of passage. She said they've never before seen old men try and hang with the youths.

What's that?

Who is Panda?

LOL!!! Panda is Black's aunt, Tonya and Bruce's mom, and y'all, she is a mess.

After talking to Bria this afternoon, I instantly felt homesick. She filled me in on all that I'd missed in two days, while telling me how good God was for letting me kidnap the older, richer brother instead of the younger insignificant brother. Then she told me not to mess nothing up because we were set for life.

And when she said *we*, she meant *we*, as in *her* too. Before I got off the phone with her, she said she was going to come visit and snag one of Black's security guards because she had heard from Betty that some of them were fine.

Anyway, after talking to her I was homesick. That was until I met Panda. Panda materialized after Black and I had lunch. He informed me that there was a car waiting outside for us, but that he would not be coming with us because he had a meeting upstairs with the she-bat, her husband, and a few more of his executives. Apparently, he had an office over the restaurant.

The restaurant was in the Greenville area and had plenty of stores and boutiques surrounding it. He told Panda and me to shop for enough clothes to fill my side of the closet and to carry back the things Rain and I would need for the next few days, and have the other items sent to the Big House.

Of course, I put up a fuss because my closet was just fine at *home*. But he'd only looked at Panda, handing her his credit card and gave her his orders, orders that she'd followed to the t. But she was so crazy, and had *the tea* on everybody, I'd not even noticed how the time had flown by. She'd subtly held a bunch of outfits, shoes and even a few pair of boots up to me asking me what I thought about them.

I balked at a few prices, I'd never paid so much for clothes, but she only waved away my concern.

"Please girl, you're the King's future wife. Are you kidding me? You really need to be getting on a plane to go shopping, maybe somewhere in Paris. I don't know if I'm all that impressed with what the *supposedly* best boutiques in South Carolina have to offer." And then she held her nose up in the air and huffed at the woman who had been watching us on the low since we walked in the store.

See what I mean? She was crazy!

I was thrilled when we found the Children's Place. I looooovve that store! Although most times I couldn't afford to shop in it.

But not today. Today I was able to take the store by storm. Together we picked out so many outfits for Rain I think the store clerk was ready to kiss us both. Even though I felt kind of bad about all the money that had been spent on me today, I didn't feel bad spending Black's money on my daughter. He was her uncle after all...

Panda had to remind me we had to meet Black back at the restaurant and the helicopter. By the time we got there, he was already onboard waiting for us. I thought he was going to be angry because everybody said he didn't like to be kept waiting. Panda was a nervous wreck the whole way back. But he wasn't angry, he just smiled at me and asked me if I got everything I needed.

When we got back to Hosea's I had just enough time to change out of Kelly's clothes and into my own that fit way better. I chose a beautiful multi colored maxi skirt. It was perfect for a festival because not only was it full of vivid colors, it flared around my ankles like smoke when I walked. I partnered that with a white off the shoulder peasant blouse.

The blouse was one of the items I balked at, although I secretly loved it, it cost more than three months rent. But it was simply amazing. I loved it because with it being off the shoulder, I didn't have to worry about trying to hide bra straps, it came with a bra stitched inside that held the girls in place perfectly. I guess it should, seeing as to how it cost a small fortune.

Anyway, Black and Hosea went to the festival ahead of us. By them being the tribe's Chief and Medicine Man, they sat on the judges' table for most of the contests. Tonya had taken Rain hours ago, so that left me in Panda's capable hands.

She had me dying laughing as we walked around the festival. She would smile and wave at someone, but after we passed would fill me in on all the dirt she knew about that person. I swear, it was like she was a Black Seminole version of Bria-Bria.

I can already tell that she and I were going to be good friends. I don't know why, but I attracted these kinds of people.

"Look at him, mad at that baby because his old ass done threw out his back. Stop cheating!" She yelled at Big Troy from where we stood next to the wooden fence overlooking the field of corn.

"Where are you from, you don't talk like anybody here." She talked like she was straight from the ghetto, but I didn't want to be rude and say that.

She laughed. "You mean I talk ghetto, huh?"

I shrugged. "No not...I mean, you just don't talk like the other Black Seminole here."

"That's because I'm the only one who's lived in the ghetto. When I was sixteen, I fell in love with this dope boy from Chicago. Against my daddy's wishes I ran away with him. I spent ten years living in K-Town. Hell, probably still be there today if Black hadn't come and got me and my kids."

I frowned. "Why did he come and get y'all?"

She turned back to look at the field. "My baby daddy didn't know how to keep his hands to himself. I hid it from my family long as I could, but one day he beat me so bad, I couldn't get up from my bed. Because he didn't want to go to jail, he didn't let me go to the hospital and wouldn't allow anybody to call for help." She was staring at the ground ahead of her as she relived that horrible night.

"I thought I was going to die. I could feel blood in my lungs. Somehow Bruce snuck away from the house and called Black. The next thing I know, my nephew was at my bed lifting me in his arms." She shook her head.

"If not for my baby risking his life to sneak away from his maniac of a father, I would have died." I rubbed her back.

"I'm so sorry you had to go through that."

Don't ask the question you're thinking about, Earth! Don't you dare ask that question!

"What happened to your baby daddy?" *Hardheaded!*

She shrugged like it wasn't a big deal. Her head lifted on her shoulders. I could tell she didn't feel no way bothered by what happened to him.

"His car blew up. Police said it looked like he had a faulty alternator."

Faulty alternator my ass. My gaze flew to Black where he stood leaning against the fence waiting on his turn. I sucked in my breath. He was watching me with that predatory look on his face. Just then he pulled on his cigar and blew out a cloud of smoke. He never looked away from me, he didn't even try to hide his predatory nature.

It was so hard to believe that this was the same man who'd sang on my balcony last night, or the one who stalled getting chewed out by drinking orange juice under the guise of replacing his electrolytes. The Black that watched me was a killer. He was Holata's heir. How is it possible he can be two men in one?

Or maybe he wasn't, maybe he pretended to be human around me.

"I'll be right back." I told Panda. "I'm going to go check on Rain."

"Girl, she alright, Tonya has her. She is so thrilled to be working for you, it's all she talks about."

I smiled. "I know, I just need some air."

If she thought it was strange that I needed air outside she didn't say anything. She just returned my smile and nodded. "Okay, hurry back, Horse getting ready to take his turn and he's worse than Big Troy."

"Okay." I told her already heading away from the gaming area. I didn't want to see Black. Something very frightening was happening to me. I was falling in love with the kind of man Sis. Dinah always warned me about.

I knew she liked him when she met him, but she didn't know him like I did. She didn't know that underneath all that charm was a stone-cold killer, one that had super powers and would not hesitate to use them. Hosea said his powers came from God and I believed him. But he also said the devil was fighting for Black's soul and winning, and I believed that too.

I walked over to the area that was set up to entertain the children. It looked more like a carnival over here. There were rides and games to win prizes. There was even a petting zoo. I found Tonya helping Rain mount a pony.

"Mommy look at me, I'm getting ready to ride this horse!" She waved at me excitedly.

I smiled waving back at her. "I see you, baby. Make sure you hold on tight."

"You're just going to keep breaking your promise, huh?" Black leaned on the petting zoo fence facing me.

I didn't look away from Rain. "I don't know what you're talking about."

"Look at me, Earth."

I rolled my eyes and looked at him. He pointed at me. "That right there. You promised you would never look at me like that."

"Like what?" I snapped.

I don't know if it was my attitude or what, but something angered him. He stood up straight dropping his cigar to the ground stepping on it. Then he crowded my space big time. I refused to cower away from him, he was a damn bully and I wasn't going to let him bully me.

"Like I'm a f***ing monster that's what!" He growled those words in my face before he took my arm and pulled me toward the trees. He wasn't hurting me, but he gripped my arm in a way that if I pulled it would definitely make it uncomfortable.

I didn't make a scene because I didn't want to upset Rain. And nobody we passed dared to say anything to him in this mood, not even Hosea who appeared at the edge of the trees. He just watched his grandson with a displeased look on his face.

When we got a good distance from civilization, I snatched my arm from him. "What do you want from me, Black?!" I didn't care that I was yelling. I was fed up with him messing with my emotions and causing me to question the way I viewed the world.

"You want to just come in my life and change everything, like I wasn't doing just fine without you."

He stopped and began to pace angrily in front of me, making me feel as if I was watching a big caged cat. "I want you to stop looking at me like I'm the f***ing boogie man. One minute you were sitting there enjoying yourself and the next you're staring at me like I ate your f***ing dog."

I folded my arms. It was unreasonable for him to expect me to act normal around somebody like him. Faulty alternator... Please!

I wondered how many people he's killed.

"Why does it matter to you what I think? Why the hell were you watching me close enough to see my moods change anyway? Damn!"

He whipped to face me. "Because you're mine!" He yelled back. "And I can f***ing notice your moods all the f*** I want!" He began pacing again.

"I notice every f***ing thing about you! I know that you rub your right ear when you get sleepy, and if Rain is close by, you'll rub hers instead. You like French vanilla cream in your tea." He frowned his face.

"I don't know why, it's f***ing gross, but you do. You're ticklish on your lower back. If you can't find both slippers, you'll put on another shoe just so your feet won't be cold, but instead of taking off the slipper like any sane person would do, you'll leave the one slipper you can find on and then slide your other foot in a Timberline or some sh*t." He stopped pacing and turned to look at me.

"I know that you're the most beautiful when you wear yellow. For some strange reason, during that time, you're the most beautiful girl in the whole world. I know that you need me, just like I need you, whether you're woman enough to admit it or not."

Whatever the hell I was about to say just flew right out the window. This man was such a conundrum. Everything inside me wanted to believe him. It was my life experiences that had me slowly shaking my head.

"Melech…" My words were quiet. "Can't you see this is wrong. I am your brother's wif—"

The flames roared to life in his eyes. "You are not his wife!" He growled through clenched teeth as he closed the space between us. "You were never his! You have always been mine! Always!"

Now afraid he was going to set the trees on fire, I went to step back, but he wrapped his strong arm around my waist pulling me closer. Not able to look into his eyes that looked too eerie for my nerves to take right now, I looked at the trees over his shoulder.

"Don't run from me. Get use to this! Look at me until you're no longer afraid of it. The fire is a part of me, it's not going anywhere. Just like you and Rain are now a part of me." He paused for just a moment. "Look at me, baby…please."

I don't know if it was the raw desperation I heard in his voice or what, but I lowered my eyes until I was staring into the flames that still burned in his.

"I need to be the one you look at and see everything. I need to be the one to chase away all those bad memories and replace them with good ones. I need to be yours and I need you to be mine."

He lifted my hand and slowly brought it to his face. "Can't you feel it? Our souls come together and make one. Can't you feel it?"

I nodded as tears came to my eyes. "I can…and it scares me to death."

He frowned. "Why, baby? Why does the thought of us scare you? Why are you looking for every excuse you can find to push me away?"

"Because everybody that I love always leaves me." I shook my head. "If you left, it would kill me."

He palmed my face. "I'm not your mom or your dad. I'm not Mitch. I'm your man, baby. When God created me, he took you from my ribs. I'm not going anywhere. Me and you…we're going to grow old together."

I palmed his face with my hands. "How do you know that?"

He grinned. "The father of our people told me."

And then he was kissing me. It felt so good to have his mouth back on me, I stood on my toes wrapping my arms around his strong neck so that I could get closer to him. He growled into my mouth and lifted me off my feet, feeling the desperation that was causing havoc inside of me.

The sudden attack on my lips coupled with the powerful words he'd just said to me was my undoing. It had been too long since last we touched and tasted. I wrapped my legs around him, needing to feel his hardness pressed against my center. His hands hastily moved all the layers to my maxi skirt out the way so that he could feel my heat. And…

Mmmmm, he did not disappoint. He was ready for me and I was ready for him. Only the thin layer of my panties and his jeans stood in our way.

I broke off the kiss and desperately drew air into my lungs, his mouth didn't stop, it lowered to devour my neck. His strong hands palmed my soft bottom underneath my skirt, kneading it, pressing me closer to his hardness.

When his hungry mouth made it to the top of my peasant blouse, he brought an impatient hand up and yanked it down so that my right breast was exposed to him. I inhaled sharply. When my breast sprang free the tip of it came to rest against his lips.

He groaned before his hot, warm mouth closed over my tender flesh pulling strongly. My head fell back against the tree as he fed from me. My moans became louder and louder as I submitted to him. I wanted to feel him inside me right n--

Somebody cleared their throat behind us and it was like being splashed with a bucket of wake-up juice. The good thing was whoever it was could not see my breast because Black's big body was blocking me from view.

The bad thing was that the fire was back to roaring in Black's gaze. He was not happy about the interruption. I lifted my blouse to cover my flesh, Black watched, that little muscle ticking furiously in his cheek.

"Hey, Cuzo!" It was Bruce.

He whipped his head around to look at him, when his little cousin saw the flames burning in his eyes, the younger man didn't think, he just reacted, diving to the ground like somebody was getting ready to shoot at him.

"Cuz! Wait, cuz, don't cook me!" He yelled damn near balling up in the fetal position. "Mama, help me!" His screams were muffled because his face was pressed into the dirt.

It was too much, I lowered my head to Black's shoulder and cracked up. Big bad Bruce was on the ground crying like a little girl. Seeing him like that had even made Black chuckle. Shaking his head, he let my legs slide down his body to the ground. Gently, he rested his forehead against mine.

"Can you turn those off?" I whispered.

A sexy grin appeared on his face. "I'll do anything for you, Minx."

Entranced, I stared into his eyes and watched as the burning flames slowly faded from his gaze. He pressed his lips to mine, giving me one last kiss, it was the sweetest caress I'd ever received.

"We cool?" He asked.

I lifted one side of my mouth in a grin. "For now."

He groaned. "Damn, baby, you're not going to be easy, are you?"

I shook my head. "Nope, not at all."

He picked up my hand and brought it to his lips. "I wouldn't have it any other way." He nodded his head toward his little cousin who still lay balled up on the ground.

"Let's go put his mind at ease before he sh*ts himself." I tried to muffle my laughter, but I couldn't. When Bruce heard it, he peeked up at us. Seeing that the flames were gone from Black's eyes, he shamelessly jumped to his feet dusting his clothes off, grinning at us as if he wasn't just crying like a girl.

Black chuckled. "You okay, lil cuz? You seemed mighty frightened a minute ago."

Bruce shrugged. "Naw, I'm cool. I was just playing."

Black wasn't going to let him get off the hook that easily. "You sure you were playing? 'Cause it sounded like you called for your mama."

"What!? No! I said *one more*. As in, you should give her *one more* kiss before I put this hurtin' on you and she don't look at you like a man anymore."

I held my head back and laughed. Bruce fit right in with his big cousin and his crew. He talked just as much garbage as them.

Black shook his head. "Naw, that ain't what it sounded like. It sounded like you said, Mommy, help me! Please!"

Bruce pretended to think about it. "Yeah, I don't know how you got *mommy help me* from what I said, but none of that matters. I came to get you to let you know it's time for the main event. Me and you, brother. Let's see who's gonna be calling for their mommy at the end of *this*."

It was Black.

In fact, he handled losing to Bruce worse than Big Troy handled losing to Bruce's little friend earlier. He called foul, accusing the referee of cheating for the younger man. And at one point even threw his bundle of corn at his little cousin and tried to trip him.

The object of the game was really simple. In keeping with the spirit of harvest time, the players had to harvest the corn, stalk, roots and all, and tie them in bundles of twenty. Then they had to run with their bundles to the bins that were about a half block away and put the bundle in the bin.

The player with the most bundles at the end of thirty minutes wins. Simple, right?

Except Black and his men were out of shape like Hosea said. All the running was not their friend. By the time Black came out the corn field with his fifth bundle, he was clutching his chest, feeling that last cigar he'd smoked.

He held up his hand to call for a time out, but the referee told him there were no time outs. He then proceeded to fall out on the ground and yell at the man that he was having a goddamn heart attack. Bruce, with like his ninth bundle of corn, took the time out to run laps around Black, who was on the ground faking like he was having a heart attack, laughing at him.

"Who's on the ground crying for his mama now?!"

That's when Black tried to trip him, but Bruce with the spring of youth, artfully dodged his legs. Goodness, I couldn't remember a time I laughed so hard. It was just a shame what these kids were doing to these *old men*.

Yes, I said *old*. That's exactly what they all looked like, out there calling foul, clutching at their chests, ankles and backs. It was ridiculous. The only two that gave the youths any competition was Shiloh and Shappa.

Something I did notice throughout the games was the number of women, both Native and Black Seminole who was very quick to run to Melech's aid. But there was one in particular who was always underfoot, a very beautiful Native girl that looked to be about my age. She and Black talked like they went way back, but she would do things like laugh and under the guise of being so tickled, put her hand on his chest where she'd rub it around just a little, feeling all that hardness under her palm.

"A word of advice." Panda said coming to stand next to me to lean on the fence. "Bruce told me you and Black are on rocky ground. But if I were you, I would be the one rubbing Bengay on those old muscled shoulders tonight. Because if you don't, there are many who will, if you get my meaning."

I smiled at her, she was so much like Bria it was funny, only older. She is what Bria will be like in her forties. I shook my head. "Naw, I don't know what you mean."

I said that just to see what would come out her mouth next. She cocked her head to the side really sassy like.

"Well, let me spell it out for you. Don't be no fool and go push all that man into one of these thirsty heffa's hands." She grinned aware of what I was doing. "What about now, did you get my meaning?"

"Mmmmhhmm, I got you the first time, baby."

"Alright now, my girl." She held up her hand for a high-five. "I'm so glad my nephew chose a girl from the hood. I thought he was going to eventually bring home some snobbish heiress of some vast fortune, who can't tell her ass from a seashell."

My laughter spilled out across the field, getting Black's attention. He grinned and winked at me, as if he knew we were over here talking about him.

Oh! Yes! Panda and I were going to be good friends indeed.

"So, tell me, who is Miss Thang over there that keeps on smiling up in my man's face, finding every excuse under the sun to touch him."

"Girl, that's Kitty, Ms. Lily's niece, she was around Black a lot when they were kids, so quite naturally she thinks she got him in the bag. I love Ms. Lily, she's so sweet, some of the best cooking I ever had. But her niece…" She shook her head. "She one of those types that will suck, freak, and do anything to get your man. So, if you know like I know, you'll keep him away from her."

I didn't answer, I just looked back to where Black was standing still complaining to the referee, Ms. Kitty not too far away. She may be the type to do anything to get my man, but if my man is stupid enough to mess up what he has at home for such a fickle type, he deserved the consequences that came from such an action. I promised myself I would never live with such a man again.

And that was one promise I will keep, no matter what.

That being said, later that night after I laid Rain down for the night, I found myself sitting on Hosea's couch with Black's big body between my thighs, as I rubbed those old muscled shoulders. Abner lay by his side gently purring as Black lazily ran his hands through his coat.

I mean, yeah…I ain't going to put up with him cheating on me, but I ain't going to just push him into no other heffa's arms either. If somebody is going to be rubbing these capable shoulders, it for damn sure is going to be me.

"Can you rub my shoulders next? I'm out there killing myself for your hand in marriage too." Bruce said from where he lounged on the floor not too far from Black. You can tell he admired him. Like Abner, he was never too far from him.

"Only if you're ready to die, little brotha." Black moaned as he let his head fall back. I dug in deep applying pressure to his stiff muscles.

"Come here, sweetheart, I'll rub your sore shoulders for you." Horse said in a fabulous voice as he reached for Bruce.

"Eww! Naw man!" Poor Bruce nearly leaped to the other side of the room.

Panda laughed from where she sat cuddled up next to Big Troy on the other couch under the guise of being cold, needing his big body for heat. I mean don't get me wrong, the night had gotten a little brisk, but I was noticing something about Panda and Big Troy.

She was always joking with him saying stuff like, *if you were just a little older, I would do this, or that.* And he'll respond by saying something like, *any time you want me to prove to you I'm old enough to handle you and your needs just let me know.*

Panda is a beautiful woman. She looked like an older version of her daughter. Hell, she looked like she could be Tonya's older sister. I only prayed I looked that good when I got in my forties.

All I'm saying is, I think there was something brewing under the surface between her and Big Troy and one or both were too afraid to explore a little deeper to see what it is. My gaze went to Horse who was texting someone on his phone. Judging by the look on his face it was a woman.

I had pretty much nailed Horse's personality back at the bookstore. He was a manwhore. According to Panda, outside of Melech and Michael, he was the most sought after bachelor here. But where Melech and Michael had to be wise about the relationships they started here at the reservation, seeing as to how they are a part of the ruling family, Horse had no such obligations and tried his best to sample all the beautiful women that came his way.

Watch Bria-Bria come here and fall hard for him. Just mark my words.

Crush sat quietly on the stairs running a stone against his knife sharpening it. I wondered if there was somebody for him. He was not a bad looking man. In fact, he was quite handsome, in a very rugged kind of way. He didn't speak much and when he did, it was in short bursts.

He was a bigger mystery than Melech in my opinion. The fact that his mind worked different from the rest of ours was only the surface of all that made up Crush. He had a form of autism that enabled him to be able to read people in such a way that you didn't always have to be vocal with him for him to know what you needed or wanted him to do.

Earlier this evening after the festival had began to wind down, I began trying to make my way to Rain, but the crowd of people kept me from getting to her as quickly as I'd liked. I don't think I showed any outwards signs of distress, but one minute I saw Crush watching me, and the next, he disappeared in the crowd.

Seconds later, he reappeared with Rain in his arms, heading toward me. I relaxed instantly. He does stuff like that all the time. I'll give you another example. After sitting there watching the games chatting it up with Panda, I began to get a little thirsty. Without moving from my spot, I looked around to see if I could spot a place selling water. I wasn't big on soda pop and all the other sugary things most commonly sold at a fair.

I didn't see anything, so I kind of just let it fade to the back of my mind determined to just wait till I get back to Hosea's. A few minutes later, Crush was walking past me because it was his turn to go into the battle arena. As he passed, he stopped and held out his hand. I was shocked to see a bottle of ice-cold water in his big palm. He didn't speak. When I thanked him, all he did was grunt and continue on into the corn field.

And he wasn't just that way with me either, he was also that way with Black, Horse, Big-Troy, Bruce, Tonya, Rain, Panda, Tocho, Hosea, Shiloh and Shappa. He was even that way with Abner. Every time he came around the big cat, he had a chunk of smoked meat for him.

Panda says he's like that because he sees us as his family, and he takes care of his family. I could only imagine what he would do for a woman he loved. He's the kind of guy that will bring a single flower home every day, just because he knows it's your favorite. Or--

The front door flew open interrupting my thoughts and Dan ran in.

"Pop is sitting in front of the fire and old Yona is playing his flute!" After he made his statement, he dashed right back out the door.

There was only a moment pause before everybody jumped up and followed him. Black held his hand down for me, pulling me up off the couch. At the same time, he snagged the multi-colored throw blanket.

"What is it? What's happening?" I cried as we ran out the door, the sound of the flute made its way to our ears. It was as if it traveled on the wind.

"Pop is getting ready to tell one of his legendary stories. It's been nearly four years since the last one. Trust me, you've never seen anything like it."

By the time we made it to the fire, a huge crowd had gathered around Hosea. However, a spot had been saved for the chief right up front. Black sat on a log and this time it was I who sat between his legs. He wrapped the throw he'd grabbed around my shoulders incasing me in its warmth.

When I looked across the fire at Hosea, I gasped. His eyes were completely white. He stared straight ahead seeing something that only he could. Black wrapped his arms around me, pulling me into his embrace.

"It's alright." He whispered in my ear. "He's a griot...he sees, try and hear."

When Hosea began to speak, every nerve ending in my body stood on alert. It was as if I was bracing myself for an impact that was sure to knock me off my feet.

Only...

For the first time, I wasn't' holding myself up alone. Black's solid body was planted firmly behind me. He wrapped his arms tighter around me, letting me know that he was here to hold me up should I get weak.

Why did he need to hold me up? You ask...

For some reason, Hosea decided to tell a story about me...

"In a beginning, the Ancient of Days created the heavens and the earth, a tale we all know all so well."

The older man on the flute stared at the flame as he played. Somehow his tune wrapped around Hosea's words to caress our ears. Black was right, I've never heard storytelling done this way. Hosea turned to look at me with his white gaze. I stiffened in Blacks arms, but he just squeezed me tighter.

"I'm here, baby." He whispered close to my ear.

"Did you know, child, there was once a garden. And in this garden the most beautiful music was made. He who created this music was the most beautiful himself. Ohhhh!" He moaned clutching at his hands as if the beauty that only his eyes could behold was more than he could bear.

"So beautiful he was. In that day the Ancient of Days was pleased with him and his beautiful music. This Meleck..." he paused. "Meleck mean's messenger, or what you would call angel. Did you know that?"

I shook my head.

He smiled. "Yes...it's why I gave my grandson that name. He's destined to do great things. But he is not alone..." He waved his hand. "But that has still yet to be seen. Anyway, I was telling you about the beautiful one. The Meleck of music. He wanted to create an instrument that would play music to equal his beauty. Music that would transcend space and time. He knew that this would please the Ancient of Days greatly."

"But first he needed to find wood. Not just any wood. Wood that will never crack or need to be cleansed and polished. You see? Only perfect wood would do. And all the Meleckim knew that there was only one tree in all the garden with wood such as this."

"So, he went to that sacred tree. A tree not as beautiful as he. In fact, this tree was rather plain for the eye to behold. But for what this tree lacked in looks, it made up ten-fold in the fact that it was the only tree in the garden whose wood was perfect and whose fruit was the kind that gives life."

"That Meleck, that beautiful clever Meleck knew that this plain, unappealing tree would please the Ancient of Days beyond any other tree in the garden. For this reason, that beautiful Melek began to have hate in his heart, and iniquity was born."

"He could not understand how he could be standing before the Most High perfect in both looks and skill and be loved second best to a tree that was as plain as plain could get. Every other tree in the garden thought so. In fact, they all praised that beautiful Meleck on his looks and his music. Even they couldn't understand how that plain, unappealing tree still held the love of The Most High."

Hosea leaned forward as if he was going to tell us a secret, holding his hand to his mouth. "I'll tell you guys a little secret. The Ancient of Days always roots for the underdog. Always, yep...every time. Just sit back and take a look throughout history. Notice the choosing patterns. The devil chooses the most beautiful and the most talented. And the Ancient of Days, the rejected, the broken hearted..." He paused for just a moment as his eyes settled back on me.

"The forgotten..."

At this point I was squeezing Black's hand so hard I knew I was going to leave a mark.

"Now, our beautifully clever Meleck took of this wood that will never need to be cleaned, or polished, because it was perfect and formed it in a shape that none of the other Meleck had ever seen. Because it was two-fold he shaved a chunk of the wood away to make a bow. He then traveled deep into the abyss and found a creature never before seen by the eyes of men, and traded a few strands of his hair for a simple kiss from the Meleck that was known all over to be..." He pointed at the audience.

"The most beautiful..." We all supplied.

He smiled. "That's right, you guys are catching on." His white gaze came back to me. "When he got back to his workshop, he began to create this instrument, an instrument that only he could see in his head. He worked doggedly on it. So intent was he, he didn't notice the days and the years that went by. When he finally emerged from his workshop, it was to find that a new element had been added to the garden. He came closer to get a better look, because the other trees were talking. They said the Ancient of Days loved this new element so much, that he formed it himself with his own hand. Do any of you know what that element was?"

"Man." Melech said from above me.

Hosea nodded. "Yes, man..." His gaze came back to me. "Like a spoiled-rotten child he tried to play his new instrument, he wanted all the Most High's attention, and when he didn't get it, he formed a plan. Can any of you guess what his plan was?"

"To kill man." Crush answered surprising all of us.

Hosea smiled at Crush through tears. "Yes, my friend! He devised a plan to kill man. And not only that, he wanted to show the Ancient of Days how unperfect his creation was. How flawed man is. Because remember, he was..." He pointed at us, although there was a smile on his face, tears ran from his white eyes.

"The most beautiful..." We all said in unison.

"He rushed back to his workshop needing to hear the beautiful music that only this instrument could play. Only...it would no longer sing for him. When he asked it why? It said because iniquity was found in him, and he had become unclean to the Ancient of Days. That Meleck, that beautiful Meleck still didn't understand why it wouldn't sing for him, seeing as to how he was its creator. But it reminded him that he may have formed it, but its wood came from the Tree that gives life and that it will never sing for the unclean. Ohhh!!!!" Hosea clutched at his chest.

"He mourned the lost of such beautiful music many days. The iniquity in him only grew with his hate. When finally he realized his instrument will never play for him, he put an ancient curse on it, a curse so simple in its making. He cursed it to watch! Forcing it to watch his wrath forever. Forcing it to watch his destruction of the Ancient of Day's perfect creation."

Tears were now running down my face. I remembered the feel of its pain. I remembered feeling it gnawing at my insides until its pain became mine. I remember clutching my stomach crying out.

"And although the instrument was forced to watch evil generation after generation, it still would only play for the chosen. One person is chosen in a whole generation. And only that person will it sing for."

He stood and walked around the fire, squatting down before me. Gently he took my hand in his.

"Did you know, it chose King David? Only he would it play for. But soon it began to show him things, things that forced him to cry out. It was he who named it Earth's Cry. Did you know that?" I shook my head as I wiped at tears that wouldn't stop falling.

"Why me?" My words were so low that only he and Melech heard me.

He put his finger underneath my chin, lifting my face so that I was staring into his white gaze and then he smiled.

"Because like King David, sweet child, you're the underdog."

20

THE TALENTED MR. BLACK IS BACK

EARTH

DAY 2 OF THE GREEN EAR FESTIVAL

This morning I woke up in Black's arms. I lay awake for nearly an hour just thinking about Hosea's words to me last night.

"Because like King David, sweet child, you're the underdog." He'd told me as he gently held my chin. "You have been chosen to be the Earth's Cryer for this generation."

I shook my head. "Hosea...I—" I felt ashamed admitting my weakness in front of all these people, but if there was any way he could help me, I needed to try.

"I can't do it. A mistake was made. I'm not strong enough to take what it showed me. I just can't..."

He chuckled as he stood. "You'll be amazed what you can do when the life of someone you love dearly depends on it."

I frowned at his back as he slowly walked around the fire to take his place. "What do you mean?"

He didn't speak for a moment, just stared into the fire with that white gaze. "A threat is coming to someone you love. In order to save them, you must face your fears. In that hour, you will know what to do."

Later that night after everyone had gone home and the house was quiet, Black and I lay on the couch staring into the fire he'd built to knock the chill off the room, lost in our own thoughts.

"I have to tell you something." He whispered close to my ear.

I turned to straddle his lap, I could tell by the worry in his eyes that what he had to tell me was heavy.

"My pop is a griot, so a lot of his stories are just parables, not to be taken literally. Instead, the message is only heard by those who are meant to hear, to everyone else, it's just a catchy tale."

I gently massaged the back of his neck with my fingertips. "Why are you telling me this?"

"Because the father of our people came to see me. When he speaks, his words are always to be taken literally." He picked at one of the ruffles on my skirt staring down at it as he thought about his words.

"He told me something very similar to what my pop told you. He said that if I didn't learn to make fire come from a sword he'd given me when I was a kid, then…" His gaze rose to mine.

"Somebody I loved dearly would be hurt."

"But you can make fire come from anything, right?"

With a lost look on his face he shook his head. "I thought I could, but for some reason I can't. It's as if the sword is of a different place, a place my fire can't reach."

Right in that moment, Hosea's words when he and I first met came back to me. He basically said that temptation was standing in Black's way.

"Maybe you need to face your fears as well."

He shook his head. "There is nothing that I'm afraid of."

I lay my head on his shoulder as he wrapped his arms around me. "Maybe, maybe not. I guess the both of us will soon see."

I could not have imagined how true my words would prove to be.

Early that morning, I left Black sleeping on the couch as I made my way upstairs to Earth's Cry. It still sat on its stand in front of the window. I was almost afraid to touch it. Hosea wasn't lying about the wood. It never needed to be cleansed or polished...It never split or bulged, it was perfect wood.

I remember when I was a little girl my mother told me to always sit it in front of the window so that it could see out to the world. I never questioned her and always sat it in front of the window. I was so fearless back then. I used to sit right next to it with my side resting against it, needing to touch it and look out at the world with it.

But now the only thing I could do was hug myself, tucking my hands underneath my arms. Even now, my being longed to play it. It was calling out to me, it needed me to let it sing. I shook my head as tears came to my eyes.

"I can't...I can't!"

Strong arms came around me and I turned into his embrace. "Shhh, baby. Everything is going to be alright."

"How do you know that?"

"Because we're not going to worry about this thing until the festival is over. And then I'm going to find the father of our people and get some real answers."

I lifted my head and looked up at him. This was his third time mentioning the father of his people.

"Who is this man? Who is the father of your people?"

"The Preacher."

I frowned. "He's a preacher?" I didn't mean to sound disheartened, but...Yeah, that was kind of disappointing. If I had a penny for every crooked preacher out there, I would be a billionaire.

He chuckled shaking his head. "No, not in the sense you're thinking of. Nobody really knows his name. He never tells anyone. When asked, he simply tells people he's a Quheleth, nothing more, nothing less." He sat me down on the bed.

"I think he won't tell us who he is, because he knows that if the world knew the truth about him, they would make a god of him. And he's real big on all praise going to The Ancient of Days and The Son of Adam?"

I was confused. "But why would people try and worship him. Who is he?"

He shrugged. "There are a lot of speculations of course. My grandfather thinks he's Lazarus."

My eyes widened. "Lazarus? As in the man the Messiyah rose from the dead?"

He nodded. "One and the same. But there are others who think he's Enoch."

"Who is Enoch?"

"Enoch was a man who lived before the flood. He was Adam's great, great, great, great, grandson. I think…Scripture say's because he was a good friend to The Ancient of Days, he was blessed not to see death."

Okay, now he was starting to freak me out. "Are you saying that you think this man, the father of your people has lived on the earth since before the flood? That's impossible."

He lifted and eyebrow. "Is it? Do you believe in the Bible?"

"Of course." I felt like I was experiencing deju vu. I'd just had this same conversation with his grandfather.

"Well, in the book of Matthew, chapter sixteen, verse twenty-eight, the Messiyah tells his disciples that there are some standing there amongst them who shall never see death at all until they see the Son of Adam coming in His reign."

I stared at him with my mouth hanging open. I could not believe he'd just quoted scripture to me. He's the biggest heathen I know.

"Wow! I'm amazed that you know the Bible so intimately."

He chuckled. "Please, Hosea is my grandfather. I'd read it twice front to back before I was ten."

My mouth dropped even further. "Are you kidding me?!"

A grin came to his handsome face. "See, I'm not as bad as you thought I was, huh?" The only thing I could do was shake my head. I'm not going to lie, I was looking at him in a different light. I've been telling myself for the last ten years I was going to read the Bible front to back. Sis. Dinah had been trying to get me to do it since I was twelve. And I hadn't gotten around to doing it yet.

And here Melech...Casino boss Melech, has read it twice. What the world! When you think you know somebody!

"Good, I'm glad I could leave you speechless, all those hours of being forced to sit still and read the Good Word has paid off. Anyway, back to the black cowboy."

I grabbed his arm. "Did you say, black cowboy?"

He nodded. "Yeah, the Preacher...He wears this black cowboy hat and long black duster, cowboy boots, spurs and all."

"I know him!" I put my hand over my mouth. I didn't mean to yell that. It was still very early and the house was still asleep. In my excitement my volume kind of got away from me.

It was his turn to frown. "You know the Preacher?"

I could not stop the laughter that bubbled up from my throat. What is the irony?

"Yeah, I know him. He helped me kidnap you."

"Really?"

"I kid you not. Bria and I was having a hard time getting your big body in the car once you fell asleep. The Preacher appeared out of nowhere and asked us if we needed help. Then he just walked to the car and lifted you in the passenger seat for me."

He chuckled, shaking his head. "Figures…"

"So, you're telling me that he's Lazarus, the one the Messiyah loved so much he brought back from the dead?"

"I'm not telling you anything. Our people have been trying to guess at his identity for as far back as our records go."

"But is he the same man that has existed since as far back as your records go?"

He nodded his head. "His appearance has never changed. My grandfather saw him when he was a child and he looked exactly the same, hasn't aged a day."

I shook my head. "Had I known all the supernatural baggage you came with I would have never kidnapped you. My life was simple before you came in it."

He chuckled pulling me close in a one arm hug. "This coming from the woman who owns the Devil's violin. Or did you forget that before you started throwing stones."

I gave into my laughter and it felt good. "Touché."

"Listen." He said holding my head in his hands looking into my eyes. "I know what my grandfather said was troubling. But I don't want you to worry, I will handle this. I want you to enjoy the rest of the festival. Nothing bad is going to happen."

"How do you know that?" I muttered picking invisible lint from his jeans.

"Because I'm not going to let it happen. No matter what I have to do, I'm going to keep you and Rain safe. That's my word." I stared into his eyes.

I believed him.

I believed he would do whatever it took to keep us safe. What that would be, I don't know. But I believe he would do it.

"I have a question."

He grinned. "What's that?"

I looked back at that invisible lint I was picking off his pants so that he couldn't see the laughter in my eyes.

"Who's going to keep you and your men safe from Bruce and his friends?"

Mock fear came to his eyes. "That's a good damn question."

And it was…

The answer…

Nobody!

For the next three days, Bruce and his friends continued to administer a butt whipping on Black and his men. We laughed so much that it was easy to forget Hosea's dire warning. Black and the fellas didn't just lose, they were the sorest losers on this side of heaven.

They accused Bruce and his friends of cheating and accused the referee and Hosea of showing favoritism. Black at one point, got so mad that he accused everybody including me of plotting on him to make him look bad during an obstacle course that involved wall climbing, crawling through mud, walking a tight rope, and numerous other obstacles designed to test one's endurance.

And look bad he did. After that race he threw away all his cigars. Said he was done smoking. He was smart enough to know that they were the reason he couldn't keep up with his eighteen-year-old cousin without feeling like he was getting ready to lose a lung.

That was also the night he made love to me again…A night I will never forget for as long as I live.

So, pull up a chair and grab yourself a glass of wine, for you out there who don't drink, now is the time to cuddle up with a nice steaming cup of tea. I'm going to tell you how that amazing night went down…

EDWINA FORT

EARTH

DAY 5 OF THE GREEN EAR FESTIVAL

After we all got back to Hosea's from the festival that night, Black pretended to pout because the next day Hosea would be announcing the winners of the games, and it was no secret that Black and his men were not it.

Of course, the fellas were teasing him pretty good, telling him that tomorrow he was going to lose his girl to his little cousin. Even Bruce had gotten in on the fun, asking me where I wanted to live once he and I got married.

And although Black in good nature put up with all the teasing, I sensed something else under the surface, and I wanted to reassure him that he didn't have anything to worry about. At least that's what I told myself.

But between me and you, I was h-o-r-n-y.

You see over the last couple of nights, Melech and I have slept either on Hosea's couch or on the floor in front of the fire. Because that little twin-size bed upstairs was not big enough for Black, let alone the both of us. And he'd told me flat out that he wasn't sleeping apart from me another night. He said the night he had at the casino, had been miserable.

So, because I hadn't been ready to go home with him, I agreed to sleep with him here in Hosea's living room, and it's only so much a girl can take. Lying next to all that muscled, chocolate goodness night after night has taken its toll on me.

And it didn't help that at some point during the night last night, our lips ended up battling in that dance as old as time. Things got pretty heated. The only thing that kept it from going all the way was the thought that Hosea was sleeping in a room not too far away.

Needless to say, he and I had some unfinished business.

Now there was an art to this. I couldn't just walk up to the man and say, hey brotha, I need you to finish what you started this morning. No...I had too much pride for that. It had to seem like it was his idea.

Yep, you guessed it, I needed to *play* hard to get.

Well... at least harder to get. I had my pride to think about after all.

So, this is how I did it. Folks around these parts were tired of fair food, so I came back a little early to make a big pot of chicken alfredo, garlic bread and a huge salad. But first, I jumped in the shower and washed all the dust from the fair off me. Then I moisturized myself with my body butter that made me smell edible.

I put on the cream-colored lace panty and bra set that Panda insisted I get. So glad I'd listened to her. Then I slid into this cream colored boho maxi dress that had cost Black a fortune but looked amazing on me. It fell loosely on my body in a way that would accentuate my curves deliciously, but classily. Plus, it buttoned up in the front for easy access.

Hey! Don't judge me... Y'all just don't know how badly I need this man's loving right now. Hell, I didn't even know what had come over me. I just woke up this morning with a burning need that only he could extinguish.

I didn't bother putting on any shoes, I felt my sexiest barefoot. When I was all put together, I moved on to the next stage in operation drive Black insane with lust while playing hard to get. A good meal...

But first I made a quick sandwich for Kelly. The little heart was always too sick to leave her bed. Once I got her squared away, I put together the meal. I'd thought I made too much, but when Black and his crew walked through the door, joined by Bruce, Hosea, Rain, Tonya and Dan—

Poor Dan, let me pause my story to tell you guys about what happened to poor Dan really quick. I found out from Kelly that Dan didn't like me too much. I had noticed he was very short when we passed each other in the hall and what not, but I hadn't thought too much about it.

She said because of me, Black was sticking around the house longer than usual. And he was. He rarely went back to the Big House. If he did, it was just to change or something like that, but then he would come right back here to Hosea's.

She asked me why I was staying here in this dump when that great big fancy mansion was waiting for me. I told her I didn't know, for the time being I just felt more comfortable here. She said everybody feels that way around Hosea. It was something about him that attracted people, but she told me I needed to be brave and go back to my own house.

I laughed and asked her what the big deal was. She said with Black being around so much, it has forced Dan to go out of his way to avoid him. Still laughing I asked her why he needed to avoid him. She said if Black knew that Dan was sitting around playing on the PlayStation all the time instead of getting a job to take care of her and the baby, he would beat him to within inches of his life.

I laughed really good after that, 'cause I didn't believe it was that extreme. I know Hosea and Bruce had joked about it, but I just didn't believe it was as big of a deal as they all were making it out to be.

Boy...was I wrong.

Yesterday, as I was walking up to the door, poor Dan came flying out to land on the ground on his neck.

Black stormed out the house after him looking madder than a junk yard dog, those flames blazing in his eyes.

"Let me find out you sitting on your ass again and I will kick the sh*t out of you!"

Dan lay balled up on the ground shivering in fear, in the same position Bruce had been in the other day. But hey, I didn't blame either of them. It was scary as hell being on the other end of those eyes, not knowing if your body was getting ready to go up in flames.

"I'm sorry, cuz…I'm sorry!"

"Get your punk ass up and go get a job. You got one month to have a place for your girl and your baby, or I'm gon' do her a favor and get rid of your useless ass, so that maybe she can find the real thing and not have to spend the rest of her life in love with a piece of sh*t like you!"

He looked at Horse who had been leaning against his car sweeting talking a woman that had two little babies with her. "I don't want to see him again till he has a job." And then he turned and stormed back in the house.

I knew he was mad 'cause he didn't even acknowledge me. I was beginning to learn something about those eyes. When them bad boys were blazing, the best thing to do was to let Mr. Man cool on off.

Anyway, Dan wasn't completely useless. Apparently, he was really good at fixing cars. The local mechanic has been trying to get him to come and work at his shop since he was sixteen, but as you know, our little friend Dan would rather play video games.

However, that's not the case anymore. Can you guys guess where he's working? Yep, you got it. He's now the not so happy employee of the local mechanic…

Okay, where was I?

Oh yes, dinner…

I'd thought I'd made too much food, but I hadn't. By the time all those folks got done there wasn't a noodle left.

During dinner I kept feeling Black's eyes on me, he watched me shamelessly and he didn't care who saw him. Every opportunity he got he was touching me. I was standing by the fridge when he opened it to grab a bottle of water and put his big warm hand on my lower back when he did.

But it wasn't until I stood at the sink finishing off the dishes that I found out what he really was thinking. Strong arms wrapped around me from behind and Black's delicious cologne filled my senses, waking up the feelings that had been impatiently lying dormant inside me all day. His big body blocked out the rest of the house, it was as if he'd drawn a cocoon around us.

"Thank you for the food, baby, it was really good." He kissed the spot just below my ear. Mmmm...that felt so good.

"Why don't you let Bruce and Tonya clean the kitchen and you rest a bit."

I shook my head. "Naw, I need the distraction."

Y'all see that...You see what I just did?

He moaned in my ear. "Rumor has it, I'm going to lose my girl tomorrow."

I had to bite my bottom lip to tame my grin.

"Have you heard the rumor?" He asked me.

I shook my head. "Nope, but if I was you, I wouldn't worry about it."

"I'm trying not to worry about it, because I know my girl. She won't leave me for a kid. It's just that..."

He let his words trail off as he opened mouth kissed that spot just below my ear. I stifled a moan as I squeezed my thighs together. Whatever I was holding in my hands slipped through my fingers and my sudsy hands clutched the sink.

"Wh—" I had to clear my throat. My voice was thick with lust. "What can your girl do to reassure you that you have nothing to worry about?"

He moaned in my ear again before he took my lobe in his mouth. My eyes drifted closed. I was trying to hold it together, seeing as to how there were a bunch of people in the living room. And although they couldn't see what he was doing to me, Hosea's opened floor plan still enabled them to see Black's back, and the fact that he had me pressed against the sink.

"Maybe if my girl let me take her back to our house and make love to her in our bed, maybe then my heart will be at ease."

I licked my lips to cover up the smile of success that tried to break through. When I had it under control, I turned in his arms so that my breasts were pressed against his chest. Looking up at him with inviting eyes I shrugged. Right then my dress fell off my shoulder, I couldn't have planned that as perfectly as it happened.

His heated gaze lowered to my exposed skin.

"Maybe she could do that. But what are you going to do to reassure her? Why should she be doing all the reassuring?" I pouted my lips like a little girl.

He grinned…Damn, he is so fine!

"I'll be willing to do a number of things to reassure her, the first would be making sure she comes apart for me repeatedly until she begs me to stop because she thinks she's going to die if she comes again."

I lifted an eyebrow. "Wow! That's quite a feat. Do you think you can pull something like that off?"

His grin turned to pure wickedness. "I don't know. It's been so long since I held a woman in my hands. Maybe I've forgotten what to do."

I held my head back and cracked up. He needs to quit it.

"Then why should she take the risk, if you may not be able to deliver all that you've promised?" I asked when my laughter died down.

"Because I'm a f***ing overachiever, always have been. If I can't make it happen, I'll die trying." He said the last in a 50 Cent voice that had me laughing again.

He leaned down and kissed my exposed neck. "I love to see you laugh."

My laughter turned into a moan. I put my hand on his chest and pushed him back a bit. I was tired of him teasing me, I was ready to feel the full storm that was Melech's lovemaking, enough was enough!

"I think that's good enough for her. Let's do it!"

His devious grin let me know he was very aware of the turmoil that was happening inside of me, and he had set out to tease me into admitting my hunger for him. Oh well...so much for playing hard to get. He took my hand and when we turned from the sink, everybody in the living room suddenly got really busy doing random useless things.

Including Hosea, who was now dusting off the arm of the chair where he sat.

"Ha, very funny." Black told them as he pulled me towards the door. "Tonya—"

"Don't worry, boss, I've got this. I'm already running bathwater for Rain."

He nodded. "Good job."

I blushed because he was so focused on that door, he didn't say anything to anybody else. So I figured it was my job to do so.

"Okay...I guess I'll see you guys later."

"I guess you will." Hosea said giving me a knowing look. "Do you want me to send one of the children to get your shoes?"

"She doesn't need them." Black threw back without stopping.

"Tell Rain I said she'd better beh—" I began, but Hosea cut me off.

"Enjoy yourself, daughter. Rain is a good child. And right now, she's not thinking about you, so don't you be worrying about her."

I was ashamed to say that was true. She and her little friends had gone upstairs after dinner and I haven't seen them since. Of course I heard them, it sounded as if they were going to come through the ceiling with all the bumping…

Anyway… I waved one more time to everyone as Abner slipped out the door ahead of us. At that point I think I was a little nervous. This will be my first time going back to the Big House, the house that Melech called ours. My first time sleeping in that Japanese style bed on top of the dais. My first time being made love to on the Japanese style bed on top of the dais.

On our way to Black's truck, his arm suddenly appeared around my waist as he pulled me back against him, my feet were barely touching the ground, they actually dangled on the top of his boots.

"You not changing your mind, are you?"

Biting my bottom lip, I shook my head, trying my best to smile up at him. He studied my face for a bit.

"Why are you afraid of me?" He was beginning to frown. I quickly turned in his arms palming his beautiful face between my palms. I've learned something else about my strong man, he was very self-conscious about his gift if it caused me to look at him in fear. He really didn't like to appear to be a monster in my eyes.

"It's not you. It's the Big House."

"Minx, I know being around Pop is comforting, but we can't stay with him forever, we have a home."

"I know, it's just that, it's such a big house…"

He rested his forehead against mine. "Yeah, it is. But you can do whatever you need to do to make it your big house. I want you to be comfortable there, I want you to make it feel like your old place over the bookstore."

I smiled at him, he thought he was so slick. "My old place?"

"Mmmhhhmmm…" He leaned in and gave me a brief kiss on my lips. "Come on, let's go get to know our bedroom. After tonight, you'll feel right at home. That's a promise."

Ten minutes later, we pulled the truck into the eight-car garage, except it was like no home garage I'd ever seen. It looked like a showroom. I couldn't see what every vehicle parked inside was, but there was a royal blue one that caught my attention instantly. The doors sat open like wings.

"What?!" He asked holding up his hands, when he saw me giving him the side eye. "A man has to have toys."

Chuckling, I shook my head.

"Ohhh! There are my babies!" Ms. Lily cried as soon as we walked through the door that led into the house from the garage. She came barreling towards us with her arms opened. Black opened his arms for her, but she practically pushed him aside to get to me.

"There you are, Misses." She gushed as she wrapped me into her soft embrace. "I was so worried you didn't like me."

Black still stood where she'd shoved him with his arms open with a surprised look on his face. Laughing I remembered what Horse had told me about her spoiling him. He was genuinely shocked she had pushed him aside for me.

I hugged her back as I stuck my tongue out at him. "Oh no, Ms. Lily, why would you think such a thing?"

"Well, you were so unhappy when you first got here. And I'd spent a lot of time trying to get the house ready for you and the little Misses, but it didn't look as if you liked any of it." With her arm wrapped around me, she guided me toward the kitchen away from him.

I looked back and watched him and Abner walk toward the stairs. He winked at me before he disappeared from sight.

"No, sweetheart, I was very happy with everything, I—I was just a little tired, a lot of things had gone on that day."

Ms. Lily patted my hand. "I know, dear, I should have allowed you to rest first before overloading you with all the components of this big place." She hugged me again. "But I'm so glad you're back. I get so lonely all by myself. Can I get you some tea? Are you hungry? Would like a glass of wine?"

"Wine would be nice." I told her chuckling at her enthusiasm to make me happy. Wine was just the thing to knock the edge off my nerves.

"Red or white?"

"White…"

I didn't want to be rude to Ms. Lily, but I had to ask her if I could take my wine to go. There was plenty of time for her and me to shoot the breeze. Meanwhile, there was a very sexy man waiting for me upstairs.

Surprisingly, she understood completely, and after showing me that her room was located just off the kitchen should I need anything, sent me on my way. By the time I made it to the bedroom I had drained that glass of wine.

I knocked twice on the door before I opened it a bit and slipped in. Coming from somewhere overhead was the sound of Floetry's *Imagination*. Not fair, he knows I love me some Floetry. The lights had been dimmed in a way that made it look as if candles were lit. He'd pulled the tategu, the Japanese style screen doors open so that a nice night time breeze blew in from the private garden, as well as the sweet fragrance of jasmine and the relaxing sound of the fountains and the river.

Oh yeah, a girl could get used to that.

It sounded as if he was in the shower, so I stood at the opened tategu and looked out at the garden. It was so peaceful… And completely private. Our only audience was the raging river that was located on the other side and the big round moon in the sky. I could see myself sitting in this garden for many hours doing a number of things, reading a good book, thinking… making love.

Chuckling at myself, I shook my head. Goodness, I had one thing on the brain. Right then the shower shut off and I turned so that I could see that one thing as he made his way out of the bathroom.

Y'all, before I knew what was happening a moan escaped my lips. Black walked out that bathroom with just a towel wrapped around his waist looking good enough to eat. When he saw me standing at the opening of the garden he smiled.

"There you are. I thought I was going to have to come and steal you away from your new best friend."

I pushed off the wall and sashayed over to the bed. "Jealous?"

"Maybe." He said coming to stand right behind me as he watched my hips sway as I walk up the stairs to the bed. I slowly pulled up my dress up my thighs and making sure to arch my back so that my butt poked out really good, I crawled teasingly to the center of it before I turned on my back, reclining on my raised elbows.

Without pulling my dress down I drew my legs up and looked at him through my opened thighs. He still stood at the bottom of the stairs shamelessly enjoying the show. The hunger in his eyes was turning me on even more.

"You are such a f***ing minx." He grumbled as he followed me up the stairs. When he began to slowly crawl towards me, he reminded me so much of the big black cat that shadowed him. Speaking of Abner...

I put my foot in the center of his chest, stopping him.

"Wait!" I yelled throwing my head back. Laughter bubbled from my lips, he did not appreciate being stopped. He wanted what he wanted right now.

"What is it, Minx?" The way he growled those words was so damn hot. I think I was really enjoying teasing him.

"Where is Abner?" I blinked at him innocently.

He looked at me as if I had gone simple. "You stopped me to ask me where Abner is?"

I bit my bottom lip to keep from cheesing too hard and nodded.

"Mmmhhhmm."

"Tell me something, baby. Do you like this pretty new dress you're wearing?"

I bit my lip harder.

"Mmmmhhhmm."

"I figured you did, 'cause you look really sexy in it. However, if you don't remove your little foot from my chest, I'm going to rip the dress from your body and ravish you."

My mouth opened in mock surprise as I lowered my foot. "Shame on you, Mr. Black, I was simply asking a question."

He brought his hand to my leg and began to gently rub up, pushing my dress up along the way.

"Shame on you, Minx for thinking I'm going to allow you to get away with all this teasing you've been doing all evening."

"What are you going to do about it?"

"First I'm going to get you out this dress." Wrapping one arm around my back he lifted me to a sitting position and then lifted the dress over my head tossing it to the side. Oh well…I guess we'll use the buttons next time.

I lay flat on my back so that he could get a good look at my sexy panty and bra set. As his heated gaze raked over me, his body reacted in such a way that made me so glad I'd listened to Panda.

"Damn, Earth, you are so f***ing beautiful." His hands gently trailed down my side.

I squeaked in surprise when he suddenly flipped me so that I was lying on my stomach. And then his warm body was there over me and his lips at the base of my neck. Inhaling, I closed my eyes and gave myself up to his masterful touch.

He started kissing me at the base of my neck and began working his way down. The feel of his warm mouth on my back was so erotic. By the time he turned me over to my back, he'd somehow removed my bra and panties. His mouth was so intoxicating I hadn't even been aware he'd done it.

He took in my naked body before his gaze came back to mine. The grin that appeared on his face let me know I was in danger. "You asked me what I was going to do about all the teasing you've been doing tonight." He leaned down and gently kissed the tip of my breast.

"Tonight, I'm going to teach you a very important lesson. Don't stir up my hunger if you can't handle my appetite."

He lowered his head to my breast again, but this time there was no gentle kissing. His mouth was hungry, and he proceeded to teach me that lesson he'd spoke of. After my world shattered the first time, and he was nowhere near finished, I thought to myself, I can handle his appetite.

But then he was inside me, filling me until I thought I would burst, driving into my heat until I begged for mercy. But the Talented Mr. Black showed no mercy that night. That night, he had a point to prove. That night, he wanted me to know without a shadow of a doubt that I was his and no other's. That night, he took me until I told him that if I came again, I would surely die.

21

LET THEM WITH EYES SEE

On the sixth day, Alohim made man, perfect in Our image...in Our image, he made man, PERFECT, on the sixth day...

— GENESIS 1: 26

EARTH

DAY 6 OF THE GREEN EAR FESTIVAL

Because you guys are my friends and have hung in there with me during the telling of my story, I feel I must warn you at this point. My tale is getting ready to take a dark, gory twist, one that is not for the faint of heart. But be encouraged, from the dark shined forth a light that will forever change the way I see the world. And once your eyes are opened, they can never be closed again.

You see, Hosea was right the evening by the fire. He was not speaking in parables, but simple truths. Well, at least one part I know for sure. When he said I was going to be forced to face my fears, I just...

I'd hoped for more time...

That morning started off so *huntingly* beautiful. I say *huntingly* because there was something in the air. Like the deer sensed the hunter, I myself could sense change. That morning when I woke up in Black's arms, the scent of it was heavy in the air, lingering just at the door, waiting for just the right moment to barge in and make its presence known.

Quietly, I eased out of the bed and made my way to the bathroom to take care of a few morning essentials, including a shower. Standing under the hot water I waited for it to wash away the scent of change, but it never did, it still lingered in the air, taunting me.

And I know I wasn't crazy, because Black felt it too. He came into the bathroom and took care of a few of his morning essentials. Neither of us spoke to the other. I just stood there under the hot water begging it to wash away the smell that always brought pain to me.

When he was done, he opened the glass door of the shower and stepped in behind me. Without saying a word, he lifted me in his arms and entered me. My head fell back against the smooth warm stones of the shower wall as he loved me as if this would be the last time.

He caused my world to shatter twice before he found his release. Then still without speaking, we washed each other clean, staring into the other's eyes. You see, we both could sense change in the air, and we both knew that there was a possibility sorrow waited on the other side, but neither of us wanted to speak it out in the open, so we just used our eyes to say what our mouths were not brave enough to.

Hand and hand, we walked back into the bedroom to find

that Ms. Lily had left us two surprises, breakfast in bed, and laid out on the leather box ottoman was hand-sewn linen his and hers matching garments. There is no other word that could describe the creations but two works of art.

"These are amazing!" I cried as I picked up the note she'd left for us.

"I saw you in a dream the first night the King disappeared." I began to read. *"I was never worried like the others because I knew he had found love. In my dream you two were wearing these garments. I woke up and instantly sketched them out so that I wouldn't lose their image and the next morning, I got to work. Please accept these as a gift from me. I am honored to be allowed to serve the two of you."*

By the time I'd finished reading, there were tears in my eyes. "I don't know what to say."

Black chuckled. "How about thank you the next time you see her?"

I playfully punched him in the arm. "Noooo! Really! I was hoping for something more insightful."

He shook his head as he held up the tunic she'd made for him. It was made in the style of the chiefs of old.

"I'll leave all the mushy stuff to the two of you."

I laughed, this coming from the man who'd just made love to me as if his very life depended on it. I held up the beautiful gown to my body, although it was clearly Native in design, there was also an African feel to it as well.

"It's so very pretty. I love the bead work. It must have taken her days to do it."

He nodded. "That pattern was traditionally worn by the wife of the chief."

He was studying me. Waiting for my response to what he'd just said. I smiled.

"I love it."

He visibly exhaled. "Yeah, Ms, Lily is something of a

phenomenon when it comes to designing clothes. She could go and work anywhere she wants and be famous in a year." He took the dress out of my hands and placed it back on the ottoman next to his garments, then pulled me past the breakfast that was waiting for us to the bed.

"But she refuses to go. She says the women in her family have always known how to use needle and thread, but the true honor for them is serving their chief."

"Is that so?" I asked as he lay back in the bed lifting me to straddle his lap. His muscles flexed so gorgeously underneath that beautiful brown skin.

He nodded. "That's so."

As he spoke, he snatched our towels away and lowered me down on his strength. I sucked in my breath as he filled my moist heat, pleasure so intense shot through me.

As I looked down at his handsome face my gaze blurred with tears from the all-consuming desire.

"How can I serve you, my King?" My words were breathy as I struggled to keep from crying out.

"Dance for me, Minx."

My head dropped back and my cries filled the room as I danced for my King…

We eventually got around to eating our breakfast that had long turned cold and got dressed. Because this was the closing day of the festival, Melech had several duties to perform, including congratulating his little cousin and his team for winning the harvest games.

Ms. Lily came to help me get dressed. The garment she created was quite complicated and I was clueless as to how I was supposed to wear it. As she helped me with it, she told me what each piece was worn for and what the bead work meant.

Then she helped me with my hair. Guess what. Ms. Lily knew how to do the Pocahontas braids far better than I or Betty. She even interweaved beads that matched my dress into them. When she was finished, I stood in the mirror staring at a stranger. I looked like an African Seminole princess.

"Come, let's see what the King thinks." She said practically gushing as we left out the bathroom.

Black looked so regal in his outfit, he reminded me of the African Kings of the past. The fact that he could look so, even though he'd nodded off on the ottoman waiting for us to get finished, Abner asleep at his feet said it all.

"Men." Ms. Lily muttered next to me. I knew why he was tired. Neither of us had gotten much sleep.

I chuckled, "Exactly."

"Melech," She patted his leg. "The Misses is ready."

He opened his eyes and grinned at me. As if he'd just realized he'd nodded off, he sat up straighter coming fully awake.

Now he was really taking me in. "Wow! You look so good, baby!"

I bit my lip as a pleased grin spread on my face. I felt good.

"Hurry now!" Ms. Lily said clapping her hands together. "You two are going to be late and Hosea is going to blame me. Come now, you must be off!"

* * *

Rain finally missed me enough to give me some shugga. It was the first thing she did when she saw me.

"Mommy!" She cried breaking away from Tonya to run to me. "Where was you?"

I smiled. "I slept at the Big House."

Her eyes got wide. "Is my car still there and my princess bed?"

"Yes, sweetheart, all of your things are still there." I laughed. The cares of children.

She nodded. "I want to sleep there tonight with you and bring my friends too."

"Umm, it may be too soon for you to start having sleepovers."

"Can they at least come and play sometime?"

"Absolutely, Hobbit, your friends can come over whenever you want them to." Black said coming behind her swooping her up in his arms. She threw back her head and giggled as he loudly kissed her cheek, tickling her with his beard.

Then she wrapped her little arms around his neck. "Can Hosea and Tonya come too?"

"Of course." He told her before kissing her nose. As soon as he put her back on her feet she ran off toward the children's area. But this time she stopped and turned, giving us one last wave before disappearing. We waved back at her and Tonya who ran after her.

Let me tell you guys something about Tonya, she was worth her weight in gold. I needed to talk to Black and see what he was paying her. Whatever it was, he needed to double it. She was very good with Rain. She kept up with her and played with her. She even read to her before bed.

I've never had anybody help me out with Rain like that. Never thought I would be the one to have a nanny. But now that I had Tonya, I'll fight to the death to keep her. LOL!!!

Naw, I'm only kidding.

Or...am...I?

"Here daughter, I brought your violin." Hosea said coming to sit next to me where I'd been sitting watching Black hand out medals for the biggest squash competition. He was such a good leader, although I knew he was bored out his mind studying the different vegetables his people were so proud of, you couldn't tell one bit. He gave each vegetable and its owner his undivided attention, listening carefully as they rattled on about their different growing techniques and thought very carefully before he chose the winners---

Wait! Did Hosea just say he had my violin? I turned to look at him and sure enough, he was holding Earth's Cry. My hands reached for it instantly, taking it from him.

"But why? I didn't need it." I couldn't help the fact that there was irritation in my voice.

I threw the strap over my shoulder securing the violin to my back. This was habit, seeing him touching it had almost given me a heart attack. I was suddenly very irritated. Why did he even feel a need to bring it in the first place?

"Be calm, child." He said placing his hand on my arm. I wanted to slap his hand away. "Be calm, Earth."

As if he could feel my irritation, Black looked at me from the judging table, he narrowed his gaze when he saw Earth's Cry strapped on my shoulder. Then his angry gaze shot to his grandfather.

"I know the two of you do not understand now, but before the sun goes down this evening, you will have thanked me." And then he got up and disappeared into the crowd.

"He doesn't know how to mind his business." Black growled a little later as we made our way to the area where the harvest game winners were going to be announced. "Do you want me to take you back to the house so that you can put it away?"

I shook my head. "No, it's here now, might as well leave it."

He stopped, taking my face in his hands. And just like that, a whole fairground of people disappeared as I stared into that dark gaze of his.

"You sure? I want you to be happy. If that violin makes you unhappy, we can run it back to the Big House."

I stood on my toes and gently kissed his lips. "Earth's Cry does not make me unhappy. It's a part of me, like your fire is apart of you. It's just that every time I touch it, I think about what it showed me the last time I played it."

"What did it show you?"

I opened my mouth to tell him, but right then, Horse and Big Troy joined us.

"Sorry to interrupt, but they are calling for us up on the dais." Horse put his hand on Black's shoulder. "Come on, brother, we're not making this walk of shame alone."

Black leaned in and kissed my lips. "I'll be right back..."

"Go ahead. I'll tell you later!" When he was sure I was okay he nodded and walked away with his friends.

"Hey, Earth! Over here!" Panda called from where she had saved me a seat on the bleachers right in the front.

"Girl, y'all look so cute in y'all matching outfits. Ms. Lily made those, didn't she?"

I chuckled as I eased unto the bleachers next to her. "Yeah, how did you know?"

"Girl please, everybody and they mama trying to get Ms. Lily to make them an outfit. I've been trying to get her to design a dress for me. But, noooo! She can't do anything for anybody but her precious Melech." She lightly tapped my hand and smiled.

"And now, apparently, his precious Earth."

Laughing, I shook my head at her as they began the ceremony. By this being the main event, there was a whole program set up around the judging. Black and his men, and Bruce and his friends all sat on a slightly raised dais as drummers and dancers that wore elaborate feathered headpieces and deer-skinned costumes performed for them.

The next part of the ceremony I think was a surprise to Black. The Board of Elders, including Hosea stood in front of the dais and one by one told him how proud they were of his leadership and how it was an honor to serve him.

But it was as Hosea was speaking that it looked as if his eyes watered.

"Grandson, I know it seems as if I'm always nagging you. A benefit only I am allowed since I am grandfather to the chief." He cut his eyes at the other board members causing the audience to chuckle.

"But I do it because of what the father of our people told me when I was only a boy."

Wow!

The other night Black told me that outside of being reprimanded for referring to him as the Great One, Hosea had never told him what else the Preacher said to him when he'd visited him as a boy. And now after all these years, he was finally getting ready to tell him.

"He told me I would raise a great warrior who will guide our people through the troubled times. He said a ravisher was coming that will destroy all, and that you will be the one to lead us out of this destruction." Hosea shook his head.

"But that first, you will be tested to the very limit of your endurance." He turned to the chair behind him picking something up from it. When he turned around, he held a big sword in his hands.

At first Melech looked shocked that Hosea had the sword, but then his grandfather started speaking again and this is where it looked as if his eyes watered.

"I look at you son and I see hope for the future. I know that evil will not win, no matter how hard it tries." He put the sword in Black's hands, but he didn't let it go. Instead he stood looking directly into his grandson's eyes.

"I believe in you. I believe that you will do what it takes to become the man we *all* need you to be. I am so very proud to be your grandfather."

The crowd cheered, touched by Hosea's words. I stood to my

feet clapping. I believed in him too! I believed that he was going to conquer whatever it is that was standing in his way to achieve his ultimate greatness.

Panda whistled, coming to her feet next to me. "That's my nephew!" She yelled. Soon the whole crowd joined us on our feet, cheering for their chief.

A smile broke out on Black's face before he wrapped one arm around his grandfather pulling him into a hug. Hosea hugged him back for a while before he threw up his hands silencing the crowd.

"Okay! Okay! Now, that's out the way. It's time to get to the nitty-gritty…What we've all been waiting for."

The crowd let out another round of cheers. Hosea reached out his hand toward me.

"Come, daughter."

Blushing, I quickly shook my head, no. But Panda wasn't having any of that.

"Aww, don't get shy on us now!" She said trying to pull me up from the bench. I refused to budge, but the crowd began to encourage me to go to him.

Hosea grinned. "You might as well come on up here, we can't proceed until you do."

"Okay!" I cried.

And I do mean cried. I stood pouting like Rain. The last time Hosea had me in front this crowd he embarrassed the hell out of me. It felt like fire was on my neck as I walked toward the raised dais with all those people staring at me.

Hosea turned to look at the men that were seated on the dais. "Why are you still here? Scram so that the lady can sit down."

Black and his men, and Bruce and his friends all stood, taking their chairs with them. Then a make-shift throne that looked as if it was a creation of Hosea's little ones was brought to sit in their place.

"Daughter…" He said holding his hand out for mine, when I took it, he guided me to the throne. "Please be seated."

Black and his men stood lined up in a straight line going diagonal to the right of Hosea, Black standing closest to him. Bruce and his friends were lined up in a straight line going diagonal to his left, Bruce being the closest to him. It kind of reminded me of how the bride and groom's wedding party lined up for the wedding.

I bit my lip, looking at Black for help. He smiled nodding his head slightly as if to tell me I had this.

"As you know, our two great warriors were competing for the hand of this fair maiden." Hosea began to speak causing the crowd to erupt in cheers. He held up his hand bringing silence once again.

"And as you know, it didn't go so well for one of our warriors." The crowd began to boo. Black held his head back and laughed as Horse gave him a pitying pat on the shoulder.

"There was an obvious loser of these games." The crowd began to boo Hosea louder. He held up both hands.

"There, there…I'm not a complete monster. As stated before, the choice is in the hands of our beautiful maiden. She could redeem this warrior today…and spare him a great deal of embarrassment." I bit my lip to keep from laughing. Hosea is a mess. Meanwhile Black was now giving me the puppy dog eyes.

"Of course, there is only one way. She could very well choose to marry him. Because we all know he didn't win her hand in these games in any way." The crowd booed Hosea again…

"Alright, have it your way." He told them. "I'll step to the side and give this unfortunate warrior the opportunity to redeem himself."

The crowd shot to their feet cheering. Bruce ran to the stand and retrieved a black suede box from his mother, then ran back to stand in his place, box in hand.

What the world? I looked at him trying to determine what that was all about, but right then, Black began to walk toward me looking like the King he was born to be. When he got to the dais in front of me, he went down to one knee. The crowd was now going crazy cheering him on.

He tried to tame his smile as he reached for my hand.

Oh God! Oh God! This thing was happening!

At first, he didn't speak. He just stared down at my hand that he held in his, gently rubbing the back of it with his finger.

When he lifted his gaze to mine, all traces of humor were gone. Instantly he pulled me into that gaze, causing everybody to disappear. What kind of voodoo is that? He's the only one that has ever been able to do that to me. At this moment it felt like it was just he and I.

"Did you know that before you came in my life, I can't remember the last time I laughed." He shook his head as he thought about it. "I'm sure I laughed at some point, I just can't remember when."

I wasn't going to make it… Tears were already beginning to fill my eyes and the man had just begun to speak.

Damn! I am such a crybaby.

"Before you, my world seemed gray. You came into my life splashing yellow paint all over everything, and I realized that yellow paint was light…your light. And now…" He shook his head as his eyes began to plead with me.

"And now, I don't know if I can survive without it. Please baby, don't make me go back to my gray world, please. I need you to help me stay in the light." He paused for just a moment.

"Marry me, Minx…and make me the happiest man on this planet."

I was shaking so badly by the time he was finished, my teeth were chattering. How was it possible this man had penetrated all my walls and made it to my heart? He may have really sucked at these harvest games, but he was the conquering warrior here, because he'd done what no man ever did, not even his brother. He'd conquered my mind, body and soul.

I loved him...

"Yes..." I cried through my tears.

"Yes?" He asked as if he couldn't believe it.

I nodded... "Yes, baby...I will marry you!" The crowd went nuts as he jumped to his feet snatching me out of the chair and into his arms.

"Thank you, Minx!" He repeated as he planted about a hundred kisses on my face. Somebody cleared their throat next to us. We parted to see Bruce standing with the black box in his hand.

"Yeah, I almost forgot!" Melech said with a huge grin on his face.

He opened the box, laying there on a red silken bed was a beautiful gold arm cuff. And it wasn't small, he needed two hands to lift it out. The sunlight caught the diamonds in a way that caused them to wink brilliantly at all who watched.

"In our culture, when a man becomes engaged to a woman, he gives her a bracelet as a seal that she now belongs to him."

Completely transfixed at the beauty of the bracelet, I watched as he carefully wrapped the gold around my upper arm. I don't know what it was about it, but I instantly felt like a queen, I lifted my arm so that I could get a closer look.

"It's beautiful." I told him.

The bracelet was designed in a vine pattern. There was a diamond in each cut, putting one in the mind of flowers. And there had to be at least twenty-five cuts. It fit like a sleeve, from elbow to shoulder the delicate gold flowed up my arm as if it had been especially made for it. I narrowed my eyes when I saw that there was something written in fine script going up the golden vine.

"For as long as I have breath, I will love that girl in the yellow dress. Black's Earth…Forever." I read out loud.

It was made especially for me! I threw my arms around his neck and held him close, I didn't mean to cry into his neck and wet up his nice tunic, but it was too much… I couldn't believe God had blessed me this way. And here I thought that change I felt this morning was going to be bad.

"Let us celebrate the union of our King and Queen!" Hosea yelled causing the crowd to jump to their feet again and the drums began to play. Black stepped away from me and amazingly, he began to dance. Only… it was not a dance, it was more like a chant with movement. His men and Bruce began to do the movements with him.

It reminded me of the Hulu dance that's performed by the Hawaiian men. Black was leading it, speaking a language I didn't understand, there were some chest pumping and feet stomping.

"What are they doing?" I asked Hosea who came to stand next to me.

"The chief and his men are honoring his future bride and pledging their allegiance to her."

"And what should I do?"

"Nothing, stand there and allow them to honor you."

And honor me he did. He looked so handsome doing his tribal dance. Like the big crybaby, I am, I cried all the way through it. I don't think I will ever forget what it felt like in that moment to have this powerful man, this man that everybody wanted a piece of honoring me this way.

Little old me. Earth, the girl whose parents didn't even love her enough to stick around. Earth, the forgotten… Forgotten no more.

"It's true what he said to you." Hosea said leaning closer so that I could hear him over the drums.

"What?" I asked nodding my head to the beat.

REDEMPTION: EARTH'S CRY

"He didn't smile that much before you came along." Although I didn't look away from Black, I was listening intently to Hosea.

"Seeing him let go and have fun like he done the other night he sang to you on your balcony…" He shook his head. "I hadn't seen him so carefree since he was a kid."

"I thank you, Ms. Earth for shining your light into his dark world."

I turned then to look at Hosea, but Black was pulling me into his arms. As the people continued to celebrate around us, he held me close looking down into my eyes.

"You set all this up, didn't you?"

A grin came to his face as he nodded, causing me to drown in his gaze. "I'll never let you go."

"I don't want you to ever let me go."

The smile suddenly left his face as he slowly lifted his head to look at Crush who stood over by the fence. Crush nodded his head toward the trees. Frowning, I followed his gaze.

"Is that a… clown?" I asked as what I was pretty sure was a clown popped out the trees and began to wave at us.

He did some kind of silly dance before he put one hand over his mouth as if he had done something wrong. But then he turned back towards the trees and beckoned somebody forth to join him. Abner suddenly appeared next to Black, growling low in his throat as he watched the clown, he hunched down on his legs as if he was ready to pounce any minute.

Another clown popped out the trees. He and the other clown hugged as if it had been a long time since, they saw each other. The music and the celebrating had come to a halt as everybody now watched the clowns that were clearly putting a show on for us. Folks had even begun to head toward them.

"Life has a way of throwing us into situations that will either kill us or make us stronger." Hosea said, but it seemed as if his voice came from a distance, although he still stood not too far away from us. He didn't look at the clowns, his gaze was trained on Melech, and there was sorrow in his eyes.

"The time has come for you to choose life or death, my son." Those words were barely over a whisper.

That feeling I'd felt this morning came back with a vengeance. Here was that change I'd sensed earlier. Both Black and I stared at Hosea for a moment before our gaze went back to the clowns that had now been joined by more clowns.

The children began to run towards them. Panic shot threw my heart when I saw Rain headed that way as well, Black noticed at the same time I did. I felt his muscles tense as he prepared himself to sprint after her, but before he took one step, Crush scooped her up in his arms.

The crowd gasped as out the trees came what looked like a full circus act. Several clowns walking on the tallest stilts I'd ever seen came out the trees, joined by clowns that rode on huge bicycles with crazy big wheels. Beautiful women in bright red sparkling leotards began to flip from the trees while some was being carried in big swings.

It was overwhelming.

"I don't like this." Crush grumbled as he stood Rain on the ground next to me. I was relieved to see that Tonya was now standing by her mom and had not run toward the clowns.

Horse spit on the ground. "Me either."

"Mommy, I want to go see!" I grabbed Rain's hand keeping her from dashing off.

"Not right now baby, stay here with mommy. You know I'm afraid of clowns." I told her. I wasn't lying. I was terrified of clowns. Rain nodded and held my hand tighter.

"It's okay, I'll keep you safe."

Black was in a serious discussion with all of his men as well as the town's sheriff trying to figure out who was behind this. But right then the clown on the tallest stilts came to a stop in front of us. Abner was growling so viciously in his throat Black had to stop talking to his men and give his pet his attention.

He squatted down next to him, speaking calmly to him, but Abner would not be comforted.

"Is your pet friendly?" The clown asked from nearly twenty feet in the air. Black stood frowning fiercely at him.

"Who hired you?" He spat, not even pretending to be cordial

The clown laughed down at him. "Will you look at there...his master isn't all that friendly either. Maybe the both of you can use a little kiss of happiness." He lifted his hand to his lips and kissed his palm before blowing the kiss down towards Abner and Black.

Too late we realized there was something spraying from his hand, some kind of dark fluid. The frown grew on Black's face as he watched the stuff spray all over him. I recognized that acrid smell.

"Oh God! It's blood!" I cried at the same time Abner and Black sprang into action going for the clown's stilts...

He let out a loud laugh before his eyes flashed red, and right there before our faces, clown and stilts disappeared. Black was grabbing air.

In fact, all the clowns and the performers' eyes flashed red before they too blew billows of blood in the air that rained down on the crowd and the ground. The blood resembled fire as it filled the sky to cover everything. The people cried out trying to escape it, but it was everywhere. And just like the clown on the stilts, once they'd blown their blood, they too disappeared.

"Mommy!" Rain cried clutching my legs. I held her close as I looked around as all the children began to run for their parents...

My gaze went back to Black. He stood there looking down at the blood that had been splattered on him...his hands were shaking badly. There was something wrong with him. There was something seriously wrong with him. I felt it like I felt that change this morning.

Slowly his stunned gaze lifted to mine. There were tears in his eyes.

"It's gone…"

His words were so low that if I hadn't been looking at his mouth, I would not have known what he said.

"What's gone?"

"The fire, Earth. The fire is gone!"

22

STRANGE FRUIT

Southern trees bear strange fruit, Blood on the leaves and blood at the root, Black bodies swinging in the southern breeze, Strange fruit hanging from the poplar trees

Pastoral scene of the gallant south, the bulging eyes and the twisted mouth, Scent of magnolias, sweet and fresh, Then the sudden smell of burning flesh

Here is fruit for the crows to pluck, For the rain to gather, for the wind to suck, For the sun to rot, for the trees to drop, here is a strange and bitter crop...

— BILLIE HOLIDAY

EARTH

The sound of a man's laughter coming from the trees drew everyone's attention from the blood. Black's whole body went tense and a growl came from his throat when a tall, handsome Native man dressed in an expensive white suit came from the trees with a huge smile on his face. He held his arms open as if he was expecting everyone to rush to him and hug him.

He wasn't alone. A small army of about thirty men, maybe more spilt out the trees behind him. These men were dressed for battle, army fatigues, combat boots, guns in hand raised and pointed at us. They broke off into two groups. One group stayed with their leader, guns raised and pointed at Black and his men.

And the other group started directing the people back to their seats, threatening to shoot them if they so much as blinked the wrong way. Several black SUV's screeched to a halt in the parking lot and more men spilled out of them, guns raised. We were being besieged.

I clutched Rain to me as my heart rate accelerated to a dangerous level. I felt crippled with my fear. Rain buried her face in my leg that she held for dear life. I stroked her hair willing her to remain calm. The last thing I needed was for her to start crying and draw the man's attention to her.

However, I needed not have worried; he only had eyes for Black. He looked at him with so much hate, he seemed obsessed with it.

"What did you think of my little production, little brother?" He asked as he approached us. "It's called an optical illusion. I made you all believe there were clowns, but guess what." He put his hands on his mouth as if he was going to tell us a secret.

"There were never any clowns. It was awesome, wasn't it? You should have seen your face."

He turned to his men and made a face that was supposed to resemble Black's, and his men joined him in laughter. The Native man was laughing so good he had to wipe away tears. Black looked at Crush, he didn't say anything, he just looked at him, Crush nodded before he gently took my arm and pulled me and Rain back away from Melech.

The man in white sobered instantly as his gaze fell on Crush. "Hold on, my retarded friend!" Crush stopped and I could feel the tension going through his body.

"I see my little brother still has a special place in his heart for the handicap."

It was taking everything within Crush not to reach for that gun that I knew was just inside his jacket. There were at least three guns trained on him alone, if he reached, he'd be dead before his hand could even touch the metal.

"No need to hide her, this whole contest is about her, isn't it? Come, my beautiful sister-in-law." The man in white called to me. One of his men that stood closest to us pointed the gun at me and signaled for me to get to moving.

"You must have a death wish to show up here!" Black growled as he stepped in front of me, preventing me from going any farther.

It looked as if Abner was going to leap, but Melech lowered his hand giving him the signal to stop without looking away from his enemy.

The man feigned confusion. "I don't know what you're talking about. I am the rightful chief of these people. Why wouldn't I come back and claim what's mine? You are a damn thief, who spooked my father into leaving you my inheritance." He pointed angrily at Black.

Wow! This must be Hawk. That explains the hate and obsession in his eyes for Melech. Panda had told me all about how ugly things had been between the two of them during their childhood. She said once Hawk realized his father was looking at Black to take over after him, he continually tried to kill him.

"You're not the rightful chief of sh*t, let alone our people."

"We'll see about that, little brother." He turned to look at the crowd. "I've come to challenge my stepbrother to my father's seat and rightful place."

A gasp went through the crowd as they began to mutter amongst themselves.

Hawk's eyes settled on me and my hand instantly lifted to the strap of Earth's Cry's case, drawing comfort from the instrument.

"After I kill my brother, I will do the rightful thing and marry Mitch's widow." My hand squeezed the strap as more muttering rolled through the crowd.

It was Black's turn to laugh. "You crazy as hell if you think I will let you anywhere near her."

Hawk turned back to face Black. "How will you stop me when you're dead…" He lifted one side of his mouth in a knowing grin. "Tell me, brother, do you still feel that fire down in your bones?"

The muscle ticked furiously in Melech's cheek as his hands balled into fists at his sides.

Hawk poked out his bottom lip and pouted. "No? Did your Power go bye-bye?"

"I don't need my Power to kick your sorry a**."

"Now that's where you're wrong!" Hawk yelled before he held up his hand and a sword appeared in it. The crowd gasped, as like I, they wondered if their eyes were playing tricks on them. The sword just appeared in his hand as if by magic.

"You see brother, you made a fatal mistake. You received your Power from flighty God, a God the does not like filth of any kind. A little pig's blood, and then poof, he's gone with the wind, and you're left standing here facing true power by your lonesome."

So that's what they spewed out over everything, pig's blood.

"We live in a filthy world, Black." He continued. "If you want true power in this place, you must go to the God of this filthy place. I've achieved something that even Holata had not mastered. I've connected with the God of this world and he has blessed me greatly!"

"So what, you can do a few magic tricks, I'm not impressed." Black sounded bored.

His attitude angered Hawk, but he covered it with a chuckle as he began to circle us, wielding the sword artfully. His men had not moved from where they stood pointing their guns at us.

"It goes far beyond magic, my black brotha. You see, when I left all those years ago, I was determined to find power. I searched the world for it sparing no expense. Would you like to know where I found it?"

Black exhaled. "Not really."

Hawk's eyes flashed with his anger, Black's nonchalant manner was driving him mad. "I'm going to tell you anyway." He spat. "I found true power between the thighs of a Pakistani whore. She told me that in order to receive it, I had to kill someone that I loved." The smile grew on his face as his eyes now sparkled with excitement.

"I waited till my father and his black whore were on their way home from the airport and rammed them with my truck causing them to fall over the cliff. They died on contact and power filled my veins." He spoke as if he was telling everybody he'd just won the lottery.

The crowd gasped and Hawk whipped around to face them. "Is this not our way? Do we not reward the most savage!? Who is King of Savages now? But wait!" He cried as his evil gazed came back to Black's. "I'm not finished yet."

I clutched the back of Black's shirt just to let him know I was here for him. Dear God, this man had just admitted to killing his mom. Black was so angry his body was vibrating with his rage. I could hear him grinding down on his teeth. He wanted to kill Hawk. If he still had his Power at this moment, Hawk would be burning.

"I found out a little secret about the one who supplies my power." Hawk continued not fazed one bit. "He's a greedy bastard, and the more I feed him, the more he feeds me. So, I killed Mitch the same way I killed my father and your whore of a mother. And he made me even stronger."

My knees nearly gave out. All this time we'd all thought what happened to Mitch was an accident. He'd been killed... And by his own brother! I lifted a quivering hand to my lips to hold in my cry. This man Hawk was pure evil.

"Enough with the talking!" Black barked. "You want my seat...let me see you take it mutha f****!"

I tightened my fist in his shirt. "You can't do this!" I cried desperately. I wasn't thinking clearly, I was just reacting off of a need to keep him safe.

He turned to me palming my face between his big hands. For just a moment he didn't speak, he just stared down into my eyes, drawing me in, causing everything else to fade.

"I have to do this, Minx." His words were low. I shook my head.

"No, you don't! You can just give him what he wants and we can go back and live over the bookstore." I didn't care that I sounded frantic. I didn't want to lose him. I loved him. I'd rather he walked away than lose his life.

"I know what your temptation is." I continued, pleading with him to hear me. "It's the money. The devil came and tempted you with unlimited wealth to keep you distracted. And it worked! Don't you see? It worked! Your heart is divided, it's the reason you can't get the fire to come from the sword. But we can walk away from it. We don't need it. I promise I'll keep you happy. You don't need the money!"

This was a suicide mission. The pig's blood had caused Black's Power to leave him. Hawk was clearly some kind of high-level magician. He'd made a mirage of circus performers come out the trees and a sword appear in his hand from thin air. I didn't have a good feeling about this.

Black shook his head. "These are my people. They depend on me to do what's best for them. I cannot walk away and leave them in Hawk's hands. He will destroy them."

Oh! God that was true! I hadn't even thought of that. Black couldn't just walk away, he was chief here. Using his thumb, he dried away tears I hadn't even been aware of shedding. This was all happening so fast my mind had to race to get ahead of it. He'd just proposed to me, he said we will be happy together.

I grabbed a hold to his hands that palmed my face and squeezed them. "You better not lose! You promised you wouldn't leave me."

He leaned down and kissed my lips. "You love me, don't you?"

Biting my bottom lip, I nodded. "Very much so…" My voice quivered.

His kissed my lips again. "I love you too, Minx."

He squatted down in front of Rain and she threw her arms around his neck.

"Don't fight him, daddy! He's a cheater!"

Black chuckled as he wrapped her in his arms. "He is a cheater, baby, but he's a sorry fighter. Your daddy is going to kick his a**."

"You promise?" Her little voice quivered with her tears.

He nodded. "I promise."

When he stood, Bruce wrapped his arms around him. "Cuz, just burn that punk up and be done with it! Why even give him the time of day?"

"Awww, look at that! Black has a *mini me*." Hawk mocked. "*No doubt he's eyeballing him to rule in his stead. Is this what's to come of the Great Holata's legacy?! Is everything my great-grandfather worked for to fall in the hands of a bunch of niggers?*"

The muscle ticked furiously in Black's cheek as he snatched his sword up from where it had been sitting against the big tree that was next to the raised dais. Hosea stood by the tree, there were tears in his eyes.

"Do you even know how to wield a sword?"

Black shrugged. "I know enough to beat that sorry son-of-a-b****."

Hosea shook his head. "You wrestle not against flesh and blood, but against principalities, against authorities, against world-rulers of the darkness of this age, against spiritual matters of wickedness in the heavens." He closed the gap between him and his grandson.

"The being that now possess Hawk's body cannot be destroyed by you alone. Without your Power you will die." He put his hand on his shoulder. "Maybe you should have listened to your woman and sat this one out."

Black stepped away from his grandfather's touch. "You know as well as I there is no walking away from this."

After he spoke those words his gaze came to me one more time, and it was then that I realized Black was walking to his death, Abner and his men right by his side.

"It's about time, I nearly fell asleep during all that mushy sh*t. Wow! Bro, that woman has really made you soft. I don't remember you being so..." he paused as if he was searching for the word. "Sentimental..."

Black chuckled. "I'll be sure to cry over your grave."

The smile left Hawk's face. "Tell your men, especially the big dumb one if they so much as blink, they're dead. This is a fair fight..."

"Fair!?" Black interrupted. "Is that why you sprayed me with pig's blood...to be fair?"

Hawk chuckled. "Well, I had to make it sound good for the crowd." And then he lunged at him with his sword.

Black barely got his up in time to parry. Hawk looked surprised. "Look's like someone has been practicing. And here I was going to take it easy on you." He grinned. "Not anymore!"

And then he attacked with gusto. Black wasn't a bad swordsman, but he was no where near as good as Hawk. After only a few minutes, it was clear that Hawk was toying with him. A gun shot filled the air, when Black turned to look, Hawk's sword slashed up his chest cutting through his tunic and his flesh.

My hands flew to my mouth to stifle my scream. Melech's men hurried to Crush who lay crumbled over on the ground. A very muscular man with a blond crewcut had shot him.

"He moved." Was all he told his boss when he looked at him.

"What the f***?!" Black roared clutching at the open gash in his chest.

Hawk grinned… "He moved. I told that retarded bastard if he reached for his gun, he was dead…But you need not worry about him, you're soon to join him!"

He began to swing with a whole new burst of energy. I went to go to Crush, but Hosea grabbed my arm.

"Not yet…"

"But Crush is hurt, he needs help!"

He shook his head, watching the fight closely. "Not yet…"

It was torture standing there watching Hawk have fun with Black. He sliced his arm and his leg. It was when he nearly cut his throat that Abner disobeyed his master and lunged for the man he fought. Hawk's eyes flashed red before he let the sword roll in his hand till it was facing up just as Abner was coming down, a loud cry filled the air as the animal's belly was impaled.

"Nooooo!" Black yelled before he threw his sword to the ground and charged Hawk with his fists.

I went to go to Abner, but once again Hosea grabbed my arm stopping me. When I looked at him, he just shook his head without looking away from the fight.

"No yet, daughter!"

In his rage, Black got ahold of Hawk's throat and began to squeeze the life out of him. If Hawk had been normal and not possessed by the devil like Hosea said, Black would have easily defeated him. He was bigger than Hawk and stronger. But because Black was not wrestling with flesh, he didn't see Hawk hold his hand out to the side and a knife appear in it much like the sword had.

"He's got a knife!" I cried...but it was too late. Hawk imbedded the knife in Black's stomach, the same as he done Abner. Crying out I clutched my own belly, feeling it as if it was my wound.

There was screaming inside my head as Melech stumbled back surprised at the blow. Hawk now grinned at him like one of the clowns he'd made magically appear then disappear.

"What's the matter, bro? You feeling kind of weird? That's called death."

Black went down to his knees and his men left Crush's side to go to him...

"Ah! Ah! Ah! Another step and you all die!" Hawk said as he joyfully watched his brother die in front of him.

He turned to face the crowd. "Look at your leader! Look at the one my father called the most savage! Look at him...down on his knees bowing to me, your true leader!"

You could hear a pin drop. Everybody including me stared in shock at Black who had fallen to his knees clutching a gut wound that will surely kill him.

Hawk pulled his sword out of Abner's body, causing the big cat to cry out as it began to shake uncontrollably. He wielded the sword as he approached Black, ready to deliver the death blow.

"Do you know how long I waited to see you in your rightful place, on your knees in front of me?"

"F*** you!" Black grumbled before he spit a wad of blood on Hawk's white snake skin boots.

Hawk backhanded him, but Black didn't fall like he'd hoped, instead, he turned his head to the side and spit another wad of blood on his other boot.

"Like I said…F*** you!"

Hawk drew himself up visibly getting control over his emotions. "I am going to enjoy this."

I couldn't explain what made me look up toward the trees. Maybe it was a gentle whistle that drifted to me on the breeze, or maybe it was the way the air seemed to shift. But my gaze went up toward the trees and crouched down on a really high limb like a black bird of prey was the Preacher. I couldn't see his eyes, his hat cast the whole top of his face in shadow, but I could feel them looking at me…

He nodded…

"It's time…" Hosea said from my side.

"Time for what?"

He turned to look at me for just moment before his eyes settled on Earth's Cry. "It's time to face your fears."

And suddenly I knew what I had to do…His words from the night we all sat by the fire came back to me.

"A threat is coming to someone you love. In order to save them, you must face your fears. In that hour, you will know what to do."

There was no hesitation in me. Black was dying, I would do anything to save him, no question.

I took Rain's hand and tucked it into Hosea's. "Stay here for Mama, okay?"

Tears came to her eyes. And although she said okay with her mouth, she shook her head no. I smiled as I rubbed her little cheek. "I love you so much, baby…"

And then I turned back to face my fate…

"Wait!" I cried out, causing Hawk's arm to freeze just as he was bringing his sword down to take Black's head off.

When he saw it was me that had called out to him, he smiled. "Yes, sweetheart, is there something I can do for you?" My skinned crawled at the way he called me sweetheart.

I nodded as I slowly made my way to them.

"Dammit! Earth...go back to my grandfather, he can keep you safe!" Black growled before he spit out more blood.

I shook my head. "I just want to be able to grant you one last wish."

Hawk's eyebrow lifted as he rested his sword on his shoulder. "This sounds interesting, please explain."

I took the violin off my back and sat it down on the ground. "He asked me several times to play my instrument for him and I always told him no." When I opened Earth's Cry's case, Hawk whistled.

"Look at that beauty."

I looked at Black and even now that he was dying, his gaze had the power to cause everything else around us, including the psychopath in the white suit to fade to black.

Tears blurred my vision. "I think it's time I played a little tune for you."

It took him a minute, but finally he nodded. I lifted my gaze to Hawk.

"If he's going to die, may I please play on song for him? I will never be able to live with myself knowing I'd denied him this one thing."

Hawk had not looked away from Earth's Cry. "I don't give sh*t if you deny him anything, f*** him. However, I am suddenly very interested in hearing you play." He held his hand out towards the area of ground in front of him. It just so happened to be the only area of ground where there was no pig's blood...

Hmmm...What's the odds?

My gaze went up to the top of the tree where the Preacher silently watched. Right then, the wind blew and his coat opened enough for the sun to reflect off the sword handle at his waist. I had a feeling that he could come down here and end this all…But he didn't because it was something we had to work out for ourselves.

I lifted Earth's Cry out of its case. As soon as I touched it, relief flowed through me. It was as if my limbs have been starved for only what it could feed. When I lifted the bow out the case, I felt complete. How could I have done this to myself? Why has it been so long since I touched it, played it?

I walked to the area of the earth that was not covered in blood. To block out the many eyes that were looking at me, I closed mine. As soon as I did, the tune came to me. My limbs were now operating as if they had a will of their own. I felt my arm raise the violin until the tip of it lay on my left shoulder, my chin came to rest against the chinrest.

Mmmm…that felt so right.

I began to sway to the tune I heard in my head before my hand lifted with the bow and I began to fiddle out the tune. A rush of relief flowed through me, seeming to supply fresh air to my lungs that I didn't know had been starved. You see, I needed to play Earth's Cry like I needed to breathe. The bow fit perfectly in my palm as if it was made just for me.

At first, I was in control of the tune, but that didn't last. Earth's Cry took over, embedding itself inside of me, taking over my nerves and muscles until I could no longer tell how much was me, and how much was it. Its energy flowing into my body felt like cool water.

The first flash of memory shook my soul, it was of a hunter dressed in strange clothing that made him strong. His skin was so dark it looked as if he had been burnt in a furnace. Like Melech, he had a regal appearance and was extremely handsome.

He was king in this place. In his hand was a golden bow and arrow. He was very good with his weapon. When he turned to look at me, the blood lust in his eyes was breathtaking.

In the very next flash I was standing on a field of blood. The hunter's eyes were no longer human, the Ravager had taken over his soul, his thirst for blood and destruction was unmatched by anything the world had ever seen. There were piles of dead animals that the hunter had murdered surrounding him. He hunted animals to extinction. So high was he on their blood that he began to dance in it, covering his body in it.

That was the longest memory, memories that were not my own. After that, fragmented flashes of recollections began to happen before my eyes one behind the other. In a matter of seconds, I saw every war that was ever fought on the surface of the earth. I clutched my stomach as I watched my children die. I was covered in their blood.

Flash

Toxic chemicals buried deep in my womb killing me. Toxic death dumped into my womb killing me. They were draining my blood...drinking my blood. This Ravager and his insatiable hunger for destruction killing me...

Flash

They're taking my children away in chains. My precious babies who were led astray and did not keep the covenant. They're taking them away in chains, away to be punished. I cried for them, the Ravager was after them, and he was getting drunk on their blood...

Flash

In a desperate attempt to hold on to my reality, I opened my eyes to try and see Rain and Melech one more time before I slipped away completely, but it was already too late, my eyes were not my own. I stared at the huge tree that stood next to the raised dais. There were black bodies hanging from trees, their blood sprinkled on the leaves.

Tears came from my eyes. Standing around the tree were men dressed in their Sunday best, their bodies had become hosts for the Ravager. In their hands were torches. They approached my pregnant daughter whose legs shook as she struggled to breathe around the rope that was cutting into the flesh of her neck, its burning strap more painful than anything she had ever felt.

One of the men pulled out a knife and cut her dress away from her beautiful body that shined like copper in the torch light. Although she was dying, she pleaded for the life of her unborn child with her eyes. With hands that shook I reached for her, but my feet didn't move. My only job was to watch.

To always watch...

The men laughed up at her before they took the knife and stabbed it violently into the top of her womb. My scream mingled with hers. I felt the pain as if it was my own. I wanted to look away, but Earth's Cry kept singing her song, showing me all the horrors she's seen.

Using both hands the man put all his weight into cutting down her belly. Another scream ripped from my throat when her baby fell from her stomach. They let the baby hang from its mothers' cord, wrapping it around its neck so that it strangled it.

Flash

The scene changed, but the tree stayed the same.

Well...

The roots stayed the same. The crown of the tree had been cut off to form a stake. There was a man being led to the stake. Like my daughter, his skin was the color of burnt copper, but his hair was white as snow.

This man was the exact opposite of the mighty man with the golden bow. This man was not attractive. He dressed simply, he dressed like my children who were hanging from the tree. Everything in my soul grieved at what they were doing to this innocent man.

The people cursed him. They were angry with him. They hated him. But it wasn't them, it was the spirit of the Ravager that urged them on. It hated this man, this simple man who had done nothing wrong but be a perfect servant. It hated him because inequity was not found in him.

I reached for him wanting to protect this innocent man, but just then he turned to me, and looked at me across space and time. His eyes were ancient. In his gaze I saw so much. He was a reflection of the condition of the people. In his gaze I saw the death of the Ravager.

They beat him until he bled.

Only... his blood the Ravager could not touch, because in his blood was his death found. When they lifted him and impaled him, I yelled out feeling the pain as if it was my own side.

I wanted to look away, but Earth's Cry wouldn't let me.

He never cried out as his blood began to run into the roots of the tree. And then something amazing happened. Water began to come from his wound, mixing with the blood that ran into the roots, and the tree began to grow a new crown. Strong branches came from the roots more beautiful than the ones that were there before. The leaves that appeared were like nothing I had ever seen.

And then...

It began to bear lovely fruit.

MELECH BLACK

In my vanity I'd let down my people, my woman and myself. I thought I understood what this life was about. Although the paranormal has been a big part of my life, I still had no understanding of the Power that had possessed me or its enemy.

I had foolishly thought my greatest accomplishment was picking up where Frank had left off and growing the business. I had fed that part of me, completely ignoring the spiritual part of me, and now I was here on my knees dying while my woman was being presented to my worst enemy.

This was all my fault…

She was so afraid as she walked into the center of the field. I wanted to go to her, but I no longer felt my legs. I was dying.

She closed her eyes and began to sway to music that only she heard. I took in her beauty and embedded it into my memory, determined to take it to the grave with me. When she finally began to play, I was stunned at her skill. I must admit, I thought she didn't play because maybe she wasn't that good.

But she was past good…She was amazing!

I recognized that tune…What was it? Hmmm…

What…is…that…tu---

Strange Fruit!

She was playing Strange Fruit…

There was something happening to her, her body jerked as if it was being inhabited. When she opened her eyes, I had to clutch at my chest. A light came from them so bright and pure it was overwhelming. I instantly felt unclean in its presence. I wanted to look away, but I couldn't. The light dimmed as she closed her eyes getting lost in the music.

She continued playing Strange Fruit, but in a way that it has never been played before. The sound she made come from the instrument was so complexed it was impossible for a human to do. The tune was hypnotic, wrapping around us all, holding us immobile while it told us a story. My grandfather was a minor griot compared to what we were seeing now.

Her body jerked as she played, then suddenly she opened her eyes again casting us in the bright glow. Seeing us, but not...

"For it is written says יהוה, every knee shall bow to him, and every tongue shall confess to Alohim." Her voice was not her own...The voice that came from her body was like the sound of many waters. It was the voice of Power. The bright light of her gaze fell on Hawk.

"Bow, abominable spirit!"

Hawk's body was hit by something that caused him to shudder, he yelled out as he was forced to his knees. Clenching his teeth, he tried to fight it and stand again but couldn't. He opened his mouth to say something...

"I will not permit you to speak." Was all she said as an invisible hand covered his mouth. Nothing but grunts came through, but she was not finished with him.

"I bear witness against you, unclean spirit. I've watched you ravish throughout this age, and for your crimes you shall pay."

Earth, or whatever had taken up residence in her body said before she closed her eyes and went back to playing her wraith-like version of Strange Fruit, as if Hawk was nothing but a naughty puppy she'd put in its place.

When the hand that held the bow stilled and her eyes opened again, we all jumped as that bright light washed over us, bringing the stench of our uncleanness to our noses.

"He came to his own and they rejected him..." She called out, looking toward the big oak tree that sat next to the dais. I turned my head to follow her gaze, but there was no one there. Who was she talking about?

"He came to his own and yet his own did not accept him." She repeated, still staring at the tree. There was a look of such grief on her face. Then suddenly she clutched her stomach as if she was in the heights of labor pain.

"Creation mourns you, Master!" She yelled before she cried

REDEMPTION: EARTH'S CRY

out in pain clutching her stomach again as a spasm shot through her body. I couldn't take it. I couldn't stand to see her in such pain. The sound of her agonizing cry pierced my soul.

I tried to stand to go to her, needing to help her in some way, but my grandfather put his hand on my shoulder keeping me on my knees, he shook his head.

"She must be allowed to mourn, son."

As soon as he said that, another agonizing wail tore from her body, it was such an unbearable sound that it brought tears to my eyes. She was grieving like a mother who had lost her child.

"No!" I growled as I tried to rise again. "I can't see her this way!"

Just then she stopped clutching her stomach and turned to look at me. The bright light from her eyes making me feel weak. My limbs wanted to collapse under the weight of it, but it felt as if something or somebody was holding me up. Her gaze held me captive as she lifted her bow and began to play Strange Fruit in that hypnotic way.

Slowly she approached me, her gaze dissecting me, seeming to take me apart and put me back together again. It traveled through my body leaving no part of me unstudied. I wanted to look away, but I could not. She paused in her playing moving her head to music that only she could hear….

"They said to let the blood of the innocent one be on the heads of their children." Her voice rang out seeming to echo throughout the mountains. She pointed her finger at me.

"Fire Bearer! See what I see!" I gritted on my teeth as something that felt like electricity hit me hard taking me across what seemed like space and time.

I was still on my knees, I could still feel my grandfather standing next to me. I could still hear the sound of the violin as it played its song of mourning. Only I was in three different times, if that made sense. I looked down and my knees were on three different kinds of grounds. The grass from my time, my space. But there was also a dirt road and another road made of stone.

The sounds of a chanting crowd blared over the violin. I looked up just in time to see an old black man being violently shoved past me or rather right through me. He fell to his knees that already bled from where he'd fallen before.

The people around me couldn't see me. They all chanted for the death of the little old man. His back was open from where he had been badly whipped. The chains around his wrists and ankles rubbed his flesh raw. He was in so much pain that he couldn't carry what looked like a wooden post…or stake.

Every time he fell to the stones one of the uniformed guards kicked him in his side. I tried to get to my feet and help him, but my grandfather's hand kept me on my knees. I looked up to see if he could see what I saw. But he couldn't, he didn't even look in the direction the old man was being led, his eyes were on the Earth Cryer.

As the old man got back to his feet, one of the guards grabbed a man out the crowd to help carry his stake. And even though he was beaten beyond recognition he continued to walk toward his death without uttering a word.

"The people said to let his blood be on the heads of their children!" The Earth Cryer's voice came to me.

And right then the sounds of what sounded like the chanting from an old chain gang began to cross time. It was as if their chants and the sound of metal striking metal was in time to every step the man took toward his death.

I turned toward the chanting and saw the dirt roads. As far as the eye could see, there were black men, women and children being led down the dirt road in chains, the same chains that the old man wore. And just like his chains, they cut into their flesh. Some of their backs were almost identical to his, big gaping wounds from being whipped.

They faded a bit and I was back in the strange street watching the one the Earth Cryer called innocent being led to his death, I wanted to stop it, the people had cursed their children. I tried to warn them, but my voice couldn't be heard over the chanting of the crowd and the chanting of the chain gang. I squeezed my fists together trying to use all my strength to get to my feet.

I had to stop this!

"Be at ease, Fire Bearer, for this has to happen." The Earth Cryer said to me. I didn't want to watch it, I didn't want to see them kill him.

The chanting of the chain gang grew louder. Their voices harmonized perfectly as they sang about their heavy burdens, about how they worked till they died. It didn't make any difference whether the sun was up or down. They were destined to work to the death. They sang about their women and children that they will never see again. They called out for the Ancient of Days. They didn't know why this was happening to them.

"They told them to let his blood be on the heads of their children." Earth's Cry's sorrowful voice came to me, but this time, her words were barely over a whisper. I felt my grandfather slide the handle of the sword back into my hand.

The chanting of the crowd drowned out the chanting of their children. I yelled out when they picked him up and drove the stake into his side, clutching the metal of my sword in my palm as pure uncut rage shot through me.

Standing next to me was a group of women who could not see me. They wept for the innocent one. Their cries could be heard over the chants of the crowd.

The innocent one stopped and looked at them.

"Daughters of Yerushalayim," His voice sounded like many waters. "Do not weep for me, but weep for yourselves and for your children. For look, the days are coming in which they shall say, 'Blessed are the barren, and wombs that never bore, and the breasts which never nursed!'

The chanting of the chain gang drowned out that of the crowd as the sound of the metal striking metal could be heard in tune with their song. The scream of a woman pierced the air. The sound was full of so much anguish that it split my heart in two. I was forced to watch three small children that clung screaming and crying to their mother's legs be ripped away from her. She pleaded with the men not to take her children away from her. She pleaded with her master not to sell them, but he just shoved her away from him and shook hands with the man he had just completed his business with.

Earth Cryer yelled out as she clutched her womb reeling in pain. As if her life depended on it, she went back into playing Strange Fruit. I felt helpless in this place between three times, forced to watch the gravest injustice to ever happen in the history of man. And it angered me.

No, it past angered me, I was almost blinded with my rage. Just then, the sound of the violin crossed space and time to drown out the chanting of the people for the death of the innocent one, and the chanting of their children to sooth me.

The one hanging closed his eyes as if he too could hear it. When he opened them, he was looking directly at me, in his eyes I saw the fire. As the chanting of the chain gang got louder, I realized he wasn't looking at me, but through me, across space and time. He was no longer looking at the people that called for his death but at their children, and great pain showed on his face.

He grieved for them. He loved them. He was dying for them. I turned my head to follow his gaze. This time they were leading a group of runaways to the hanging tree. They hung them in groups of twenty-five. As their bodies shook, the one whose blood covered them held his head back and yelled...

"Power! My Power! Why have you forsaken me?" With tears

he watched their bodies shake from his own stake. Then when they failed to move anymore, he uttered.

"Father into your hands I commit my spirit." And like those who hanged from the tree, he closed his eyes and breathed his last breath.

"No!!!!!!" I yelled as a rage came from the soles of my feet and made its way up through my veins feeling like fire. No, it was the fire…It was back. But not like before. The fire inside of me was the wrath of the Ancient of Days.

As if the street could feel my rage, it began to shake violently and crack apart around me. The sky got completely dark. Thunder rumbled through the ground so loud it drowned out the sound of everything else.

My rage paled in comparison to the rage that now gripped the earth. The people that had called for his death realized too late their mistake. They began to run and try to hide themselves, but the earth was full of rage for the death of the innocent one, and the bodies of the dead began to come up through its surface. Creation itself called out at the injustice of such a death.

The son of The Ancient of Days had given his life for the people.

"Come back to me, Fire Bearer." Her voice pulled me back across time, that wrathful fire came with me. When I opened my eyes, she was standing right in front of me.

"If they do this to the green tree, what is going to be done to the dry tree? For they have taken crafty counsel against thy people and conspired against thy hidden ones. And thy people die from lack of knowledge." As she spoke the light was dimming in her eyes.

"I cannot fight this battle for you, warrior, choose today who you will serve. One path leads to death, and the other to life."

The light faded completely from her eyes and it was my Earth that stared back at me. She opened her hands and the violin and bow fell from her fingers. When she spoke, it was with her own voice and not with that of Power.

"Choose wisely, beloved, or we all will die." She whispered before her eyes rolled to the back of her head. Quickly I held out my arms and caught her before she hit the ground.

When my gaze rose, the only thing I could see was fire…Rage like I never felt before washed through me as I made my choice. On this day, I choose life…

Something hit me hard in the chest…. I closed my eyes and roared as it tore me apart on the inside, killing the man I used to be. When I came together again, I came as a vessel. I opened my eyes and looked down at the burning sword in my grasp…

23

THE TRUE INHERITANCE

You are of Alohim, little children, and have overcome them, because He who is in you is greater than he who is in the world.

— *1 JOHN 4:4*

THE NARRATOR

The force that was holding Hawk bound and gagged released him when Earth fainted. Quickly he scrambled to his feet reaching for his sword so that he could complete the job. He didn't make it this far going through hell and back to fail now.

He would prove to his father, to Holata, to that bastard Melech and all his people that he deserved to hold the title of the King of Savages. He had studied many years to become a sixth level mystic. He traveled to the darkest, foulest most uninhabitable parts of the earth to find his spirit guide, the one who instructed him on the ways to greatness.

It was he who told Hawk that if he made Melech unclean with the blood of a black pig he would cause his Power to leave him.

No... Hawk had come too far to fail now. Once he had his sword in his hand, he turned to face the thief that stole his inheritance.

Melech was still on his knees with his eyes closed, his tunic covered in his own blood, the little witch passed out in front of him. When he was done with Melech, he would slit her throat for her deception. She had embarrassed the sh*t out of him, forcing him to his knees, muting him. Now was not the time to wonder what happened to his spirit guide then and why it was Earth held so much power over him.

"Like I told you, little brother, your Power is weak in this place. You made the wrong choice."

He raised the sword over his head and came down with all his might, determined to cut the bastard in two. But just as his sword was getting ready to make contact with his head, Melech's hand with his sword in it shot up, blocking the blow. It hit so hard sparks flew.

Black opened his eyes and Hawk nearly pissed his pants at the sight of the fire burning with a vengeance in his gaze.

"No brother, it is *you* who've made the wrong choice!" He growled right before his sword's blade burst into flames.

"Greater is He that is in me, than he that is in the world!" He flawlessly came to his feet, he and Hawk now face to face... sword to sword.

"Shoot him!" Hawk called to his men without looking away from Melech. "Shoot him!" He yelled again when no one moved to obey.

The first round of bullets came from his right, moving faster than what was humanly possible, Melech spun away from Hawk using the sword in a way that made everyone gasp because they had never seen such swordsmanship, not even on TV. He wielded the sword with great speed and accuracy, causing it to move in an arc around his body. The burning sword moved so fast it could not be seen by the eye.

Each bullet that touched the arc sparked before it flew back to the one that shot it as if from a gun, causing Hawk's men to start dropping like flies. Everyone sat stunned, including Bruce and Melech's men, with mouths hanging open as they watched their chief literally use his sword to dodge bullets. And not only that, he sent the bullets back to the ones who shot them.

A growl pierced the air before a loud scream followed. Abner was back on his feet and in his eyes burned the same flame that was in Melech's. He took the man down nearest to him with one powerful swipe of his sharp claws shredding his face before ripping his throat out. By the time the man's body finished twitching, he was on to the next one. They were shooting at him, but not one bullet touched him as he continued to use his claws and powerful teeth to destroy.

All that shot at him burst into flames as soon as the bullets left their guns. The fire that consumed them was so hot their flesh was burnt away from the bone in a matter of seconds. Realizing they were up against a force more ferocious than anything they've ever seen, Hawk's last remaining men threw down their guns and made a run for the trees. They didn't make it far before columns of fire shot down from the sky consuming them completely.

Quicker than anyone could have fathomed, there were none of the enemy left but Hawk. He called on his spirit guide, trying to create another optical illusion, but nothing happened. The spirit that had aided him to this point had abandoned him, leaving him to face Melech's wrath alone.

"Brother, think about what you're doing. You don't want to

kill me in front of my father's people." He said as he began to take a step back for every step Melech took forward.

A low deadly growl came from his right. Viciously baring his teeth that were covered in the blood of Hawk's men, Abner was crouched low ready to attack, the flame in his eyes consuming his whole pupils.

Melech stood for a moment taking in his brother, then he turned and walked away from him as if he wasn't impressed.

"Abner." He called without looking back.

Still growling in his throat Abner slowly turned away from Hawk to follow his master. Hawk exhaled, not believing he'd actually turned his back on him, this was too easy.

He reached inside his suit coat and pulled the gun out of its holster. And to think his father thought that weakling was more savage than his own son.

Before anyone could bat an eye, Hawk had his gun out and—

He never got a chance to point it. A loud BOOM filled the air before the ground around where he once stood was littered with his body parts.

Black never turned around. The people, Bruce, Hosea, and his men all stared at their leader in a mix of awe and horror, their gazes going back and forward between the carnage he and Abner had just reaped by themselves and his retreating back.

He was more powerful than he'd been before. The flame that burned in his eyes was fiercer than it had been before. It coupled with the great burning sword he held in his hand and the big black cat that walked by his side, whose eyes also burned, were more than they knew what to deal with.

Melech didn't speak to anyone; he walked to where Earth still lay on the ground unconscious and scooped her up in his arms. Rain broke away from Hosea and ran to him grabbing a hold of his shirt as he began to carry Earth down the road towards the Big House, Abner and Rain by his side.

It took everyone's mind a moment to catch up with what they'd just witnessed, when they did, Horse and Big Troy jumped into action running for the trucks. Horse drove a pick up and Big Troy an SUV. They agreed to split up into two groups, half of them would help Big Troy get Crush to the hospital, and the other half would ride with Horse to get Melech and his family home.

By the time Horse caught up with Melech he was a good distance down the road. He didn't speak to his boss. He just pulled ahead of him throwing the truck in park. Quickly he, Bruce and Shiloh got out and opened the tailgate on the truck. They still looked at him in awe. They'd just witness him take out a small army of men with just him and his pet in a matter of minutes.

With Earth cradled in his arms Black climbed in the back. Sensing that Rain didn't want to be separated from her family, Bruce lifted her into the back with them, Abner hopped up after. Black eased down against the back window with Earth in his arms. Rain squeezed in next to him; lifting his arm he circled it around her pulling her close. Abner settled down against his stretched-out leg.

For a moment, Horse just stared at his boss and his family. Whatever happened to them today happened to them as a unit. It bonded them together stronger than any wedding ceremony ever could.

Today, they had become one...

Horse watched the fire fade from Black's gaze, when it did, his eyes rolled to the back of his head as his body went lax in unconsciousness.

"Come on, let's get them back to the Big House. Ms. Lily will have them both as right as rain in no time."

Bruce nodded. "Yeah, my mom and my sister are on their way as well."

"And I'm sure Hosea will be coming with them." Horse said as he climbed into the passenger seat.

High up in the tree the Preacher gave thanks to the Ancient of Days. Two more of his children had crossed over. He exhaled feeling more tired than can be imagined. It seemed as if his whole life had been spent preparing for the coming battle, and now that it was just upon the shores, he felt hard pressed for time.

The forces of evil never slept, never stopped, and never gave up. So he could not sleep, stop, or give up. He had to continue to push forward to help his children who were meant to follow the Way. It was the reason he had been made the way he was. And it was a job he did not take lightly…

THE EPILOGUE

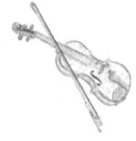

EARTH

3 MONTHS LATER...

"You know, people say it's bad luck for the groom to see the bride before the wedding." I told Black as I slowly walked to him.

He looked so good sitting relaxed on the ottoman in our bedroom, dressed in his royal maroon and gold tribal garb. Abner sitting on his hind legs next to him. Ms. Lily had been working on our wedding garments for the last three months and they were simply amazing.

She had infused more of an African flavor into these than our engagement day outfits. I was dressed in a maroon and gold work of art. The sleeveless top half of the dress was fitted and hugged my breasts and stomach in a way that accentuated my small baby bump. The bottom half of the dress was layers and layers of fabric that let out into a long beautiful maroon and gold Afrocentric pattern tail.

The golden engagement arm bracelet Black had given me went perfect with the gown. Both Ms. Lily and Bria had spent hours doing my hair. After they were finished, they'd carefully secured the gold crown Black had gifted me with last night on top. It was so beautiful and looked as if it matched the bracelet.

At the same time they did my hair, Panda did my make-up and nails. Tonya and Betty helped to get Rain dressed and had already left with her to go to the hall where there were over two hundred people waiting to see Hosea marry Black and I.

I had expected to be stressed out today, but surprisingly everything was going smoothly. The final days leading up to the wedding had been kind of stressful because I was studying for my final exams while taking care of last-minute wedding plans. However, I feel as if my sleepless nights have paid off because I think I did very well on them. I won't know for sure until after winter break.

But I was determined not to think about it till then. Plus, Black and I were going to Jamaica for two weeks for our honeymoon and I will be entirely too occupied to think about anything other than my husband.

Rain wanted to stay with Bro. Abraham and Sis. Dinah while we are gone, but she didn't want to leave Hosea, Ms. Lily, Tonya and her friends. So, Sis. Dinah and Bro. Abraham agreed to stay here with her while we were gone so the little misses could be surrounded by all her favorite people while her parents were away.

Black helped me climb up on the ottoman next to him, carefully as not to mess up my hair, I rested my head on the spot between his head and shoulder, and then I exhaled. This was one of my favorite spot's to be.

"I don't give a damn what people think, I was not waiting any longer to see you. It was bad enough Bria and Panda took you out to a strip joint last night." I playfully tapped his chest.

"It was not a strip joint, it was a spa resort. We spent all evening getting massages and facials…the works."

He grunted. "Close enough…" I shook my head.

Black was something else, y'all…

"I don't say anything when the Preacher ships you off to Chicago and I have to sleep in that big old bed by myself."

He chuckled. "You can come any time you want…you know that."

Yeah, I knew that. The thing is, I wanted to finish school and have my degree by the time our son is born in June. That way, I'll be ready to accept the teaching position down at Seminole Territory grade school when I wean him. They were getting ready to introduce a new preschool program that I was going to be heading up.

"I wish I could." I told him. "I would love to meet Lyon and Nuriyah…Ohh! And Gideon and his beautiful wife SaafiYah. You talk about them so much, I feel like I know them already. They really sound like nice people."

He grunted again. "Nuriyah and SaafiYah maybe. I've thought about running Lyon over with my truck. You've glamourized the Lyon's Den, but it's become a place of torture for me. That man is a drill sergeant. He's relentless…I swear, he never gets tired. If I didn't know any better, I would think he wasn't human. And Gideon is no better. That brotha got serious personality issues." I chuckled as he went on complaining about his new teachers.

After that day Melech killed Hawk, the Preacher came to see him and told him it was time for his training to begin. He said that day on the field Melech had become a vessel for the Spirit of the Most High. While being used by the Spirit he became a freaking super hero, as the people of Seminole Territory witnessed themselves when they watched him take out a small army, just him and Abner.

Goodness, I wish I had been able to see that. It was all everybody talked about around these parts On that day Black had become a legend to his people, he now had a higher standing than even Holata.

Anyway, the Preacher said nothing can stop Melech when his body is being used by the Ancient of Days. However, he was going to train him to be able to fight just as well when his body was not being used.

Melech thought the Preacher was going to be doing most of the training himself, but he'd been wrong. He took him to a place called the Lyon's Den, located deep in the heart of a Chicago ghetto and introduced him to two men he called his brothers, Lyon and Gideon. And then told him that his brothers will teach him to fight both physically and spiritually.

Some of the things Melech has told me about these guys are nothing short of *amazing*. He said both Lyon and Gideon each had the strength of a thousand men. At first, I didn't believe him, but when he did not smile or say he was joking I became dumbfounded.

Of course, I shouldn't be surprised seeing as to how my new husband can cause people to catch on fire just by looking at them, but hey, to hear there were two men in the heart of the ghetto strong enough to throw cars across a parking lot was a little much to take in in one sitting.

By the way…the cars in the parking lot is a true story. Melech said there was another man being trained with him at the Lyon's Den named Gabriel. Gabriel was very strong like Lyon and Gideon, but like Melech, he was young and new to being a warrior of the Ancient of Days.

He said after a full day of training, he and Gabriel were practically laid out on the gym floor near death. Lyon and Gideon, who were also best friends believed in pushing one's body until there was nothing left. That's how their training sections went, period.

Now, the reason I told you guys they were best friends was because Melech says they're the oddest best friends he's ever seen. I asked him how so…He said they were odd because they didn't care for each other at all.

Then he told me about an altercation the two of them had gotten into when trying to determine what they were going to eat for dinner that day. Melech said he and Gabriel didn't care they just wanted to feed their depleted bodies.

But Lyon and Gideon who both wanted spaghetti got to arguing about whether fried fish should go with the spaghetti or fried chicken. Apparently, Gideon felt that fried chicken should go with spaghetti, but Lyon felt fried fish should go with spaghetti.

Melech said the argument actually came to blows…and that Nuriyah who is Lyon's wife was tired of them destroying the gym and yelled for them to take it out to the parking lot. The chance at seeing these two powerful warriors battle caused both Melech and Gabriel to find the strength to hurry off the floor and out to the parking lot for front row seats.

Once out there the fight got so heated that Lyon ended up picking up a car throwing it at Gideon, who barely escaped getting crushed by it. He said that Gideon in retaliation threw a car back at Lyon, but the car missed him and slammed into the gym, putting a big hole in the wall.

Both men stood looking at a steaming Nuriyah on the other side and only then did they realize their fight was stupid. Apparently, they fought about stupid things all the time, they literally could not stand each other. Melech said even though they were tired beyond belief, Lyon and looked at him and Gabriel and told them to patch up the hole.

But then my husband would get a look of wonder on his face. "Although they fight like cats and dogs, when they come together, there is no force on earth that can stop them. Watching them fight the enemy is something you'll never forget."

And get this...Melech said Lyon actually has a pet lion named King and Gideon a big black pet wolf named, well... Wolf. Yeah, he was really original with that name. Melech said nobody batted an eye when he walked through the door with Abner. Well, all except Gabriel, who felt cheated because he didn't have a pet that he had a special bond with like the others.

Lyon tried to explain to him that everyone didn't have pets. There was another brother who trained with them sometimes named Solomon. He was a big-time lawyer for the poor man, and when he wasn't in court, he was there at the gym with them. Gideon said Solomon can vanquish evil spirits with his mind. He said demons were very afraid of him.

Anyway, Solomon didn't have a pet. However, Solomon was not Gabe's favorite brother. So he still was not comforted in the fact that he didn't have a pet. Gideon tried to explain to him that those with pets have them because the pet found them, not vice a versa. Gabe was not satisfied with that and continued to feel cheated because he didn't have a pet.

It got so bad that in order to shut him up about it, Gideon told him his pet will find him soon. Then he and Lyon got together and told him that they knew where to find his special pet. Gabe got really excited. Melech said Lyon and Gideon made a big to-do of presenting his pet to him. All of Lyon's men came together to witness it as well as Gideon's. They told Gabe his pet sat waiting for him underneath a huge box in the center of the boxing ring there at the gym.

Melech said Gabe was so excited he was literally cheesing as he walked to the ring. All the fellas were patting him on the back congratulating him for finding such a special gift. When he finally got to the center of the ring and lifted the box, it was a baby turtle underneath.

Melech said they all fell out laughing at Gabe...who just stood there with a really salty look on his face.

"Oh...Okay, I see y'all got jokes." Was all he said causing everybody to erupt in another fit of laughter. Needless to say, after that day, poor Gabe let the topic of his special pet drop.

"What the hell is going on in here?" Bria screeched interrupting the peace and quiet Black and I were enjoying and my thoughts as she burst into our bedroom door.

Melech inhaled, clearly annoyed at her action. I reached up and patted his chest. "Don't you even think about it." I whispered.

"She needs to learn how to knock..." He grumbled angrily under his breath.

I chuckled. "I don't care, you better not burn my friend again."

"Are y'all over there whispering about me?" Bria asked in her extra loud voice as she walked into the bathroom to look at herself one more time in the mirror.

Dear Father, why is my friend so loud?

"I don't know, did you knock on that door like we discussed?" Black called after her.

"Behave." I mouthed.

"Oops! I'm sorry, I forgot. Next time I'll remember."

"Yeah right..." He grumbled under his breath.

She came out the bathroom. "Oh my God! Why are y'all just sitting here chilling like there ain't a bunch of folks waiting for y'all at the hall?! Girl, you should see how auntie Dinah is staring at Larry's crazy a** with that big old Rastafarian hat on." She laughed shaking her head.

"Can't take his a** nowhere." Her eyes snapped to us. "Come on, Crush just pulled the car out front." And then she sailed out the room leaving the door wide open behind her.

"Let me just heat up her shoes…"

"No!" I laughed getting up from the couch.

Like Larry, Black didn't care for my friend that much. He too thought she was simple-minded.

Okay, so since we're on the topic of Bria, let me tell you something before I get out of here. My time with y'all has come to an end. But no worries, because my sistas have wonderful stories to tell, and they can't wait till they get their chance to tell you guys all about their amazing journeys to love.

Remember when I told y'all that Bria was going to come here and end up falling for Horse?

I was so wrong…so very wrong!

Y'all will never believe who she fell for…Go ahead, try and guess, while Black helps me put on the beautiful white fur hooded cape that was the finishing touch to my ensemble.

Did you guess the answer?

All of you out there who said Crush would be right.

Yep, she had fallen for the big silent giant. Apparently, her simple mind and his complexed one somehow worked. And from what it looked like, worked well. He barely talked to anyone, but to Bria, he opened up like a flower.

And she was fiercely protective of him too. You say something about her man and she went straight ghetto crazy on you. I asked her what was the deal. I'd never seen Bria love a man, what was it about Crush? And I kid you not, she told me she'd never had a man make love to her like him. She said he was a beast in the bedroom…her words.

Anyway, that's my time…But before I go, I want to tell y'all that I no longer deny myself Earth's Cry. When the mood hits me and she needs to sing, I play. I have seen some terrible things, but I have also seen the most beautiful.

For all of you out there who see the days darkening, be encouraged, trouble don't last always. And neither will this darkness. Evil will not win, no matter how hard it tries to convince us that it will. For it was written, and the Words of the One who wrote it always come to pass... Selah

THE END

COMING FOR WHAT'S MINE

I

BONUS CHAPTER 1

INTRODUCING THE LAW BOYS
SERIES

ABOUT COMING FOR WHAT'S MINE

You think you know how the game is played. You have no idea...

In my world, the ganstas on the street are feared. I had no way of knowing that once I accepted a Botany Scholarship at Georgetown University I was going to be unwittingly thrown into the savage biosphere of politics. I've come to learn that here in D.C., the politicians are the real ganstas, and that they are far deadlier than anything we common folk could ever imagine.

However, I would soon find out just how dangerous the political milieu can be. It is a place of glamour, lies, and power. Trust the wrong person, and you can end up dead.

I gave into the senator's son one night, allowing him to take what I had never gifted to another. It was the single most amazing thing I would ever experience.

But that one night of unbridled passion would send my life spiraling into uncharted territory. The fruit of which I carried in my womb while fleeing to protect my unborn child...

I knew she was too innocent to be pulled into my world. A world that was more treacherous than a pit of vipers. However, I could no sooner quiet my hunger for her than I could the roar of an oncoming tornado.

She gave me my taste, and I found my new addiction. But then she fled from me and became my new obsession.

Now, nothing will stop me from Coming for What's Mine...

1

COMING FOR WHAT'S MINE

AND THE FATHER IS...

JOURNEY

I was just trying to better myself. I wanted to make my mama proud, so that she could say at least one of her kids graduated high school and even went to college.

"What we gon' do?" My mother asked looking back at me with desperate eyes before turning to look through the peep hole again. The pounding on the door came again but this time louder. I should have just gone to a local college. The University of Illinois had an excellent botany program. Why didn't I just go there? Why did I have to go to Georgetown? Why did I listen to my roommate and take that secretary job at the senator's office? Why...dear God why did I have to catch the eye of the senator's only son, who was so very brutal and also the youngest Senior Special Agent with the Federal Bureau of Investigation? Who would probably one day, if his father had anything to do with it, become president of the United States.

"Open up, Ms. Reevers!" I closed my eyes as that deep voice washed down my spine. He wasn't supposed to be here. This wasn't supposed to be happening. How had it come to this?

"Journey! What we gon' do?" Tears were running down my mother's beautiful face. I looked back towards my younger brother Rob's bedroom. He and my older brother whose apartment is upstairs were frantically trying to flush their product down the toilet, but because they were going so fast pills were everywhere.

Rome, my older brother and the head of our family ran back into Rob's room before coming back out with three pistols. He looked around trying to decide what to do with them before going to the window, opening it and tossing them out. We lived on the third floor; please God don't let any children be down there to get a hold of one of them.

This was all my fault. That night should have never happened. I should have never slept with him. I knew how vicious he was. I had heard the stories. Putting my hand on my face I tried to stifle my screams when the pounding came louder. He hit the door so hard it caused it to shake on its foundation.

I should have never run from him!

"Get back away from the door!" Joseph yelled.

My mother stumbled back just in time to avoid being hit by it as it crashed in busting the lock.

"Freeze FBI!" The two officers with the man that has haunted my dreams for the last nine months yelled as they hurried in behind him pointing their guns at us. Rome and Rob threw what drugs they had left in their hands and ran out the back door.

"Where you going boys?!" Jo yelled after them with a huge grin on his handsome face. Although he smiled, it didn't reach his eyes. I knew him, he was pissed! My heart as well as my legs was frozen in fear. This was a nightmare! He wasn't supposed to be here! Why was he here?

"What's up, Journey? You look like you see a ghost!" He stared at me with that intense angry gaze of his. He had a way of looking at me that made me feel as if he didn't see anybody else in the room, only me. But I couldn't help but be confused, why was he so angry?

And yes, I did feel as if I was looking at a ghost. A dangerously handsome ghost! A powerful ghost that was well out of my league! He was the son of a senator! And as Alice his mother told me the day she came to pay me to disappear, destined to become the second black president of this great nation. Why was he here?

My mother wrapped her arms around me trying to pull me out the way as several more agents came in through the back door. She and I both cried out when we saw that they had both of my brothers in handcuffs. One of the officers carried the three guns Rome had tossed out the window with him. They forced them down to their knees on the kitchen floor.

Seeing my brother Romeo, who was something of a legend around these parts forced down to his knees was a bit of a shock to me. My heart was beating so loudly in my chest that it was causing my vision to vibrate with its force. Heavenly Father, please let Ayana stay asleep. There was a good chance he still didn't know about her.

"Search the place, bring me my baby!"

"No!" I cried breaking away from my mother to run to my bedroom. But I never made it, Joseph moved then, so suddenly he startled my mother. He grabbed me around my waist lifting me off the ground. Complete chaos erupted! Both of my brothers shot to their feet when they saw him grab me.

"Hey man, get yo' hands off my sista!" Rome yelled charging at us, but two of the agents tackled him, wrestling him back to the ground. Another agent took down Rob, both of my brothers continued to fight trying to dislodge them.

I went wild in Joseph's arms, but it was no use, he was so strong. If my memory served correctly, underneath that custom made suit was a plethora of chocolate covered muscles that he kept toned up every morning in his home gym.

"Let me go! Don't touch my baby!" I yelled towards the room where the agent had disappeared.

"Calm down, Journey!" He hissed in my ear. A shiver raced down my spine as tears came to my eyes. My body had begun to betray me already. I don't know if it was because I gave this man my virginity or if he was just that skilled of a lover, but he had a way of manipulating my body and mind to get me to do anything he wanted me to do.

I was trying to talk, trying to ask him why he was here and what he wanted with my baby. But my emotions were such a wreck; I couldn't even form a sentence around my crying. My gaze went back to Rome, who was now being choked on the ground by the agent.

"Stop resisting!" He hissed at my brother as he continued to choke him.

"You choking him!" I managed to get through my sobs. "Joseph! They choking him! Please tell them to stop!" Visions of all the recent deaths of black men by law enforcement raced through my head.

"Please!" I cried out. Rome was the rock of our family; he was what held us all together. If something happened to him I will never forgive myself.

"Let him go!" Rob yelled as he tried to get to the officer that was choking Rome. "You cowards take them handcuffs off him and let him defend himself!" Rome's eyes rolled to the back of his head.

"Please God!" My mother cried collapsing to her knees. She had her hands together and was praying through her tears.

This was all my fault!

"Joseph!" I cried, pleading for mercy to a man that it was no secret had none.

"Calm down and I'll tell him to stop!" I did, instantly. He threw me on the couch and then signaled for the man to let Rome go. When he did my brother began to gasp, greedily sucking air into his lungs. I shot off the couch to go to him, but Joseph grabbed me around my waist, throwing me back on the couch.

"Don't move!" He yelled.

He was so angry! I had never seen him like this.

The agent came out the room holding Ayana, he had taken the time to wrap her in her blanket. Instinctively, I stood to take my baby from the strange hands, but Joseph's angry gaze shot back to me and I eased back down on the couch. I was such an emotional wreck, I was shaking. On one hand, the life of my brother, who was the pillar of our family was at stake and on the other hand, strangers were handling my three-month-old baby. I wanted to scream, never in my life feeling this trapped.

Another agent came through the front door carrying a silver case in her hand. She sat it on the table before opening it. Inside the case was what looked like a mini-lab. Quickly she put on a pair of latex gloves before removing two big cotton swabs. When she walked towards Ayana with them, Rome shot off the floor again, but was soon tackled back to the ground.

"Don't touch my niece!" He hissed. My gaze shot up to Joseph.

"What are they doing to her?" I asked clutching the couch on the side of my legs so hard my knuckles turned white. It was taking everything in me to stay seated. Joseph didn't answer, he just looked down at me as if I was the dirt underneath his expensive Italian leather boot.

The woman gently ran the swab just inside Ayana mouth, who instantly begin to make the sucking sound causing my milk to come down. When the woman removed the swab, my baby started to fuss, now ready to eat. To my surprise, the agent that was holding her handed her to Joseph, who gently began to rock her, causing her to drift back to sleep.

When he looked down at her, that anger and hate that he looked at me with disappeared. He looked at her with a mix between curiosity and wonder. Something in my very being revolted at seeing him cradling her. He paid to get rid of her; he wanted me to have an abortion. Why was he now holding her as if she was the rarest thing on earth?

The female agent gently put the swab in a little canister that had blue jelly like liquid in it before she walked to Joseph.

"Open up, Boss." Without looking away from his daughter Joseph opened his mouth. After she took the sample from it, she put the swab in another canister of blue jelly. Then she went back to her make-shift lab and put both the samples in some kind of device that began to shake them so rapidly they could no longer be seen by the eye. Moments later her hands were flying across the keyboard.

Everybody sat and watched her. Even my brothers and mother had calmed down once they realized what was happening. The anger on Rome's face let me know that I was in big trouble, but his anger paled in the presence of Joseph's, who was older than my brother and more powerful. I wanted the floor to open and swallow me. I already knew what the results were.

Joseph was the only man I had ever slept with and it had only been for one night, after going out drinking with Michelle, my roommate from school. I shook my head. I blamed *her* for all of this. She was the one that told me about the secretary position at the senator's office. She said it would be perfect if I took it, because she was interning there.

I was at Georgetown on a scholarship for their botany program. And although Rome was sending me money on a regular, I'd figured getting a job on my own would be the grown-up thing to do. I was spreading my wings after all. It was the first time in my life I had been from under my brother's protective covering. And it felt good to be making decisions on my own.

I had been working in the office for two weeks before I saw Senator Warren for the first time. He was a very busy man and a big deal in D.C. Michelle told me that his family was one of the richest black families in the world. I felt like a fish out of water working there. I was the only one that didn't come from a prestigious family. The only one from the ghetto. The only one in the office with locs and the only one that wore colors. Everybody else dressed in black and white, and every now and again dark blue. Everything I owned was warm oranges, bright yellows, and vivid reds.

So, you can imagine my surprise when one day while I was filing away some things in the file cabinet, I looked up to see Senator Warren's only son that up until that day I had only heard about, who was an even bigger deal than his father standing there watching me as if I was the most beautiful thing he had ever seen.

Because he scared the hell out of me, being too big, too old, and way too handsome, I turned away as if I didn't even notice. And I did an excellent job at avoiding him for a while, but Michelle called me all kinds of fools.

"Girl, are you nuts? There ain't a woman in all of Washington that wouldn't give their left breast to have that man sending them flowers and candy." She ran her hand through her long hair that she spent hours each morning flat ironing.

"I've been trying to get him to notice me for the last two years.

Nothing! I can't even get him to glance my way. One time I bumped into him determined to get him to look at me, that joker didn't even look away from his phone, just muttered excuse me and kept on walking."

I stood there holding the beautiful bouquet of flowers that had just been delivered to the office in my arms, more flattered than I had ever been and more afraid.

"I don't know Michelle, he's a bit much don't you think?" She waved that a way.

"So what he's older than you? What difference do a few years make?" I looked at her as if she had gone loco.

"A few years? The man is thirty-two, I just turned nineteen!"

"Pst! That just mean you'll have an experienced lover for your first time. Do you know how many of us wish a man with experience could've been the one to take our virginity? Mine was taken by a thirteen-year-old that had no clue of which hole he should have been aiming for." My mouth dropped.

"Thirteen? Oh, my goodness, how old were you?" She waved that question away.

"Once again my sweet eclectic friend, you're missing the point completely." I chuckled. Michelle was a crazy gal, she was attending Georgetown to become a lawyer, which was why she was interning with Senator Warren, who had been a judge before taking office.

"Oh sorry, I wasn't aware that you were trying to make a point." She narrowed her eyes.

"Well open your ears 'cause I am. The point I'm trying to make is, aren't you at all curious as to what it would be like, to be with that type of man? He's so powerful and dangerous. Wouldn't you like to see what sex would be like with a guy that could make you and your whole family disappear like that?" She snapped her fingers.

I frowned trying to see what the appeal was in that. She waved my look away.

"Plus, he so fine. Oh, my goodness he looks just like that guy..." she snapped her fingers as she thought about it.

"What's that guy's name...?" She continued to snap her fingers. "You know the one that use to be a real estate agent but then he became a model..." she continued to snap her fingers.

"The one that looks like he could be related to Idris Elba..." Snap... Snap... "Oh goodness, what is his name? It's on the tip of my tongue." Right when I motioned for her to get to the point her eyes brightened with recognition.

"Donnell Blaylock, Jr.!"

I shook my head. "Never heard of him."

"Girl... he is a tall, fine, piece of chocolate sin on legs." As she spoke she frowned up her face as if it hurt her mouth to even speak on it. "Just like Joseph. If I were you I would get over that shyness, stop avoiding his phone calls and accept his invitation to take you out to dinner." I exhaled.

"Michelle you know a man like that will never take somebody like me seriously." She looked at me as if I had grown a lump out of my head.

"What do you mean by that?"

"I'm from the westside of Chicago. My family don't have a name. We don't have a lot of money. He's not looking for a commitment he's looking for a little young play thing, and I'm not in the market for that."

"Why not?!" She yelled causing the people that were waiting to meet with Senator Warren to look up. I smiled at them before hissing for her to control her vocal levels.

"Because," I said very quietly hoping it would encourage Michelle to follow suit. "I have a lot going on right now. I need to focus on my studies—" she cut me off before I could even finish speaking.

"Aww Journey, give me a break! You study plants. Boring plants! I'm sure a little rendezvous with the Senator's boy ain't gon' come in the way of all that excitement. Besides, don't you think it's time you gave up your V-card? I swear you're the oldest virgin in the world right now." She slid that in before she turned and sashayed away. I chuckled at her as I put the flowers in a vase.

That had been the fifth time he's sent me flowers. I didn't tell Michelle the truth as to why I was avoiding Jo. The truth was he scared me to death; he was just too much. Because of Rome I had come up fairly sheltered. None of the guys on the block would dare try to step to me. In my neighborhood, Rome was the boss and everybody knew how overprotective of his family he was.

And Rob, only being a year older than me was no better. He kept the guys from approaching me at school. I mean sure, there were a few boys that tried to sneak and have a relationship with me, but it only got so far before their fear of one of my brothers finding out would eventually become a turn off. So, as you can see, it was safe to say that Rome and Rob were the reason I was still the proud owner of my V-card.

Anyway, that being my first time from under their protection, it felt as if Joseph was a raging storm. I had never encountered a man like him. I was used to the guys that I had grown up with. Like I said, Rome is the boss in the hood, but Joseph expanded further than the hood and my understanding. He was well-traveled and just felt more advanced that what I could handle.

I couldn't help but feel that if he ever got me, he would devour me and leave me lost and turned out somewhere. It wasn't that I didn't think I was good enough for him; being the only girl and the baby, I had come up the princess in my household. Between Rome and my mother, I was quite spoiled. It wasn't much that I wanted that Rome didn't make sure I got.

No, that wasn't the issue.

Joseph was just too…too…

Aggressive!

I'll tell you what I mean. *I was in the office cafeteria making* myself a cup of tea one morning. It was early and I thought I was in the office alone. I heard the front door open, but I just assumed it was Michelle, so I didn't turn around when I heard the cafeteria door open and then close.

"Good morning, Beautiful." The deep voice scared the hell out of me, I whipped around with my hand on my chest to see him standing there looking exactly as Michelle described him, a piece of chocolate sin on legs.

"You scared me," I said trying to laugh it off. But the truth is the way he was looking at me was causing my girly parts to come to life.

"Did you get any of my messages?" I turned back to my tea facing the cabinet. I knew it was a cowardly thing to do, but this man was breaking me down.

"Mmmhhmm..." I said taking a sip of my hot lemony beverage.

"So why didn't you return my call?" I nearly jumped out of my burgundy boots. Somehow he had silently crossed the floor and was standing right behind me. I whipped around again and my breath fled my body before slamming back in. He was standing really close, so close that I could smell his expensive cologne. And he was very tall too. I had on heels and the top of my head barely reached his shoulder.

"Ummm..." Oh God, I was having a major break down. I had never had a man invade my space before. "Ummm...I...umm!"

He grinned and I had to bite my lip to keep from moaning out loud! Somebody call the law, because it had to be illegal in several states.

"Ummm, what? Cat got your tongue?" As if under a spell, the only thing I could do was nod.

"Lucky cat," although he spoke in a low tone, his deep voice seeped into my being causing serious havoc in my belly. "I'd give all I own to trade places with him." He continued.

Wow!

So caught under his spell I was, I didn't notice that he had been stepping closer to me, until I felt both of his hands on the counter on each side of me, and realized that I was now in the circle of his strong arms.

"Why won't you return my calls, Journey?" I swear I was drowning in his deep dark gaze. The way he said my name almost made me moan again. I'm pretty sure when my mother named me Journey, she never meant for it to be said in such a way.

"I-um..." My voice came out a little choppy, so I cleared my throat. His face was so close and was slowly coming closer. My eyes as if they had a will of their own were drawn to his lips that were lined perfectly by his low-cut beard and mustache. He licked them.

Oh, Dear God!

"I didn't call you back, because--" I searched my mind for a legit reason for my coward-ness. When it came to me I smiled. "I have a boyfriend." Beautifully done, Journey. I was so busy patting myself on the back, I didn't notice when his gaze changed. He looked down for a minute and chuckled dryly to himself. When his eyes raised back to mine I saw it then, that ruthlessness that I'd heard so much about.

"I don't like being lied to." He muttered. "Just admit that you're afraid of me." I opened my mouth to deny it, but then snapped it back shut. Hell, he was right, why lie? I held up my fingers.

"Just a little bit!" I admitted, using my fingers to show him how little.

"Why, baby? I'm not going to hurt you." I chuckled then, shaking my head a bit.

"You don't believe me?" When my gaze came back to his, for the second time that day my breath was stolen. His eyes were serious. The smile disappeared off my face.

"No, I don't believe you." I admitted.

"Hmmm, that's a shame." As he spoke he stared at my mouth. "I guess I'll have to show you." Slowly his head lowered to mine. I was screaming to myself that you cannot let this man who for all intents and purposes was a stranger kiss you. I told myself that it was my boss's son and this would be extremely unprofessional. I told myself...

Nothing... after his lips touched mine I was lost. At first his kiss was so gentle, it didn't take long for it to draw a response from me. But as soon as I started returning his caress, he artfully swept me away in a lust filled typhoon.

I moaned as he deepened the kiss. Standing on my toes so that I could receive more of it I wrapped my arms around his strong neck. The few times I had been kissed were nothing like this, a few innocent pecks from the braver boys at school or a smooch stolen between the bleachers had all in a way just been the innocent unsure caresses of youth.

However, there was nothing innocent about what Jo was doing to my mouth right now. His lips were very sure. His dominating kiss made me want to delve into the erotic. At some point, he wrapped his hands around my waist and lifted me so that I was sitting on the counter, bringing me up higher so that he could have better access to my mouth.

This position pushed my burgundy skirt up farther around my hips as he spread my legs with his torso. For just a moment I was startled when I felt him ball his hands up in my waist length locs, controlling my head so that my mouth was in the perfect position for his ravishment. I learned something new about myself, that really turned me on.

All reasonable thought fled my mind. He had taken me to a place where the only thing I could do was feel. At the same time he devoured my mouth, he pressed his hardness against my softness in a way that had me panting.

I had no idea what was happening to me. I had no idea where we started and where we would have ended up had Michelle not walked in on us. I was so embarrassed that I ran out of there and into the bathroom and didn't come out until Michelle assured me he was gone.

That whole day I had been distraught. I could not believe I let him do that to me in the cafeteria of my job! The senator could have walked in. Oh my goodness! The man had turned me into a savage! After work,

Michelle talked me into going out for drinks with her and a few friends to help calm my nerves.

After the fourth shot of tequila, my nerves were good and calm, so calm that when I looked up and saw Joseph walking through the dancing bodies towards us I didn't even bat an eye. He held my gaze as if I was under hypnosis. Michelle leaned towards me.

"I hope you don't mind that I invited him. Maybe tonight's the night you'll unclench that V-card." She purred.

I smiled like the cat that had found a bowl of cream. Maybe she was right. I was tired of being the oldest virgin. My brothers weren't here, so why not have a little fun? I can't lie and say I haven't been curious to know what it feels like. And if Jo's love making was anything like that kiss he had given me earlier, I was in for a treat. What harm could one night be? It was time for me to become a woman.

Yeah!

When he came to the table I smiled warmly at him. That night we laughed, we danced...and we drank. He whispered in my ear that he would love to take me back to his place and prepare a late-night dinner for me.

Alarm bells were going off in my head, telling me that if I went behind closed doors with this man I was good and consumed. For a second, I got cold feet. But then my eyes crossed the table to Michelle, and she gave me the go ahead look. She even mouthed.

"Don't be a punk!"

I bit my lip as I thought about it. As if he could sense the battle I was going through, he picked up my hand and kissed the back of it.

"We don't have to do this if you're afraid." I turned back to look at this fine chocolate specimen, smiling through my nervousness. I was tired of being afraid.

"No, I want to."

True to his word, he prepared us a tasty meal of spaghetti. As we ate we drank more wine. That's when I admitted to him that I was a virgin and would love for him to teach me how to make love. Right at that moment, a look came over his face that could be described as nothing less than that of a predator. But thanks to the liquid courage I continued, although my good senses were telling me not to.

Had I known all the drama that night was going to lead to I would have stopped him. Hell, had it not been for the tequila making me feel braver than I was and Michelle making me feel like a freak for still being a virgin, I would've never been there in the first place.

But I guess fate was determined to see this through, because I was there willing and ready.

He made love to me, taking my virginity gently and lovingly. When he broke through my barrier and I cried out, he stopped and planted sweet kisses on my face, telling me that was the last of the pain. I don't think I will ever forget the look in his eyes in that moment. He kissed my lips and began to slowly move again.

At first, I was a little stiff as he continued to fill me, waiting for the pain I was feeling to get worse. But true to his word, the pain didn't get worse. In fact, the pain began to subside, although I felt as if I couldn't take all of him. He was gentle with me until I got accustomed to him. He made the pain fade completely and an intense pleasure that I never imagined I could feel took its place. And with no barrier between my most secret place and his, his loving became aggressive and relentless, like the kiss he had given me earlier. And just like earlier, it turned me savage.

That's when I learned that Jo had no mercy. Sounds that I didn't even know I could make came from between my lips. I used my nails in ways I'd never thought I would. Goodness! I didn't recognize myself. It wasn't till morning that I realized my tragic mistake. Not once did he use a condom. No...not once.

FALLING FOR ROME

I

BONUS CHAPTER 1

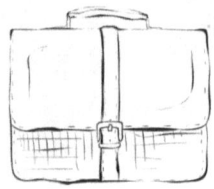

THE BEAUTIFUL ASSASSIN AND THE INGENUTIVE THUG

ABOUT FALLING FOR ROME

Take a sneak peek into upcoming novel by Edwina Fort!

Synopsis: The only child of an unloving mother and disappointed father, who wanted a son, Nakhti is determined to be the son her father always wanted and becomes a US Navy SEAL, a feat accomplished by few.

Looking to retire from a life of danger and working undercover, Nakhti is irked when she is given yet another assignment, which brings her at the doorstep of the ruthless gangbanger, Rome Reevers.

On the outside, Rome looks like your everyday thug and gangster, but within is a genius and if discovered, could make him one of the government's most coveted prizes. Will this thug genius, who's also a playa, be able to break down the walls of battle-hardened Navy SEAL Nakhti?

1

FALLING FOR ROME

BEAUTIFUL SURPRISE

I put the car in park and checked my GPS. This couldn't be the right address. The big grey building looked as if it had been one of those old industrial warehouses before it was turned into an apartment building. Several men and boys stood outside the building at the door, some looked like they were dealing, and some looked like they were hanging out with the dealers. I raised my eyebrow at a group of young girls in short skirts and shorts that walked by laughing and posing, trying to catch the eye of one of the men.

"Oh hell no." Reaching in my bag I took out my phone and pressed one.

"What's up, Nak?" The deep masculine voice came from the other end.

"What the hell, Jo? I'm in the hood." He chuckled.

"Yeah, I know. Did I forget to mention that?" I sat back in my seat leaning my head back against the head rest. I was too damn tired for this.

"Nak?"

I exhaled. "I'm here."

"Come on darling, don't give me the silent treatment. It's not that bad. I just need you to find out what information he has about me and my family, and then erase it. I don't give a damn if you have to wipe his whole system clean. Somebody has been digging real deep and my gut is telling me it's him. We are at re-election time and we can't afford any slip ups. This guy is buried in mystery, I need to know what he knows before he knows what he knows." I rolled my eyes.

"So, how am I supposed to get in there? This place is a fortress. Can you get me the blue prints to the building?"

"Already in your mailbox." Silence came from the other end for just a moment. "I wouldn't have asked you to do this on such short notice, I know I was pulling you from another assignment and you've had no recovery time. It's just that whatever system he's working with is impenetrable from the outside. I've had the best hackers on the Agency's payroll trying to crack it. It's impossible. The only way in is through the front door." I exhaled, in no mood to put up with some ignorant thug, gangsta, wannabe playa.

"And you're sure this isn't a job that Miller or Terry could handle?"

"Neither Miller or Terry will be able to get through those doors. I need the best on this one. I told you he laid out Michaels and Baker. And get this, he was handcuffed at the time. Had I not come out the room when I did, he would have snapped Tom's neck. There's not a man around that can resist that pretty, innocent face of yours. It causes them to let down their guard and then like a black widow, you strike, which makes you perfect for this job. Just look at it this way, you get in, you get out. You'll be home, wherever that is in no time."

"So, if things get out of hand with this civilian, can I kill him?"

"You have no idea how much I want to say yes to that. But alas, he's my lady's brother and she loves him. She'll be crushed if anything happens to him and I can't stand seeing her hurt. But hey, the quicker you gather my information, the quicker you can be done with it."

I grunted eyeing the man that was approaching my car with a spray bottle and a windshield squeegee that looked as if he'd *borrowed* it from the nearest gas station. Reaching in my briefcase, I pulled out a five-dollar bill before letting my window down.

"Wash your windows for you, beautiful lady?" He asked smiling, showing off his rotting teeth. The smell of alcohol and unwashed flesh singed my nose.

"I'll give you five dollars if you *don't*." He grinned as I handed him the money.

"Generous as well as beautiful. Have a blessed day." I rolled my window back up.

"Fine, but this is my last assignment." I said into the receiver. "I'm too old for this sh*t. I'm retiring." He chuckled again.

"Get out of here, you can't retire at thirty-four. I need you to have my back. I'll feel naked without you."

Dammit Jo… he knew he had my loyalty for life. He knew that there was nothing I wouldn't do for him. The man had saved my life on more than one occasion. He and I went way back to the days of being two green eared Seaman Recruits. All the way up through becoming the only two minorities in our SEAL unit.

It wasn't easy and several times I wanted to quit, but Jo never let me. He pushed me until I became the soldier that my father never was. My father who left home because I was just a stupid girl and not the boy he wanted, had tried several times to become a SEAL, but could never make it through BUD school. Not only did I make it through, I became a decorated soldier in my own right.

When Jo left the military for the Bureau, he took me with him. Again, pushing me to be more than I thought I could. Yes, I was loyal to him, unquestionably, but I was tired and he needed to know that.

"I can and I will. I'm thirty-four, but I feel sixty-four. You remember what happened last month in Libya?"

"Yeah."

"I still hear ringing in my ear from that sh*t. I don't think I will ever get my hearing back on my right side."

"You got too close to the fireworks."

"It's just the way it played out. Anyway, I said all that to say I quit after this Jo, I'm serious. The agency already fired me, why won't you just leave me the hell alone?" He chuckled, the charming bastard.

"Because you're the best man I got in the field. I won't be able to run for office unless I know you have my back." He repeated for the second time, knowing what those words did to me. I bit down on my teeth determined to stand my ground.

"Yeah well, I'm done after this."

"Nak, on a serious note…" He said, brushing off my words.

Sh*t!

"Be careful with this one. I took this kid for granted and he surprised the hell out of me. He's smarter than you can imagine. He doesn't look it, but he is. And he's dangerous. My sources tell me he's responsible for many a stiff found floating belly up in Lake Michigan. You're on his turf, everybody within twenty city miles either way is loyal to him till the death. Keep your eyes open, and whatever you do, don't take this kid lightly."

I eyeballed the hustlers standing outside of the building and farther down on the corner. It was nothing about them that appeared spectacular, just your everyday average thugs. However, Jo was the most skilled soldier I knew, so if he told me not to let down my guard, then I won't.

"Alright, I'll be in touch." Hanging up the phone I slid it back in my briefcase.

For just a moment, I sat enjoying the silence of my rental car. I had no time to rest from my last assignment for Jo, well, for his father really. The mission like most of my missions called for me to get close to a man and then kill him.

Pablo Consuela, an Argentinian drug lord had thought to blackmail the senator with some compromising photos to try and get him to vote to pass some legislation that would make it easier for him to move his product in The Gulf. I didn't know all the details, it wasn't my job to. My job was to retrieve the photos and erase them from any hard drive they may be on, and then put old Pablo out of his misery.

A job I had done flawlessly until I got too messy making my escape and ended up with a bullet wound in my side. I shook my head, this was just another sign signaling that it was time for me to walk away from this life. Jo didn't believe me, but I was going to show him, this was my last mission. When it was over and I was paid, I was ghost. I was disappearing in a way that even *he* couldn't find me.

I was going back home.

Nobody knew where my home was because I barely knew where it was. The only thing or shall I say the only person holding me there was my mom. I put her in the nursing home ten years ago under an alias. And the only way for the nursing home to contact me was through a message service that I checked from time to time, waiting for the call saying she's dead.

But I have yet to get it, so I guess she's still alive.

Maybe she was just waiting on me. Waiting to look me in the

eye one more time and blame me for being the reason daddy left. Waiting to hit me one more time for not being the boy my father wanted more than he wanted either of us. Waiting to let me know just how much she hated me before she took her last breath.

After this job, she'll get her chance if she wasn't dead. Exhaling I pushed those thoughts from my mind. Those are the kinds of thoughts that can get you killed on a mission. Those were the thoughts I was thinking when the bullet penetrated my flesh the day before yesterday.

I reached in my suitcase for a pair of eyeglasses that would complete the look I was going for and slid them on my face. Then I popped two pain pills in my mouth because my side was killing me. I hadn't even had time to get it looked at. I had to stitch it up myself, lather it with a tube of Neosporin, and slap a damn bandage over it.

Perks of the job...

When I was prepared, I stepped out the rental car and after locking it, headed toward the building.

"Daaaammmnnn!" Several of the men said as I approached, looking at me as if they had never seen a pretty woman in a two-piece fitted skirt suit carrying a briefcase.

Men...

Jo was right. For as long as I could remember, men have fallen over themselves for my face that *did* look very innocent, only to end up with their noses broken for thinking I could be taken advantage of. My face was one of the reasons the agency had hired me in the first place. They knew with my innocent looks, I would be able to slip under most people's radar.

"She look like a sexy school teacher." One of the men that was holding a red cup in his hand said. Judging by the redness of his eyes he wasn't drinking juice. I lifted my eyebrow at him checking my watch. Damn, it wasn't even ten o'clock. The smell of marijuana was also very strong in the air.

"Man, if she was my teacher, I would have stayed in school." One of the younger guys who looked to be fifteen or sixteen responded. I kept walking as if I didn't hear them. Blocking the door with both of his hands on the frame was another young man who could be no more that twenty-one or twenty- two.

He wasn't a bad looking guy. As I approached him, he passed the blunt he was smoking to another man that was much older than him sitting on the stoop. He slowly blew out the smoke as he took me in. When it was clear he wasn't going to move I stopped, but I bit down on my teeth to hold on to my temper.

Okay, so let me tell you guys why I got fired from the agency. Yes, I have an innocent face that most men consider beautiful. I look soft and approachable. Jo once described me as the girl next door. That being said…I don't have the constitution to match my looks.

I'm not friendly or soft and I could give a damn about beauty. I have a short fuse and I'm easily irritated. I may have used lethal force a time or two when pushed the wrong way. And I may have used excessive force when one of my directors thought it was alright to grab me and try to force me to kiss him one night while we were all at a bar celebrating the promotion of one of our colleagues. I was aware he was drunk, but it did little to assuage my irritation at his action.

I smashed his face into the bar, breaking it. Anyway, the agency said their hands were tied; I had too many complaints on my record to continue.

I told you guys that story to try and get you to understand what I was going through standing here in front of this civilian, allowing him to get away with his actions.

"How can I help you, sweetheart?" He asked.

"Is your name Romeo Reevers?" For a moment a look of

surprise crossed his face before he shared glances with a few of the other men. Now that I had mentioned that name, none of them were smiling anymore. The air got really tense. Even the men farther down on the block had come to attention.

Jo had been right. Whoever this Romeo was, they were very loyal to him.

"Who's asking?"

"Brenda Bonita," the lie slid easily from my lips. I had studied Romeo's file on the plane ride home. What this situation called for was a case worker.

"That's all I'm at liberty to discuss with you unless your name is Romeo Reevers." I continued.

He chuckled. "You the law?"

I reached up and pushed the curly strands of hair that hung by my ear behind it, an act that made me appear soft.

"Excuse me?"

"Police." He said losing patience with me. "Are you the police?" I softened my eyes.

"Oh no! Nothing like that." He looked at me for a minute to determine if I was telling the truth. I blinked slowly, allowing my long lashes to sweep across my doe shaped eyes.

"Aight, follow me."

"Yo Rob, what you doing man?" The older guy that still held the blunt in his hand asked.

"Relax, G. She cool." I looked back at the other men and they all wore a look of astonishment that he was taking me inside the building. As I followed him through the halls that were surprisingly very clean, he kept stealing glances at me.

"You look like some kind a case worker." He said, still fishing for my identity. I smiled at him. I liked the kid.

"Something like that." I told him.

He nodded. "Jo sent you, didn't he? To keep an eye on Rome?" I chuckled surprised by how astute he was.

"Something like that."

There were several children playing in the hall outside one of the apartments on the first floor. It looked as if the building had four levels. I could hear loud rap music playing from another apartment. We walked through a door that led to some stairs.

"I hope you don't mind taking the stairs. The elevator is broken and Rome's place is all the way up on the top floor." I smiled at him, yeah, I liked this kid.

"I don't mind."

When we got to the fourth level, there was a keypad on this door that wasn't on the others. Standing directly in front of it he keyed in a four-number code.

7,9,5,6...Got it.

I noted the fact that the fourth level was not open to the rest of the building. There seemed to be very little activity on this level. In fact, once we walked out of the stairwell, the door locked automatically when it closed behind us; there seemed to be only one other door that I could see. On this door was another keypad, he quickly keyed in the code.

3,2,9,7...Got it.

My eyes widen behind my glasses as we walked through the door. It was a loft, a very spacious loft, a nice very spacious loft. For the third time in a matter of minutes, I was pleasantly surprised. The tall floor-to-ceiling windows ran along the east side of the loft, they looked to be at least twenty feet tall. They were also covered by beautiful golden drapes.

The loft itself had to run along the entire length of the building because like I said, it was roomy. One could play a game of football in its open space or what you American's call soccer. There wasn't a lot of furniture, it didn't look as if Rome invested in that.

However, I now understood why I had been assigned this mission. Along the entire length of the north wall was a state of the art computer system. Secured to the lovely rust colored brick wall had to be at least twenty flat screened monitors. Although they were turned off, one couldn't help but wonder what appeared on them when they were turned on. In front of the elaborate system was a single plush leather chair on wheels.

It was a chair for a king.

A king whose throne was in front of several very impressive computer screens.

One thing was for certain, this beauty was something you wouldn't *ever* expect to find in the heart of the ghetto. My fingers twitched in anticipation of finding out what was stored on that massive hard drive. He spared no expense for it. There were million-dollar corporations that could not afford one such as it.

My guess was the owner of that beautiful system was lying in the bed that wasn't too far from it. Rob walked to a wall and hit a button, opening the curtains that were closer to the bed just a little. However, it was enough to shine a burst of sunlight into the loft. I came to a stop in front of the bed looking down at the occupants.

The man that I would assume was Rome lay sleeping on his stomach, my eyes traveled over his muscled back to the equally muscled arm that hung out the bed. He had on a pair of black jeans and expensive gym shoes. Asleep next to him completely naked was a very voluptuous young lady. Only the lower half of her body was covered with the sheet.

Rob wore a goofy smile on his face as he too stood looking down at the two. I could tell right off this kid was a rascal. His aim was to shock me with this. I looked at him and lifted an eyebrow, poor baby, it would take more than this to shock me.

"Yo Rome, you got a guest." He said hitting the man's shoe.

"Beat it, chump." The sleeping giant grumbled turning over in the bed without opening his eyes. Rob chuckled hitting his shoe again.

"Get up, nigga."

"What I tell you about using that word?" Rome mumbled without opening his eyes. He had a very deep voice. The younger man didn't respond, instead he looked up at me with that devious grin still on his face. He nodded in a way to tell me to watch this.

Rome opened his eyes and turned to look at him, sitting up slightly. "You deaf, punk?! What I tell—" his words stalled as his light brown gaze came to rest on me.

Although I didn't show it, for the fourth time since coming to this place, I was completely taken off guard.

Rome was gorgeous.

He looked at me through a pair of amber eyes that missed nothing. He'd just woke up from a deep sleep and judging by the empty Hennessy bottles and cups, it had been a drunken sleep, yet his eyes were sharp. They took me in making me feel as if he was reading me like an open book. I shifted on my feet feeling uncomfortable with that. No one has ever looked at me that closely.

He ran his hand over his head.

"What the f*** Rob." He growled. The grin on Rob's face grew wider as he blinked his eyes innocently.

"Bruh, you got a guest." He said gesturing towards me. Now that he mentioned it, I could see the resemblances between the two. Only difference being Rome was clearly older and his eyes were a lighter shade of brown than Rob's. He pointed at his little brother in a way that told him he will deal with him later.

"Hey," he said tapping the shoulder of the sleeping girl. She came awake with a smile on her face.

"Hey, daddy," she purred. I rolled my eyes, Rob chuckled.

"Get up, you gotta bounce." He told her. And for the first time she looked and saw us. With a squeak she snatched the sheet up to cover her breasts.

"Can you give us a minute?" Rome asked me, gesturing toward the other end of the loft where a living room area was. I lifted an eyebrow at his rude tone.

"Sure," I told him before turning to walk towards the sitting area.

As I did, I casually lifted my hand and slipped the bug from my watch, positioning it just right between my fingers. I used the same hand to ease down in the brown leather chair, securing the bug at the same time.

To the left of the chair I sat in was a huge brown leather couch, or what looked like a couch, but was really a modern rendition of a couch. It screamed contemporary bachelor pad. As if to confirm that, a ridiculously big flat screen TV was mounted to the brick wall to my right. In front of it on the floor were several gaming systems. There were quite a few game controllers sprawled on the floor around them.

When I looked back towards the sleeping area, it was to see Rome's amber gaze still on me. He was now sitting at the foot of the bed with his elbows resting against his knees. If I was the blushing type, I would be doing it right now seeing that he had watched me walk this whole distance. Finally, he turned to look up at his brother.

"Why you didn't take her downstairs to ma's place? Why the hell you bring her up here?" Rob, who had watched the whole exchange with that goofy grin on his face now wore a look of fake shock.

"Ma not home."

"So?!" Rome growled up at him, his face transformed in his anger.

Rob chuckled, not fazed a bit in only a way that a little brother could. "My bad, man. I just didn't think about it."

"You play too much." His brother responded standing up grabbing his t-shirt at the same time. When he brought it over his head, his muscled arms and chest flexed impressively. He was very tall as well.

"That's your damn problem." He continued admonishing his kid brother before he turned and noticed that the girl had not moved from the bed, she was in fact playing like she had just drifted back to sleep.

"Ay... Ay, shawty, you got to bounce. Get your sh*t." He called down to her. Amazingly she woke up and stretched, letting the cover fall from her ample breasts once again. Rob grinned shaking his head.

"Rome, you gon' call me?" She asked as she unashamedly slid out the bed reaching down to retrieve her dress from the floor.

I shook my head, women like her gave our whole species a bad name. If a man had talked to me the way he'd just talked to her, the only call I would be worried about is the anonymous one to the city morgue, telling them where to find his body.

"Rob, make sure Kiesha get to her car safe—"

"Tonya!" She interrupted him, finally insulted. Rome chuckled as he scratched his head walking towards the bathroom.

"Who the f*** cares." Was his only response as he went into his bathroom shutting the door behind him.

"Okay, you can call me Kiesha, just call me...Please!"

"Come on, shawty. I'll walk you downstairs." Rob told her as she angrily slid her feet in her heels.

"It was nice meeting you, Brenda." He called to me as they headed toward the door.

"Nice meeting you too, Rob." It really was. I don't know why he chose to make my job easier, but he had. Had he not brought me up here, there was no way I would have gotten through that group at the door.

And had I by some miracle gotten through them, I would have never made it past the locked door on the steps.

Well… Not this easily anyway.

Rome took his time in the bathroom, I heard the shower start. I was not delusional to think it wasn't a test when it really was. Jo was right. This man was smart. He was trying to feel me out before talking to me. I was careful where I let my gaze roam. Although I couldn't see them, I was quite certain this whole building was wired with cameras.

Slowly, I got up and walked to the nearest window. The drapes were opened slightly, allowing a perfect view of the ghetto below. My eyes narrowed at the roof of the building across the street, there was a man standing on it leaning against the door smoking a cigarette. When he caught me looking at him, he winked.

My gaze went to the corner store at the end of the block, several men stood outside talking, but when one of them noticed me looking, he winked.

What the hell?

I looked towards the opposite corner, there was a man sitting on the porch of a building there, it looked as if he was smoking a blunt. When he noticed that I saw him, he winked.

"What are you looking for?" Rome's deep voice came from behind me causing me to nearly jump out of my heels as I whipped around, stopping myself from reaching for the piece strapped to the inside of my thigh. I looked up at him half startled and half surprised. How in the world did he walk up on me without me hearing him? He chuckled as he flopped down on his couch facing me.

He smelled good. Now dressed in a white t-shirt and a pair of blue jeans, he even looked good. I was surprised to see that I was capable of being attracted to the thug type. Who knew?

"Did I surprise you?" He asked. For a minute my mouth just hung open. Damn, can he hear my thoughts?

"Yes." I told him truthfully. He was continuing to do that.

"Sorry about that. How can I help you Ms…"

"Brenda Bonita," I said walking toward him to shake his hand. He didn't reach for my hand, instead he studied me with that unnerving gaze of his. I had to force myself not to look away.

Get a grip Nak. You are not getting ready to let this young thug unravel you. Get it together!

I took a deep breath withdrawing my hand as I eased back down in my chair.

"It's common decency to shake your guest's hand in greeting." I admonished as I lifted my briefcase laying it gently on the granite table in front of me.

"It's common decency not to lie when your host asks you your name." My eyes rose to his.

"I told you my name. Why would I lie?"

He grinned then still studying me with that sharp gaze of his. "I don't know, but I'm sure I'll find out."

I removed several papers from my briefcase. One of them being a copy of the contract he signed with Jo.

"I've been sent here from Senator Warren's office. As you know, your sister a…" I looked at the name on the paper although I knew it by heart. "Journey Reevers is romantically involved with Joseph Warren, Senator Warren's son. I've been hired to make sure the senator and his son's reputation remain on the up and up." I smiled warmly. He did not return my smile. In fact, the more I talked, the angrier he became. The little muscle in his jaw was working overtime.

"Of course you have nothing to worry about, I am a professional. Half the time you won't even know I'm here. I'm sure you are a responsible young man and would not be willing to do anything to jeopardize the senator's and future senator's office, what with all the work they do for communities like this." He sat up on the couch.

"Wait, let me get this straight. You come into my house to tell me, a grown ass man, that you're my what? Babysitter?" I smiled.

"Well, I wouldn't put it in those terms…but, yes." He narrowed his hypnotic eyes at me.

"Funny, you don't come across as a babysitter. Why do I feel as if it's a killer staring at me through your eyes?"

It took every bit of my training not to break my cover in that moment. Nobody has ever seen the real me.

Never!

I looked away, shuffling through the papers to cover my momentary lapse.

"I don't know what you're talking about, young man."

"You can kill all that young man, bullsh*t. It's not doing what you're hoping it would."

"And what is that?" I asked lifting my gaze back to his, daring him to say it. He didn't speak right away. He just let his eyes travel over my body in a way that made me feel warm all over.

"Discouraging me from imagining what those beautiful deceptive eyes of yours will look like rounded in pleasure as you come apart for me over and over again." I loudly cleared my throat. He smiled when he saw he had ruffled my feathers.

"Mr. Reevers—"

"Rome." He corrected.

"Romeo, let's go ahead and get a few things straight. I will not tolerate sexual harassment of any kind. If you sexually harass me again, I will call Joseph Warren and inform him that you've breached your contract. If you give me a hard time in anyway from this point on, I will call Mr. Warren and tell him you've breached your contract, in which point, the actions that Mr. Warren discussed with you will be taken." I looked at him giving him my no-nonsense look.

"Is that understood?"

THANK YOU

Thank you for reading!

    I am Edwina Fort, The Hebrew Griot…

    If you liked this story, please leave me a message letting me know and don't forget to check out my Hebrew Griot YouTube page for many more stories just like this one…

Hebrew Griot YouTube Channel:
youtube.com/channel/UCN2wo3cuLpM20So1SUpyXzA

THANK YOU

Facebook Page:
www.facebook.com/hebrewgriot

Edwina Fort Facebook Page:
www.facebook.com/AuthorEdwinaFort

Edwina Fort Twitter:
twitter.com/Edwina_Fort

Edwina Fort Website:
authoredwinafort.com

Edwina Fort YouTube Channel:
www.youtube.com/channel/UCSKCjVKwFB- rWq_uHUuqE4Q

ABOUT THE AUTHOR

Author Edwina Fort is a writer who writes with a passion and purpose. She was born and raised in Chicago, but now resides in the South. Although she is new to many, this author has been writing for many years and has given her unique style of writing away freely at no cost to those who would receive. Her passion for writing came about at an early age and developed into what it is today based on her experience and life lessons. With her stories, she wants to redefine all that we've been taught to believe and shed light on our truths and potential. Writing is her calling and she wants to share that gift with you through the pages of her work. Each book will take you on a memorable journey you will find hard to forget.

facebook.com/AuthorEdwinaFort
twitter.com/Edwina_Fort
instagram.com/author_edwina

the griot's garden
IS LOOKING FOR AUTHORS.

Do you have a story to tell?

Submit online:

GriotsGardenPublications.com/submissions